PENGUIN CLASSICS

ENGLISH ROMANTIC VERSE

DAVID WRIGHT's *Selected Poems* appeared in 1990 and his *Collected Poems* after his death in 1994. He edited *The Penguin Book of Everyday Verse, Longer Contemporary Poems, Thomas Hardy: Selected Poems*, Edward Thomas's *Selected Poems and Prose*, Trelawny's *Records of Shelley, Byron and the Author*, Thomas Hardy's *Under the Greenwood Tree* and De Quincey's *Recollections of the Lakes and the Lake Poets* for Penguin. He translated *Beowulf* and *The Canterbury Tales*, and published an autobiography entitled *Deafness*.

English Romantic Verse

INTRODUCED AND EDITED BY
David Wright

PENGUIN BOOKS

PENGUIN BOOKS

Published by the Penguin Group
Penguin Books Ltd, 80 Strand, London WC2R 0RL, England
Penguin Putnam Inc., 375 Hudson Street, New York, New York 10014, USA
Penguin Books Australia Ltd, 250 Camberwell Road, Camberwell, Victoria 3124, Australia
Penguin Books Canada Ltd, 10 Alcorn Avenue, Toronto, Ontario, Canada M4V 3B2
Penguin Books India (P) Ltd, 11 Community Centre, Panchsheel Park, New Delhi – 110 017, India
Penguin Books (NZ) Ltd, Cnr Rosedale and Airborne Roads, Albany, Auckland, New Zealand
Penguin Books (South Africa) (Pty) Ltd, 24 Sturdee Avenue, Rosebank 2196, South Africa

Penguin Books Ltd, Registered Offices: 80 Strand, London WC2R 0RL, England

www.penguin.com

First published 1968
Reprinted in Penguin Classics 1986

060

Copyright © David Wright, 1968
All rights reserved

Printed and bound in Great Britain by Clays Ltd, Elcograf S.p.A.

Set in Monotype Garamond

ISBN-13: 978-0-140-42102-6

www.greenpenguin.co.uk

MIX
Paper from
responsible sources
FSC® C018179

Penguin Books is committed to a sustainable
future for our business, our readers and our planet.
This book is made from Forest Stewardship
Council™ certified paper.

CONTENTS

CONTENTS

CONTENTS

CONTENTS

CONTENTS

CONTENTS

INTRODUCTION

What used to be called the Romantic Revival in English poetry was sometimes reckoned to have begun with the publication of *Lyrical Ballads* in 1798 and to have more or less ended with the death of Byron in 1824. By then Shelley and Keats were dead, and Wordsworth and Coleridge mainly silent. Since most English poetry labelled 'Romantic' – which includes some of the best English poetry ever written – belongs to this period, that view was tenable, convenient, and misleading. For the Romantic Movement manifested itself before Wordsworth and Coleridge collaborated to produce *Lyrical Ballads*, and went on long after Byron died at Missolonghi. Under many and various metamorphoses it may even be said to have continued to our own day.

The term 'Romantic' obfuscates. It asks for comparison, always partisan, with its mirror-image, the 'Classical'; the first being seen as the antithesis of the second. A ding-dong battle – so far as writing about writing is concerned – has gone on between Romantic and Classical. This debate is really a side-issue – perhaps it would not be too much to claim that the Classical is an essentially Romantic concept largely introduced, so far as England is concerned, by Matthew Arnold. The glosses given to the two epithets have been many and confusing. They have become, as often happens in the field of literary criticism and poetic theory, terms of abuse. But generally the Romantic is held to signify the daemonic, subjective, personal, irrational, and emotional; the Classical to indicate whatever is objective, impersonal, rational, and orderly.

'*Klassisch ist das Gesunde, romantisch das Kranke,*' * said Goethe. For T. S. Eliot the difference between them was

* Classicism is health, Romanticism sickness.

'the difference between the complete and the fragmentary, the adult and the immature, the orderly and the chaotic'. * All of which is true enough if one is thinking chiefly of what Wyndham Lewis calls 'the extremist wing of Romanticism' to which Professor Mario Praz devoted a good deal of his well-known book, *The Romantic Agony*. Too much value has been given to the Romantic decadence, just as too much attention has been paid to the more obvious and vulgar manifestations of the Romantic sensibility – its gothic sensationalism and its later cult of the horrible. When these largely secondary symptoms of Romanticism are contrasted with an opposing temperament called 'Classical' much of the real significance of the phenomenon known as the Romantic Movement goes out of the window. And when Professor Grierson in his lecture *Romantic and Classical* goes back it would seem to the very beginning of western culture to claim Plato and St Paul as the first Romantics, against Aristotle as the first Classical, the line-up of the two teams becomes a game: e.g. Shakespeare is Romantic, Ben Jonson Classical; or if you like, Marlowe is Romantic, Shakespeare Classical, and so on ad infinitum.

Which is to miss the point. Romanticism is a historical phenomenon that should be approached as such. When did it begin? The word 'romantic' itself dates from the middle of the seventeenth century. 'The revolutionary character of the 1650's might almost be demonstrated from the history of one word – the word *romantic*,' writes F. W. Bateson in *English Poetry*. He goes on: 'Until 1650 no need seems to have been felt for an adjective for the common word "romance". But between 1650 and 1659 the word *romantic* is used by no less than seven writers. . . . On most of these occasions the word would seem to have been an independent creation.' Now, as Eliot remarked in a famous essay, it was in the seventeenth century that 'a disassociation of

---

* 'We have here, you will observe, a chronological interpretation: "classical" or "romantic" are merely names for the same thing (or person) at different stages of his (or its) career.' – Wyndham Lewis, *The Terms 'Classical' and 'Romantic'*.

sensibility from which we have never recovered' set in.
'The language became more refined, the feeling more
crude,' he says. 'The feeling, the sensibility expressed in *The
Country Churchyard* (Gray) is cruder than that in *To his Coy
Mistress* (Marvell). . . . The sentimental age begins early in
the eighteenth century.'

What Eliot noted was the first symptoms of a difference
in outlook which separates the modern from what – for
want of a better term – one may call the pre-Newtonian
sensibility.* For the seventeenth century was a watershed,
not merely in English history but in human evolution. It
was in this century that simultaneous and interacting break-
throughs in the fields of science and technology led to a
scientific and technological revolution that has been acceler-
ating in geometrical progression ever since. By the second
half of the eighteenth century, about the time Wordsworth
was born, the first fruits of those break-throughs – the
Industrial Revolution and the hardly less radical Agri-
cultural Revolution – were both under way. They made
possible the kind of conglomerate rather than organic
society we now live in, of which the nineteenth century was
to see the birth. Among other things the Industrial Revolu-
tion destroyed the family as an economic unit and converted
the working individual into an impersonal labour force to
be used, as W. H. Auden put it, 'like water or electricity for
so many hours a day'. The organic society of small towns
and villages where everybody knew his neighbour began to
be replaced by vast congeries in which individuals lost
identity. Our mass society was being born; a mass society
fed and clothed by mass-production and informed – if that
is the word – by mass-communications. Nor was that all.
Up to the seventeenth century man had believed he was
living in a stable universe with himself in the middle; since

* In his book *The Sleepwalkers* (Hutchinson, 1959), Arthur Koestler,
tracing the history of the development of scientific thought and
discovery, has remarked: 'If one had to sum up the history of the
scientific ideas about the universe in a single sentence, one could only
say that up to the seventeenth century our vision was Aristotelian,
after that Newtonian.'

when he has been pushed to the periphery of an illimitable and apparently expanding universe.

That is to say, it was the spiritual and metaphysical implications of the scientific and technological revolution which began in the seventeenth century and which was going at full throttle by the end of the eighteenth, together with the changed and changing view of man's place in the universe, that sparked off the Romantic Movement. In other words, the more sensitive and serious intelligences, which usually turn out to belong to poets and artists – 'the antennae of the race' in Pound's phrase – began to react, and in most cases to record disquiet.* The Romantic Movement, if we are to understand what it really was about, should be viewed in its relation to the Industrial Revolution and its consequences.

There was in fact no such thing as a Romantic 'revival'. It was rather a birth of a new kind of sensibility which had to do with the new kind of environment that man was in the process of creating for himself. If the individual was on the way to being regimented, then poets and artists, with as it were intuitive prescience, began to seek to balance the scale by giving the greatest value to individual consciousness. In doing so they exalted Imagination as the noblest of human faculties.

In parenthesis, one reason why the French Revolution of 1789 was a central experience to Romantic poets is that they saw it as essentially a revolution to emancipate the individual. 'The outward form of the inward grace of the Romantic imagination was the French Revolution, and the Revolution failed.'† And the realization of its failure most affected those who, like Wordsworth and Coleridge, most hoped and believed in it. Some have even claimed that this

---

* Which was not always acceptable to their contemporaries. No other period exhibits so high a proportion of poets neglected in their day who achieved *posthumous* recognition – e.g. (in England alone) Chatterton, Blake, Shelley, Clare, Keats, Beddoes; while Wordsworth and Coleridge did not begin to receive their due until long after they had written their best work. This was a new phenomenon.

† Harold Bloom: *The Visionary Company*, Doubleday.

is what lay behind the attenuation of their later poetry. Be that as it may, both wrote crucial poems whose theme was the failure or withdrawal of the imaginative vision. Wordsworth's *Intimations of Immortality* and Coleridge's *Dejection: A Letter** – the two key poems to the Romantic sensibility – were begun about the same time; some of Coleridge's poem may have been written partly as an answer to Wordsworth's. The interaction of the two poems on one another is illuminating.

But to return to the new sensibility of which Romantic poetry was the expression. It is most obvious in the new feeling for nature; a feeling which does not resemble that found in poetry written earlier than the eighteenth century. The attitudes are fundamentally different. Roughly speaking, where earlier poets – like Shakespeare or, say, Chaucer – accept and enjoy, Romantics elegize and idealize. Nature is seen by Romantics to be consoling or morally uplifting; a kind of spiritual healer. Mountains and wildernesses are admired rather than the evidences of fertility, usefulness, or of human cultivation. Nature is invested with personality; human moods and moral impulses are seen reflected from it. Romantics see nature through lenses of emotion, usually coloured with melancholy, nostalgia, regret. The favourite season is autumn.†

The change of attitude sprang from the changed relation between man and nature. Up to the seventeenth century it had been more or less a balanced partnership. After that the scientific and technological revolution gave man the upper hand and he began to dominate. He became the exploiter of nature and eventually its destroyer. When

---

* Better known as *Dejection: An Ode,* the title which Coleridge gave to the shortened version that appeared in his lifetime. The much longer original poem, in the form of a letter to Wordsworth's sister-in-law Sara Hutchinson, was first published by E. de Selincourt in 1947 and is the version printed in this anthology.

† Autumn is the theme of two of the best poems of Keats and Hood, as it is of Shelley's *Ode to the West Wind.* A curious remark by Keats about one of the Romantic forerunners is in his *Letters*: 'I always associate Chatterton with autumn.'

nature is no longer to be feared by man he can afford to see mountains and wildernesses as sublime or picturesque, instead of, as hitherto, desolate or appalling. Before the eighteenth century and the publication of poems like James Thomson's *Seasons* and John Dyer's *Grongar Hill* there was really no such thing as 'nature poetry', no cult of nature. The Romantics were in a position to feel sentimental about it, as did Cowper in the verses beginning 'The poplars are fell'd'. This well-known poem takes for theme a subject which was afterwards to be treated often enough but for which it is difficult to find a companion piece written before the eighteenth century. And it was perhaps an intuitive foreboding of the more widespread depredations which were to come that was at the back of Wordsworth's odd hobby – for his time – of intervening to save trees and even rocks and stones from destruction at the hands of his Westmorland neighbours. Certainly it lies behind the poignancy of John Clare's *Remembrances*:

And spreading Lea Close Oak, ere decay had penned its will,
To the axe of the spoiler and self-interest fell a prey,
And Crossberry Way and old Round Oak's narrow lane
With its hollow tree and pulpits I shall never see again,
Enclosure like a Buonaparte let not a thing remain,
It levelled every bush and tree and levelled every hill . . .

Nor, before the eighteenth century, is there any such imaginatively interpretive fellow-feeling for an animal, not even in John Skelton's *Philip Sparrow* or Andrew Marvell's *Nymph Complaining for the Death of her Fawn*, to compare with Robert Burns's verses to a field-mouse or Christopher Smart's portrait of his cat in *Jubilate Agno*. Not to make too much of it, one may as well remember that Coleridge's *Ancient Mariner* is about a man who kills a bird, and that the explicit moral of the poem is

> He prayeth well, who loveth well
> Both man and bird and beast.
> He prayeth best who loveth best
> All things both great and small.

The point is that with the Romantics nature is for the first time no longer taken for granted: it is valued, as we always value something we realize we might lose.

And this may be why another Romantic trait was a nostalgic looking back at the past, as if there to seek the reassurance of a ruder, but simpler, less complicated way of life than that which the present offered or the future promised. Not only was it a looking-back at a less-civilized bygone age but also an attempt at its imaginative recreation: a new phenomenon altogether. (Renaissance rediscovery and imitation of Roman and Greek art was an effort to resurrect what was recognized as a higher culture. The Romantics were less interested in noble Romans than in noble savages.) The eighteenth and early nineteenth centuries are notable, where architecture is concerned, for fake medieval antiquities, the building of ornamental ruins,* and of imitations and adaptations of the 'Gothick' – e.g. Horace Walpole's Strawberry Hill, Sir Walter Scott's Abbotsford and William Beckford's Fonthill. In painting, an entirely new mode emerged: the fashion for 'historical painting' which reached, perhaps, its apotheosis in the grandiose forgotten canvases of B. R. Haydon, the friend of Keats and Wordsworth. And Sir Walter Scott, if he did not invent the 'historical novel', certainly established it as a genre.

In poetry this tendency was reflected in the new interest in old ballads and the like. Imitations and even forgeries of Gaelic and medieval literature began to abound. Thomas Gray led off with his adaptations from Norse and Welsh poetry: *The Fatal Sisters, The Descent of Odin*, and so on. Then a Highland schoolmaster called James MacPherson made an extraordinary furore with his supposed translations of the supposed epics of a supposed Gaelic poet. His *Works of Ossian* caught the imagination of Europe.† For these 'translations' he invented a sort of incantatory prose–

---

* See Thomas Gray's *On Lord Holland's Seat, near Margate, Kent* for a satiric comment on the fashion.

† Including that of Napoleon Bonaparte, perhaps the prime exemplar of the Romantic man of action.

poetry, almost unreadable now, though in its day its effect was hypnotic. About the same time Bishop Percy brought out his *Reliques of Ancient English Poetry*, a collection of genuine but often refurbished and 'improved' folk-songs, Border ballads, and other early poetry. Though these ballads belong to the sixteenth century and earlier, it was in the Romantic period that they made their appearance as literature and exercised their greatest influence on written poetry. The publication of the *Reliques* encouraged Robert Burns and Sir Walter Scott to refashion old songs and ballads into their own poetry. But it was Thomas Chatterton, the Bristol apprentice (his short and tragic life – he poisoned himself in a garret at the age of eighteen – made him the archetype of the Romantic poet) who perpetrated the most dynamic of the poetic forgeries. He produced, manuscripts and all, the works of an imaginary medieval poet, Thomas Rowley. The Rowley poems are remarkable not because they took in Horace Walpole, but because with their pastiche of Chaucer and Spenser they pointed the way to a poetry of direct utterance, to an escape from the stylized ornamentation of eighteenth-century verse.

This was the beginning of the end of the 'poetic diction' of the Augustans; that 'mechanical device of style' (so Wordsworth called it) which was strangling English poetry.* As F. W. Bateson has observed, when one reads a typical eighteenth-century poem 'the words do not seem to be the expression of its thought so much as its translation into another medium'. Wordsworth gave eighteenth-century poetic diction a knockout blow in his famous *Preface to Lyrical Ballads*, one of the great documents of the Romantic Movement. There he laid it down that poetry should be written 'in a selection of language really used by men'. The key word here is 'selection', for Wordsworth in some respects remained essentially an eighteenth-century poet to the end. Any one canto of Byron's colloquial *Don Juan* – and Byron saw himself as the heir of Pope – contains more

* Though in due course Romantic poetry evolved a 'poetic diction' of its own, which Ezra Pound and T. S. Eliot were to demolish.

'language really used by men' than *The Prelude* and *The Excursion* put together. In this respect it may be worth noting that the poetry which most consistently obeys Wordsworth's recipe was written by people like Burns (only in his dialect poems however), Blake, and Clare. All three were self-educated.

But the clue to the Romantic movement lies not so much in the abandonment of 'poetic diction', or in the feeling for nature which culminated in the Wordsworthian pantheism (more properly, 'pan-entheism'), or in the half-sentimental half-sensational nostalgia for savage or 'Gothick' bygones. It is to be found in the Romantic accent on the individual as distinct from Man, on personal values, and in its interest in human psychology. Again the poets seem intuitively to have foreseen the threat posed by the growth of a mass-society with its necessary regimentation of the individual, or at the very least its heavy pressure towards spiritual and intellectual conformism,* though it was left to such European Romantics as Heine, Stendhal, Leopardi, and later Baudelaire to make clear the nature of this threat. But:

> I wander thro' each charter'd street
> Near where the charter'd Thames does flow,
> And mark in every face I meet
> Marks of weakness, marks of woe.
>
> In every cry of every Man,
> In every Infant's cry of fear,
> In every voice, in every ban,
> The mind-forg'd manacles I hear.

Thus Blake, whom his contemporaries, even Wordsworth,

* See Wordsworth's *Preface to Lyrical Ballads*: 'A multitude of causes, unknown to former times, are now acting with a combined force to blunt the discriminating powers of the mind, and, unfitting it for all voluntary exertion, to reduce it to a state of almost savage torpor. The most effective of these causes are the great national events which are almost daily taking place, and the increasing accumulation of men in cities, when the uniformity of their occupations produces a craving for extraordinary incident, which the rapid communication of intelligence barely gratifies.'

at best regarded as a visionary eccentric. Yet he was the great vatic poet of the Romantic movement. As Eliot has said, Blake's poems have the unpleasantness of great poetry; 'a peculiar honesty which, in a world too frightened to be honest, is peculiarly terrifying'. Blake is the most individual figure of the Romantic movement, whose leading echelon was indeed composed of minds so individual that nearly all who have been classified as belonging to it have also, to adapt Mr Goldwyn, been classified out. It is the penetrating insight of Blake's poems to the spiritual, over and above the human, condition that make them startling. Yet they are, as Eliot also noted, the poems of a man with a profound interest in human emotions, and a profound knowledge of them.

This interest in the psychology, as opposed to the behaviour, of the human being is a specifically Romantic characteristic. Coleridge's *Ancient Mariner* is on one level a psychological study, while his *Dejection: A Letter* may also be read as a piece of profound self-analysis. Nevertheless the poet whose interest in and knowledge of human emotions was as perspicacious as Blake's is Wordsworth, though this is not an aspect of his genius which is often commented on. *The Borderers* – hopeless as a play and not very much better as a poem – is remarkable as an exercise of psychological imagination in investigating the nature of evil. In it Wordsworth at one point parallels the Marquis de Sade:

> Suffering is permanent, obscure, and dark,
> And shares the nature of infinity.

Hardly less remarkable in this way is the often-derided *Peter Bell,* which is not, as most suppose, a dreary didactic 'moral' poem but a penetrating examination of the psychology of conversion.*

Again it was Wordsworth who wrote the major poem of the Romantic movement. This was of course *The Pre-*

* See Lascelles Abercrombie: *The Art of Wordsworth* (Oxford University Press, 1952) for a fascinating analysis and appreciation of this much under-estimated poem.

lude. Auden has pointed out how appropriate it is that one of its original titles should have been *A Poem on the Growth of an Individual Mind*. What else but the individual mind could be the hero of the great Romantic epic? This extraordinary work is the key to Wordsworth. *The Prelude* itself was to be no more than an ante-chapel to *The Recluse*, a gigantic *magnum opus* which he planned but, perhaps fortunately, never carried out. Not only *The Excursion* but all the poems he ever wrote were to form part of *The Recluse*, being associated to the main structure like 'little cells, oratories, and sepulchral recesses'. But what is unprecedented about *The Prelude* is its subject – the growth of a poet's mind! No less remarkable is the success with which Wordsworth handled so unmanageable a theme. And he succeeded largely because, as Lascelles Abercrombie observed, 'In Wordsworth psychology took the place and performed the function of mythology.'

The other major Romantic poem of which the individuality of the poet may be said to be hero is Byron's *Don Juan*, though at first sight nothing could be further from *The Prelude* in style, purpose, or level of operation. Yet as Auden remarked, 'Don Juan is as much the dramatized story of the education of Byron's mind as *The Prelude* is a direct account of the education of Wordsworth's.' The Don Juan of the poem is not a stand-in for Byron – but then Don Juan is not the hero of the poem. The hero of *Don Juan* is the poet himself, narrating, digressing, commenting, talking about it and about. Its true subject is the personality of Byron; the real man, presented with gaiety and detached realism; a Byron from whom the histrionic sentimentalism of *Childe Harold* has been cauterized.

Now it may be worth noting how often in Romantic poetry the figure of the Solitary – the individual man, antipathetic to what Ortega y Gasset defines as the mass* –

* In *La rebelión de las masas* (The Revolt of the Masses), 1930. He says, 'The mass is all which sets no value on itself – good or ill – based on specific grounds, but which feels itself "just like everybody" ... The mass crushes beneath it everything which is different, everything

occurs. There is a Solitary in Wordsworth's *The Excursion*, though in that poem the true Solitary is the character Words- worth calls the Wanderer: the two are indeed different facets of the same figure. (Significantly or not, the title Wordsworth intended to give to his never-completed *magnum opus*, of which *The Prelude* and *The Excursion* are but parts, was *The Recluse*.) Wordsworth may be said to have been more or less obsessed with the figure of the Solitary, who in various guises is the theme of many of his shorter poems – e.g. the Leech-gatherer in *Resolution and Independence* and the Shepherd-lord in *Song at the Feast of Brougham Castle*. Coleridge's *Ancient Mariner* is about a Solitary; the hero of Byron's *Childe Harold* may be said to be another; it is a transcendent Solitary that figures in Blake's *Mental Traveller* and *William Bond*. He is foreshadowed in Cowper's description of himself in *The Task*: 'I was a stricken deer, that left the herd . . .' and most poignantly in *The Castaway*. Sometimes the poet himself is the Solitary, as in Coleridge's *Dejection: A Letter*; or throughout the stark autobiography of John Clare – those poems written in the asylum, like *I Am, Love and Solitude, A Vision*, in which the Solitary be- comes the Outcast. In his madness Clare used to identify himself with Byron (he gave his long autobiographical poem *Child Harold* one of Byron's titles). In Shelley the Outcast-Solitary* is to be identified with the poet in *Alastor*,

---

that is excellent, individual, qualified and select. Anybody who is not like everybody, who does not think like everybody, runs the risk of being eliminated.' The figure of the Solitary begins to occur in poetry about the same time as the advent of the Industrial Revolution which produced Ortega y Gasset's 'Mass-man'. Almost simultaneously appeared the social phenomenon of the Dandy – the word dates from 1780. The Dandy asserted in dress and behaviour his uniqueness, individuality, and personality.

* This figure, either rejected or rejecting – and sometimes both – haunted the imagination of nineteenth-century poets and can be found in Matthew Arnold's *Forsaken Merman* and *Scholar-Gypsy*; in the non- sense poems of Edward Lear; in the first person singular of *The City of Dreadful Night* by James Thomson ('B.V.'). It may be that his last ap- pearance was as late as the twentieth century in the personae of J. Alfred Prufrock and Hugh Selwyn Mauberley.

the 'phantom among men' in *Adonais,* and the 'I' of such poems as *Stanzas Written in Dejection, near Naples, The Question* and *To Edward Williams.* The Outcast-Solitary finds a logical conclusion in *The Last Man,* one of Thomas Hood's best poems (alas too long to include in this anthology).

John Clare, whose stature is only now beginning to be recognized, was perhaps the last of the pure Romantic poets. Like Blake he was neglected in his lifetime (though he did have a few years of precarious fame) and like Blake much of his work was not published until long after his death. He was a nature-poet in a sense to which none of the other Romantics can lay claim: for in his work Clare displays the knowledge and observation of a naturalist as well as a poet.* Clare is unlike any other poet in this book, except perhaps Burns, in that his best work derives directly from the oral tradition of poetry: the ballads and folk songs of rural labourers, of whom he was one. (His father, a thresher, was a ballad-singer with a repertoire of over a hundred songs.) It was as if, at the very moment of change, the anonymous traditional culture of the peasantry had found an individual voice just when it was about to disappear. Clare himself was a victim of the agrarian revolution which altered the rural ways of life that had subsisted for centuries. The enclosure of the common lands and introduction of economic farming (the one prevented cottagers from grazing the livestock which formed part of their subsistence; the other made casual seasonal work scarcer) brought acute poverty to the peasantry in general and to Clare in particular. He could make a living neither as a poet nor a farm-worker; and this helped to drive him mad.

Compared with Clare's, the poetry of Shelley and Keats, two of his contemporaries who belong to what has been called the second generation of Romantics, is self-conscious. Both were masterly technical experimenters – the

* Compare Clare's *The Nightingale's Nest* with Wordsworth's *The Green Linnet*; and for good measure with Coleridge's *The Nightingale* and Keats's *Ode to a Nightingale,* all of which are included in this anthology.

prosody of Keats's odes and of Shelley's lyrics is remarkable as metrical achievement. Yet even in their most successful poems – but this is less true of Shelley than of Keats – one doesn't often come across the mint-bright freshness of vision and utterance which is present in the best work of Blake, Wordsworth, Coleridge, and Clare. Shelley had a glittering but adolescent intelligence. Ideas fascinated him. One cannot imagine Shelley exclaiming with Keats: 'O for a life of sensations rather than thoughts!' At its worst Shelley's poetry is a vaporous intellectual rhetoric, enthusiastically clothing nebulosities with nebulosities. His almost pure intellectualism sometimes tended to rarefy his poetry out of existence. On the other hand the sensuousness of Keats inclined to smother Keats's poetry in too thick a treacle.

A lushness of imagery and imagination begins to pervade the work of poets born after Clare. The poetry of Keats conveys the first hint of this over-ripeness. It is not to be found in his impromptu verse such as *Teignmouth, Dawlish Fair*, or the delightful *Hither Hither Love*, but in deliberate set-piece poems like the *Odes* or the overfurnished *Eve of St Agnes*, where one may detect behind the sensuousness a studied poesifying of experience. The Keats who wrote the letters is a greater poet than the Keats who wrote the poems. In the letters Keats has a purpose, and his eyes are bright with it; in the poems, admirable as they are, he seems rather to have designs – and literary designs at that – upon his reader. The line between poetry and poesy, between imagination and fantasy, wavers dangerously. There is a cancelled stanza of the *Ode to Melancholy* in which the macabre quality that characterizes the poetry of the Romantic decadence first reveals itself:

> Though you should build a bark of dead men's bones
> And rear a phantom gibbet for a mast,
> Stitch shrouds together for a sail, with groans
> To fill it out, blood-stained and aghast . . .

Such lines might have been written by T. L. Beddoes, whose *Death's Jest-Book* is a perfect necropolis in its imagery.

This nightmarish touch in the poetry of the epigoni of the great Romantics appears in the lives of the poets themselves. Most died young – James Clarence Mangan starved to death in Dublin, Edgar Allan Poe was found dying in the street in Baltimore; the stuttering George Darley, cut off from society by his grotesque affliction, died in early middle age; so did Thomas Hood, hounded by penury and bad health, flogging himself to death as a hack-writer; and possibly most bizarre of all, Thomas Lovell Beddoes, his leg amputated, died after poisoning himself with curare. The macabre overtones that invest their biographies invest their imaginations. Even Hood's humorous verse is often ghoulish – for example *Tim Turpin*, which George MacBeth includes in his *Penguin Book of Sick Verse*. The nightmare is unmistakably present in the work of Poe, though it comes through less effectively in his verse than in his prose. It also pervades the poetry of George Darley, particularly the intense lyricism of that unduly neglected long poem, *Nepenthe*. Above all it is to be found in what may be called the black poetry of Beddoes. The preoccupation of these poets with the macabre may have been a symptom of that general coarsening of the imagination – that crudity of feeling which Eliot noted – that was to become manifest in so much nineteenth-century verse. The imaginative numbness which they tried to defeat or camouflage by excursions into macabre sensationalism – as it were an eschatological excitation – was afterwards to evidence itself in the spiritual vulgarity which characterizes a great deal of the poetry of the later nineteenth-century Romantics, in particular Swinburne's.

But though shot through with Romantic sensationalism and gothic glooms, the macabre as such is not to be found in the poetry of Emily Brontë, with which this anthology closes.* It may be because she lived for nearly the whole of her short life in almost complete isolation from the

---

* Though she approaches the gruesome in her novel, *Wuthering Heights*, in that scene where Heathcliff digs up Catherine's body from its grave.

nineteenth century – as much isolated in her moorland parsonage as was Clare at his Northampton asylum. Both addressed poems to a private world – in the case of Emily her imagined kingdom of Angria, in the case of Clare his vision of a lost Helpston and imagined wife. But the nineteenth century, in what they saw as its cruellest aspect, was too much with Beddoes, Poe, Hood, and Mangan. By their time the mass society had been born, and Victorianism was just beginning.

For the reign of Victoria was to see the consolidation of the Industrial Revolution, whose heroic age belonged to the last two decades of the eighteenth century and first two decades of the nineteenth. In those forty years England was in the process of transforming herself into the first industrialized nation the world had seen. Such national efflorescences of energy have a way of being reflected – paralleled is perhaps a better word – in the poetry of their times. At any rate it seems no coincidence that the flowering of English Romantic poetry – the energy and incandescence of thought and feeling that burns in the best work of Blake, Wordsworth, and Coleridge – should appertain to these four decades.

Of this flowering the present anthology attempts to provide a representative selection. Nearly all the famous *pièces de résistance* will be found in it, though two or three of the more hackneyed stock-items have been avoided in favour of less familiar poems. It also tries to furnish, so far as anthology-logistics permit, a glimpse of the development of the Romantic sensibility from its beginnings to the first hints of its decadence. The poets are therefore arranged in chronological sequence of dates of birth, and their poems roughly, but not invariably, in order of composition. Not perversity but the idea of pointing up the irrelevance of the Romantic – Classical polemic led to the choice of Alexander Pope's *Elegy to the Memory of an Unfortunate Lady* to open the anthology. For all the neo-classic Augustanism of its prosody and diction, it will be seen that this poem anticipates the Romantic sensibility. Eighteenth-century harbingers, exemplars, and precursors, such as Thomson, Gray, Collins, Smart, Cowper, Burns, and Chatterton are likewise represented. But naturally the main emphasis has been given to the major Romantic poets – Blake, Wordsworth, Coleridge, Byron, Shelley, Clare, and Keats. Their successors, poets like Beddoes, Darley, and Poe, are also given room, as is the early poetry of Tennyson and Browning. Though an anthology of English Romantic poetry should logically extend at least as far as Swinburne, whose verse was in a sense its *reductio ad absurdum*, I have included no poems written after 1848. The 'year of revolutions', which saw the death of Emily Brontë and the publication of that essentially Romantic document, the Communist Manifesto, seemed an appropriate deadline.

DAVID WRIGHT, 1966

NOTE

Spelling and the use of capitals, italics, etc., have largely been brought into conformity with modern practice with the exception of the poems by Christopher Smart, Blake, Wordsworth, Coleridge, John Clare, and Emily Brontë, partly because in their case the texts here printed are mostly taken from original manuscript versions that have come to light in recent years. Examples are Smart's *Jubilate Agno*, Coleridge's *Dejection: A Letter*, the 1805 version of Wordsworth's *Prelude*, most of Clare's later poems (some of which were first printed as late as 1964) and the poems of Emily Brontë. In her case I have printed the original text of her poems as found in her MSS instead of the heavily edited and sometimes altered versions of them that were published by Charlotte Brontë.

ACKNOWLEDGEMENTS

For permission to publish poems in this anthology, acknowledgement is made to the following: for 'The Nightingale's Nest', 'Remembrances', 'The Pale Sun', 'Cowper', 'Death', and 'I Am' by John Clare from J. W. Tibble's *Selected Poems of John Clare*, to J. M. Dent & Sons Ltd; for 'Mary', 'I peeled bits of straw', and 'A Vision' by John Clare from Edmund Blunden's *Madrigals and Chronicles*, to Cyril Beaumont and Professor Edmund Blunden; for selections from the 1805 'Prelude' by William Wordsworth from the Oxford Standard Authors series, to Oxford University Press; for 'To a Wreath of Snow', 'R. Alcona to J. Brenzaida', 'Julian M. and A. G. Rochelle', and 'Last Lines' by Emily Brontë from C. W. Hatfield's *The Complete Poems of Emily Jane Brontë*, to Columbia University Press.

English Romantic Verse

ALEXANDER POPE

1688–1744

Elegy to the Memory of an Unfortunate Lady

What beck'ning ghost, along the moonlight shade
Invites my steps, and points to yonder glade?
'Tis she! – but why that bleeding bosom gor'd,
Why dimly gleams the visionary sword?
Oh ever beauteous, ever friendly! tell,
Is it, in heav'n, a crime to love too well?
To bear too tender, or too firm a heart,
To act a lover's or a Roman's part?
Is there no bright reversion in the sky,
For those who greatly think, or bravely die?

Why bade ye else, ye powers! her soul aspire
Above the vulgar flight of low desire?
Ambition first sprung from your blest abodes;
The glorious fault of angels and of gods:
Thence to their images on earth it flows,
And in the breasts of kings and heroes glows.
Most souls, 'tis true, but peep out once an age,
Dull, sullen prisoners in the body's cage:
Dim lights of life, that burn a length of years
Useless, unseen, as lamps in sepulchres;
Like Eastern kings a lazy state they keep,
And, close confin'd to their own palace, sleep.

From these perhaps (ere nature bade her die)
Fate snatch'd her early to the pitying sky.
As into air the purer spirits flow,
And separate from their kindred dregs below;
So flew the soul to its congenial place,
Nor left one virtue to redeem her race.

But thou, false guardian of a charge too good,
Thou, mean deserter of thy brother's blood!
See on these ruby lips the trembling breath,
These cheeks now fading at the blast of death;

Cold is that breast which warm'd the world before,
And those love-darting eyes must roll no more.
Thus, if eternal justice rules the ball,
Thus shall your wives, and thus your children fall:
On all the line a sudden vengeance waits,
And frequent hearses shall besiege your gates;
There passengers shall stand, and pointing say,
(While the long funerals blacken all the way)
'Lo! these were they, whose souls the Furies steel'd,
And curs'd with hearts unknowing how to yield.'
Thus unlamented pass the proud away,
The gaze of fools, and pageant of a day!
So perish all, whose breast ne'er learn'd to glow
For others' good, or melt at others' woe.

What can atone (oh ever-injur'd shade!)
Thy fate unpity'd, and thy rites unpaid?
No friend's complaint, no kind domestic tear
Pleased thy pale ghost, or graced thy mournful bier.
By foreign hands thy dying eyes were closed,
By foreign hands thy decent limbs composed,
By foreign hands thy humble grave adorn'd,
By strangers honour'd, and by strangers mourn'd!
What tho' no friends in sable weeds appear
Grieve for an hour, perhaps, then mourn a year,
And bear about the mockery of woe
To midnight dances, and the public show?
What tho' no weeping loves thy ashes grace,
Nor polish'd marble emulate thy face?
What tho' no sacred earth allow thee room,
Nor hallow'd dirge be mutter'd o'er thy tomb?
Yet shall thy grave with rising flowers be drest,
And the green turf lie lightly on thy breast:
There shall the morn her earliest tears bestow,
There the first roses of the year shall blow;
While angels with their silver wings o'ershade
The ground, now sacred by thy reliques made.

So peaceful rests, without a stone, a name,
What once had beauty, titles, wealth, and fame.

How loved, how honour'd once, avails thee not,
To whom related, or by whom begot;
A heap of dust alone remains of thee,
'Tis all thou art, and all the proud shall be!
  Poets themselves must fall like those they sung,
Deaf the praised ear, and mute the tuneful tongue.
Even he, whose soul now melts in mournful lays,
Shall shortly want the generous tear he pays;
Then from his closing eyes thy form shall part,
And the last pang shall tear thee from his heart,
Life's idle business at one gasp be o'er,
The Muse forgot, and thou belov'd no more!

JAMES THOMSON
1700–1748

From *The Seasons*

SPRING
(i)

Come, gentle Spring, ethereal mildness, come;
And from the bosom of yon dropping cloud,
While music wakes around, veil'd in a show'r
Of shadowing roses, on our plains descend.

(ii)

The blackbird whistles from the thorny brake,
The mellow bullfinch answers from the grove;
Nor are the linnets, o'er the flowering furze
Pour'd out profusely, silent. Join'd to these
Innumerous songsters, in the freshening shade
Of new-sprung leaves, their modulations mix
Mellifluous. The jay, the rook, the daw,
And each harsh pipe, discordant heard alone,
Aid the full concert; while the stock-dove breathes
A melancholy murmur thro' the whole.

WINTER
(i)

See! Winter comes, to rule the varied year,
Sullen, and sad; with all his rising train,
Vapours, and clouds, and storms. Be these my theme,
These, that exalt the soul to solemn thought,
And heavenly musing. Welcome, kindred glooms!
Wish'd wintry horrors, hail! – With frequent foot,
Pleas'd have I, in my cheerful morn of life,
When, nurs'd by careless solitude, I liv'd,
And sung of Nature with unceasing joy,
Pleas'd have I wander'd thro' your rough domains;
Trod the pure virgin snows, myself as pure:

4

Heard the winds roar, and the big torrent burst;
Or seen the deep, fermenting tempest brew'd
In the red, evening sky. – Thus pass'd the time,
Till, thro' the opening chambers of the south,
Look'd out the joyous Spring, look'd out, and smil'd.

(ii)

Lo! from the livid East, or piercing North,
Thick clouds ascend, in whose capacious womb,
A vapoury deluge lies, to snow congeal'd:
Heavy, they roll their fleecy world along;
And the sky saddens with th'impending storm.
Thro' the hush'd air, the whitening shower descends,
At first, thin-wavering; till at last, the flakes,
Fall broad, and wide, and fast, dimming the day
With a continual flow. See! sudden, hoar'd,
The woods beneath the stainless burden bow;
Black'ning, along the mazy stream it melts;
Earth's universal face, deep-hid, and chill,
Is all one dazzling waste. The labourer-ox
Stands cover'd o'er with snow, and then demands
The fruit of all his toil. The fowls of heaven,
Tam'd by the cruel season, crowd around
The winnowing store, and claim the little boon
That Providence allows. The foodless wilds
Pour forth their brown inhabitants; the hare
Tho' timorous of heart, and hard beset
By death in various forms, dark snares, and dogs,
And more unpitying men, the garden seeks,
Urg'd on by fearless want. The bleating kind
Eye the bleak heavens, and next, the glistening earth,
With looks of dumb despair; then sad, dispers'd,
Dig, for the wither'd herb, thro' heaps of snow.

CHARLES WESLEY
1707–1778

Wrestling Jacob

Come, O Thou Traveller unknown,
  Whom still I hold, but cannot see,
My company before is gone,
  And I am left alone with Thee,
With Thee all night I mean to stay,
And wrestle till the break of day.

I need not tell Thee who I am,
  My misery, or sin declare,
Thyself hast call'd me by my name,
  Look on Thy hands, and read it there,
But who, I ask Thee, who art Thou?
Tell me Thy Name, and tell me now.

In vain Thou strugglest to get free,
  I never will unloose my hold:
Art Thou the Man that died for me?
  The secret of Thy love unfold;
Wrestling I will not let Thee go,
Till I Thy Name, Thy Nature know.

Wilt Thou not yet to me reveal
  Thy new, unutterable Name?
Tell me, I still beseech Thee, tell,
  To know it now resolv'd I am;
Wrestling I will not let Thee go,
Till I Thy Name, Thy Nature know.

'Tis all in vain to hold Thy tongue,
  Or touch the hollow of my thigh:
Though every sinew be unstrung,

Out of my arms Thou shalt not fly;
Wrestling I will not let Thee go,
Till I Thy Name, Thy Nature know.

What tho' my shrinking flesh complain,
   And murmur to contend so long,
I rise superior to my pain,
   When I am weak then I am strong,
And when my all of strength shall fail,
I shall with the God-man prevail.

My strength is gone, my nature dies,
   I sink beneath Thy weighty hand,
Faint to revive, and fall to rise;
   I fall, and yet by faith I stand,
I stand, and will not let Thee go,
Till I Thy Name, Thy Nature know.

Yield to me now – for I am weak;
   But confident in self-despair:
Speak to my heart, in blessings speak,
   Be conquer'd by my instant prayer,
Speak, or Thou never hence shalt move,
And tell me if Thy Name is Love.

'Tis Love, 'tis Love! Thou diedst for me,
   I hear Thy whisper in my heart.
The morning breaks, the shadows flee:
   Pure Universal Love Thou art,
To me, to all, Thy bowels move,
Thy Nature, and Thy Name is Love.

My prayer hath power with God; the Grace
   Unspeakable I now receive,
Thro' faith I see Thee face to face,
   I see Thee face to face, and live:
In vain I have not wept, and strove,
Thy Nature, and Thy Name is Love.

I know Thee, Saviour, who Thou art,
   Jesus the feeble sinner's friend;
Nor wilt Thou with the night depart,
   But stay, and love me to the end;
Thy mercies never shall remove,
Thy Nature, and Thy Name is Love.

The sun of righteousness on me
   Hath rose with healing in his wings,
Wither'd my nature's strength; from Thee
   My soul its life and succour brings,
My help is all laid up above;
Thy Nature, and Thy name is Love.

Contented now upon my thigh
   I halt, till life's short journey end;
All helplessness, all weakness I,
   On Thee alone for strength depend,
Nor have I power, from Thee, to move;
Thy Nature, and Thy Name is Love.

Lame as I am, I take the prey,
   Hell, earth, and sin with ease o'ercome;
I leap for joy, pursue my way,
   And as a bounding hart fly home,
Thro' all eternity to prove
Thy Nature, and Thy Name is Love.

THOMAS GRAY
1716–1771

The Fatal Sisters
FROM THE NORSE-TONGUE

Now the storm begins to lower,
(Haste, the loom of Hell prepare,)
Iron-sleet of arrowy shower
Hurtles in the darken'd air.

Glittering lances are the loom,
Where the dusky warp we strain,
Weaving many a soldier's doom
Orkney's woe, and Randver's bane.

See the grisly texture grow,
('Tis of human entrails made,)
And the weights, that play below,
Each a gasping warrior's head.

Shafts for shuttles, dipt in gore,
Shoot the trembling cords along
Sword, that once a Monarch bore,
Keep the tissue close and strong.

Mista black, terrific maid,
Sangrida, and Hilda see,
Join the wayward work to aid:
'Tis the woof of victory.

Ere the ruddy sun be set,
Pikes must shiver, javelins sing,
Blade with clattering buckler meet,
Hauberk crash, and helmet ring.

9

THOMAS GRAY

(Weave the crimson web of war)
Let us go, and let us fly,
Where our friends the conflict share,
Where they triumph, where they die.

As the paths of fate we tread,
Wading thro' th'ensanguin'd field:
Gondula, and Geira, spread
O'er the youthful king your shield.

We the reins to slaughter give,
Ours to kill, and ours to spare:
Spite of danger he shall live.
(Weave the crimson web of war.)

They, whom once the desert-beach
Pent within its bleak domain,
Soon their ample sway shall stretch
O'er the plenty of the plain.

Low the dauntless earl is laid,
Gor'd with many a gaping wound:
Fate demands a nobler head;
Soon a king shall bite the ground.

Long his loss shall Eirin weep,
Ne'er again his likeness see;
Long her strains in sorrow steep,
Strains of immortality!

Horror covers all the heath,
Clouds of carnage blot the sun,
Sisters, weave the web of death;
Sisters, cease; the work is done.

Hail the task, and hail the hands!
Songs of joy and triumph sing!
Joy to the victorious bands;
Triumph to the younger king.

THOMAS GRAY

Mortal, thou that hear'st the tale,
Learn the tenor of our song.
Scotland, thro' each winding vale
Far and wide the notes prolong.

Sisters, hence with spurs of speed:
Each her thundering faulchion wield;
Each bestride her sable steed.
Hurry, hurry to the field.

Ode on the Pleasure arising from Vicissitude

A FRAGMENT

Now the golden morn aloft
  Waves her dew-bespangled wing,
With vermeil cheek and whisper soft
  She woos the tardy Spring:
Till April starts, and calls around
The sleeping fragrance from the ground;
And lightly o'er the living scene
Scatters his freshest, tenderest green.

New-born flocks, in rustic dance,
  Frisking ply their feeble feet;
Forgetful of their wintry trance
  The birds his presence greet:
But chief the sky-lark warbles high
His trembling thrilling ecstacy;
And, less'ning from the dazzled sight,
Melts into air and liquid light.

Yesterday the sullen year
  Saw the snowy whirlwind fly;
Mute was the music of the air,
  The herd stood drooping by:

Their raptures now that wildly flow,
No yesterday, nor morrow know;
'Tis man alone that joy descries
With forward and reverted eyes.

Smiles on past misfortune's brow
   Soft reflection's hand can trace;
And o'er the cheek of sorrow throw
   A melancholy grace;
While hope prolongs our happier hour,
Or deepest shades, that dimly lour
And blacken round our weary way,
Gilds with a gleam of distant day.

Still, where rosy pleasure leads,
   See a kindred grief pursue;
Behind the steps that misery treads,
   Approaching comfort view:
The hues of bliss more brightly glow,
Chastised by sabler tints of woe;
And blended form, with artful strife,
The strength and harmony of life.

See the wretch, that long has tost
   On the thorny bed of pain,
At length repair his vigour lost,
   And breathe, and walk again:
The meanest floweret of the vale,
The simplest note that swells the gale,
The common sun, the air, the skies,
To him are opening Paradise.

THOMAS GRAY

On Lord Holland's Seat
Near Margate, Kent

Old, and abandon'd by each venal friend,
  Here Holland formed the pious resolution
To smuggle a few years, and strive to mend
  A broken character and constitution.

On this congenial spot he fixed his choice;
  Earl Goodwin trembled for his neighbouring sand:
Here seagulls scream, and cormorants rejoice,
  And mariners, though shipwreck'd, dread to land.

Here reign the blustering North and blighting East,
  No tree is heard to whisper, bird to sing;
Yet Nature could not furnish out the feast,
  Art he invokes, new horrors still to bring.

Here mouldering fanes and battlements arise,
  Turrets and arches nodding to their fall,
Unpeopled monastries delude our eyes,
  And mimic desolation covers all.

'Ah!' said the sighing peer, 'had Bute been true,
  Nor Mungo's, Rigby's, Bradshaw's friendship vain,
Far better scenes than these had bless'd our view,
  And realised the beauties which we feign:

'Purged by the sword, and purified by fire,
  Then had we seen proud London's hated walls;
Owls would have hooted in St Peter's choir,
  And foxes stunk and littered in St Paul's.'

WILLIAM COLLINS
1721-1759

Ode on the Poetical Character

As once – if, not with light regard,
I read aright that gifted bard
– Him whose school above the rest
His loveliest elfin queen has blest;
One, only one, unrivall'd fair,
Might hope the magic girdle wear,
At solemn turney hung on high,
The wish of each love-darting eye;

Lo! to each other nymph, in turn, applied,
    As if, in air unseen, some hovering hand,
Some chaste and angel friend to virgin fame,
    With whisper'd spell had burst the starting band.
It left unblest her loathed dishonour'd side;
    Happier, hopeless Fair, if never
    Her baffled hand, with vain endeavour,
Had touch'd that fatal zone to her denied!

Young Fancy thus, to me divinest name,
    To whom, prepared and bathed in heaven,
    The cest of amplest power is given:
    To few the godlike gift assigns,
    To gird their blest prophetic loins,
And gaze her visions wild, and feel unmix'd her flame!

The band, as fairy legends say,
Was wove on that creating day,
When He, who call'd with thought to birth
Yon tented sky, this laughing earth,

turney: tourney. *cest*: girdle.

14

And dress'd with springs and forests tall,
And pour'd the main engirting all,
Long by the loved enthusiast woo'd,
Himself in some diviner mood,
Retiring, sat with her alone,
And placed her on his sapphire throne;
The whiles, the vaulted shrine around,
Seraphic wires were heard to sound,
Now sublimest triumph swelling,
Now on love and mercy dwelling;
And she, from out the veiling cloud,
Breathed her magic notes aloud:
And thou, thou rich-hair'd youth of morn,
And all thy subject life was born!
The dangerous passions kept aloof,
Far from the sainted growing woof:
But near it sat ecstatic Wonder,
Listening the deep applauding thunder;
And Truth, in sunny vest array'd,
By whose the tarsel's eyes were made;
All the shadowy tribes of mind
In braided dance, the murmers join'd,
And all the bright uncounted powers
Who feed on heaven's ambrosial flowers.
– Where is the bard whose soul can now
Its high presuming hopes avow?
Where he who thinks, with rapture blind,
This hallow'd work for him design'd?

High on some cliff, to heaven up-piled,
Of rude access, of prospect wild,
Where, tangled round the jealous steep,
Strange shades o'erbrow the valleys deep,
And holy Genii guard the rock,
Its glooms embrown, its springs unlock,
While on its rich ambitious head,
An Eden, like his own, lies spread:

tarsel's: hawk's.

15

I view that oak, the fancied glades among,
By which as Milton lay, his evening ear,
From many a cloud that dropp'd ethereal dew,
Nigh sphered in heaven, its native strains could hear;
On which that ancient trump he reach'd was hung:
   Thither oft, his glory greeting,
   From Waller's myrtle shades retreating,
With many a vow from Hope's aspiring tongue,
My trembling feet his guiding steps pursue;
   In vain – Such bliss to one alone,
   Of all the sons of soul, was known;
   And Heaven, and Fancy, kindred powers,
Have now o'erturn'd the inspiring bowers;
Or curtain'd close such scene from every future view.

Ode to Evening

If aught of oaten stop, or pastoral song,
May hope, chaste Eve, to soothe thy modest ear,
    Like thy own brawling springs,
    Thy springs, and dying gales;

O nymph reserv'd, while now the bright-hair'd sun
Sits in yon western tent, whose cloudy skirts,
    With brede ethereal wove,
    O'erhang his wavy bed:

Now air is hush'd, save where the weak-eyed bat
With short shrill shriek flits by on leathern wing:
    Or where the beetle winds
    His small but sullen horn,

As oft he rises 'midst the twilight path,
Against the pilgrim borne in heedless hum:
    Now teach me, maid composed,
    To breathe some soften'd strain,

brede: braid.

Whose numbers, stealing through thy darkening vale,
May not unseemly with its stillness suit;
    As, musing slow, I hail
    Thy genial loved return!

For when thy folding-star arising shows
His paly circlet, at his warning lamp
    The fragrant Hours, and Elves
    Who slept in buds the day,

And many a Nymph who wreathes her brows with
    sedge,
And sheds the freshening dew, and, lovelier still,
    The pensive Pleasures sweet,
    Prepare thy shadowy car.

Then let me rove some wild and heathy scene;
Or find some ruin, midst its dreary dells,
    Whose walls more awful nod
    By thy religious gleams.

Or, if chill blustering winds, or driving rain,
Prevent my willing feet, be mine the hut,
    That from the mountain's side,
    Views wilds, and swelling floods,

And hamlets brown, and dim-discover'd spires;
And hears their simple bell, and marks o'er all
    Thy dewy fingers draw
    The gradual dusky veil.

While Spring shall pour his showers, as oft he wont,
And bathe thy breathing tresses, meekest Eve!
    While Summer loves to sport
    Beneath thy lingering light;

While sallow Autumn fills thy lap with leaves;
Or Winter, yelling through the troublous air,
    Affrights thy shrinking train,
    And rudely rends thy robes;

So long, regardful of thy quiet rule,
Shall Fancy, Friendship, Science, smiling Peace,
    Thy gentlest influence own,
    And love thy favourite name!

Ode on the Death of Thomson*

THE SCENE IS SUPPOSED TO LIE ON THE THAMES NEAR RICHMOND

In yonder grave a Druid lies,
    Where slowly winds the stealing wave;
The year's best sweets shall duteous rise
    To deck its poet's sylvan grave.

In yon deep bed of whispering reeds
    His airy harp shall now be laid,
That he, whose heart in sorrow bleeds,
    May love through life the soothing shade.

Then maids and youths shall linger here,
    And while its sounds at distance swell,
Shall sadly seem in pity's ear
    To hear the woodland pilgrim's knell.

Remembrance oft shall haunt the shore
    When Thames in summer wreaths is drest,
And oft suspend the dashing oar,
    To bid his gentle spirit rest!

And oft, as ease and health retire
    To breezy lawn, or forest deep,
The friend shall view yon whitening spire,
    And 'mid the varied landscape weep.

But thou, who own'st that earthy bed,
    Ah! what will every dirge avail;

* See Wordsworth: *Remembrance of Collins*, p. 107.

Or tears, which love and pity shed,
　That mourn beneath the gliding sail?

Yet lives there one, whose heedless eye
　Shall scorn thy pale shrine glimmering near?
With him, sweet bard, may fancy die,
　And joy desert the blooming year.

But thou, lorn stream, whose sullen tide
　No sedge-crown'd sisters now attend,
Now waft me from the green hill's side,
　Whose cold turf hides the buried friend!

And see, the fairy valleys fade;
　Dun night has veil'd the solemn view!
Yet once again, dear parted shade,
　Meek Nature's Child, again adieu!

The genial meads, assign'd to bless
　Thy life, shall mourn thy early doom;
Their hinds and shepherd-girls shall dress,
　With simple hands, thy rural tomb.

Long, long, thy stone and pointed clay
　Shall melt the musing Briton's eyes:
O! vales and wild woods, shall he say,
　In yonder grave your Druid lies!

MARK AKENSIDE

1721–1770

From *The Pleasures of the Imagination*

                       O ye dales
Of Tyne, and ye most ancient woodlands; where,
Oft as the giant flood obliquely strides,
And his banks open, and his lawns extend,
Stops short the pleased traveller to view,
Presiding o'er the scene, some rustic tower
Founded by Norman or by Saxon hands:
O ye Northumbrian shades, which overlook
The rocky pavement and the mossy falls
Of solitary Wensbeck's limpid stream;
How gladly I recall your well-known seats,
Belov'd of old, and that delightful time
When, all alone, for many a summer's day,
I wander'd through your calm recesses, led
In silence by some powerful hand unseen.

CHRISTOPHER SMART
1722–1771

A Song to David

O Thou, that sit'st upon a throne,
With harp of high majestic tone,
  To praise the King of kings;
And voice of heaven-ascending swell,
Which, while its deeper notes excell,
  Clear, as a clarion, rings:

To bless each valley, grove, and coast,
And charm the cherubs to the post
  Of gratitude in throngs;
To keep the days on Zion's Mount,
And send the year to his account,
  With dances and with songs:

O Servant of God's holiest charge,
The minister of praise at large,
  Which thou mayst now receive;
From thy blest mansion hail and hear,
From topmost eminence appear
  To this the wreath I weave.

Great, valiant, pious, good, and clean,
Sublime, contemplative, serene,
  Strong, constant, pleasant, wise!
Bright effluence of exceeding grace;
Best man! – the swiftness and the race,
  The peril, and the prize!

Great – from the lustre of his crown,
From Samuel's horn and God's renown,
  Which is the people's voice;

For all the host, from rear to van,
Applauded and embraced the man –
  The man of God's own choice.

Valiant – the word and up he rose –
The fight – he triumphed o'er the foes,
  Whom God's just laws abhor;
And, arm'd in gallant faith, he took
Against the boaster, from the brook,
  The weapons of the war.

Pious – magnificent and grand;
'Twas he the famous temple plan'd,
  (The seraph in his soul:)
Foremost to give the Lord his dues,
Foremost to bless the welcome news,
  And foremost to condole.

Good – from Jehudah's genuine vein,
From God's best nature good in grain,
  His aspect and his heart;
To pity, to forgive, to save,
Witness En-gedi's conscious cave,
  And Shimei's blunted dart.

Clean – if perpetual prayer be pure,
And love, which could itself innure
  To fasting and to fear –
Clean in his gestures, hands, and feet,
To smite the lyre, the dance compleat,
  To play the sword and spear.

Sublime – invention ever young,
Of vast conception, tow'ring tongue,
  To God the eternal theme;
Notes from yon exaltations caught,
Unrival'd royalty of thought,
  O'er meaner strains supreme.

Contemplative – on God to fix
His musings, and above the six
   The sabbath-day he blest;
'Twas then his thoughts self-conquest prun'd,
And heavenly melancholy tun'd,
   To bless and bear the rest.

Serene – to sow the seeds of peace,
Remembring, when he watched the fleece,
   How sweetly Kidron purld –
To further knowledge, silence vice,
And plant perpetual paradise,
   When God had calmed the world.

Strong – in the Lord, who could defy
Satan, and all his powers that lie
   In sempiternal night;
And hell, and horror, and despair
Were as the lion and the bear
   To his undaunted might.

Constant – in love to God, THE TRUTH,
Age, manhood, infancy, and youth –
   To Jonathan his friend
Constant, beyond the verge of death;
And Ziba, and Mephibosheth,
   His endless fame attend.

Pleasant – and various as the year;
Man, soul, and angel, without peer,
   Priest, champion, sage and boy;
In armour, or in ephod clad,
His pomp, his piety was glad;
   Majestic was his joy.

Wise – in recovery from his fall,
Whence rose his eminence o'er all,
   Of all the most revil'd:

The light of Israel in his ways,
Wise are his precepts, prayer and praise,
  And counsel to his child.

His muse, bright angel of his verse,
Gives balm for all the thorns that pierce,
  For all the pangs that rage;
Blest light, still gaining on the gloom,
The more than Michal of his bloom,
  The Abishag of his age.

He sung of God – the mighty source
Of all things – the stupendous force
  On which all strength depends;
From whose right arm, beneath whose eyes,
All period, pow'r and enterprize
  Commences, reigns, and ends.

Angels – their ministry and meed,
Which to and fro with blessings speed,
  Or with their citterns wait;
Where Michael with his millions bows,
Where dwells the seraph and his spouse,
  The cherub and her mate.

Of man – the semblance and effect
Of God and Love – the Saint elect
  For infinite applause –
To rule the land, and briny broad,
To be laborious in his laud,
And heroes in his cause.

The world – the clustring spheres he made,
The glorious light, the soothing shade,
  Dale, champaign, grove, and hill;
The multitudinous abyss,
Where secrecy remains in bliss,
  And wisdom hides her skill.

citterns: harps.

24

Trees, plants, and flow'rs – of virtuous root;
Gem yielding blossom, yielding fruit,
  Choice gums and precious balm;
Bless ye the nosegay in the vale,
And with the sweetness of the gale
  Enrich the thankful psalm.

Of fowl – e'en ev'ry beak and wing
Which chear the winter, hail the spring,
  That live in peace or prey;
They that make music, or that mock,
The quail, the brave domestic cock,
  The raven, swan, and jay.

Of fishes – ev'ry size and shape,
Which nature frames of light escape,
  Devouring man to shun:
The shells are in the wealthy deep,
The shoals upon the surface leap,
  And love the glancing sun.

Of beasts – the beaver plods his task;
While the sleek tigers roll and bask,
  Nor yet the shades arouse;
Her cave the mining coney scoops;
Where o'er the mead the mountain stoops,
  The kids exult and brouse.

Of gems – their virtue and their price,
Which hid in earth from man's device,
  Their darts of lustre sheathe;
The jasper of the master's stamp,
The topaz blazing like a lamp
  Among the mines beneath.

Blest was the tenderness he felt
When to his graceful harp he knelt,
  And did for audience call;

When satan with his hand he quell'd,
And in serene suspence he held
    The frantic throes of Saul.

His furious foes no more malign'd
As he such melody divin'd,
    And sense and soul detain'd;
Now striking strong, now soothing soft,
He sent the godly sounds aloft,
    Or in delight refrain'd.

When up to heaven his thoughts he pil'd
From fervent lips fair Michal smil'd,
    As blush to blush she stood;
And chose herself the queen and gave
Her utmost from her heart, 'so brave,
    And plays his hymns so good'.

The pillars of the Lord are seven,
Which stand from earth to topmost heav'n;
    His wisdom drew the plan;
His WORD accomplished the design,
From biggest gem to deepest mine,
    From CHRIST enthron'd to man.

Alpha, the cause of causes, first
In station, fountain, whence the burst
    Of light, and blaze of day;
Whence bold attempt, and brave advance,
Have motion, life, and ordinance,
    And heaven itself its stay.

Gamma supports the glorious arch
On which angelic legions march,
    And is with sapphires pav'd;
Thence the fleet clouds are sent adrift,
And thence the painted folds, that lift
    The crimson veil, are wav'd.

Eta with living sculpture breathes,
With verdant carvings, flow'ry wreaths,
  Of never-wasting bloom;
In strong relief his goodly base
All instruments of labour grace,
  The trowel, spade, and loom.

Next Theta stands to the Supreme –
Who formed, in number, sign, and scheme,
  Th' illustrious lights that are;
And one address'd his saffron robe,
And one, clad in a silver globe,
  Held rule with ev'ry star.

Iota's tuned to choral hymns
Of those that fly, while he that swims
  In thankful safety lurks;
And foot, and chapitre, and niche,
The various histories enrich
  Of God's recorded works.

Sigma presents the social droves
With him that solitary roves,
  And man of all the chief;
Fair on whose face, and stately frame,
Did God impress his hallow'd name,
  For ocular belief.

OMEGA! GREATEST and the BEST,
Stands sacred to the day of rest,
  For gratitude and thought;
Which blessed the world upon his pole,
And gave the universe his goal,
  And clos'd th' infernal draught.

O DAVID, scholar of the Lord!
Such is thy science, whence reward

    chapitre: capital.

27

And infinite degree;
O strength, O sweetness, lasting ripe!
God's harp thy symbol, and thy type
    The lion and the bee!

There is but One who ne'er rebell'd,
But One by passion unimpell'd,
    By pleasures unintice't;
He from himself his semblance sent,
Grand object of his own content,
    And saw the God in CHRIST.

Tell them, I am, JEHOVA said
To MOSES; while earth heard in dread,
    And, smitten to the heart,
At once above, beneath, around,
All Nature, without voice or sound,
    Replied, 'O Lord, THOU ART.'

Thou art – to give and to confirm,
For each his talent and his term;
    All flesh thy bounties share:
Thou shalt not call thy brother fool:
The porches of the Christian school
    Are meekness, peace, and pray'r.

Open, and naked of offence,
Man's made of mercy, soul, and sense;
    God armed the snail and wilk;
Be good to him that pulls thy plough;
Due food and care, due rest, allow
    For her that yields thee milk.

Rise up before the hoary head,
And God's benign commandment dread,
    Which says thou shalt not die:

wilk: whelk.

28

'Not as I will, but as Thou wilt',
Prayed He, whose conscience knew no guilt;
  With Whose bless'd pattern vie.

Use all thy passions! – love is thine,
And joy, and jealousy divine;
  Thine hope's eternal fort,
And care thy leisure to disturb,
With fear concupiscence to curb,
  And rapture to transport.

Act simply, as occasion asks;
Put mellow wine in season'd casks;
  Till not with ass and bull:
Remember thy baptismal bond;
Keep from commixtures foul and fond,
  Nor work thy flax with wool.

Distribute: pay the Lord his tithe,
And make the widow's heart-strings blithe;
  Resort with those that weep:
As you from all and each expect,
For all and each thy love direct,
  And render as you reap.

The slander and its bearer spurn,
And propagating praise sojourn
  To make thy welcome last;
Turn from Old Adam to the New;
By hope futurity pursue;
  Look upwards to the past.

Controul thine eye, salute success,
Honour the wiser, happier bless,
  And for their neighbour feel;
Grutch not of mammon and his leaven,
Work emulation up to heaven
  By knowledge and by zeal.

CHRISTOPHER SMART

O DAVID, highest in the list
Of worthies, on God's ways insist,
  The genuine word repeat:
Vain are the documents of men,
And vain the flourish of the pen
  That keeps the fool's conceit.

PRAISE above all – for praise prevails;
Heap up the measure, load the scales,
  And good to goodness add:
The generous soul her saviour aids,
But peevish obloquy degrades;
  The Lord is great and glad.

For ADORATION all the ranks
Of angels yield eternal thanks,
  And DAVID in the midst;
With God's good poor, which, last and least
In man's esteem, thou to thy feast,
  O blessed bridegroom, bidst.

For ADORATION seasons change,
And order, truth, and beauty range,
  Adjust, attract, and fill:
The grass the polyanthus cheques;
And polish'd porphyry reflects,
  By the descending rill.

Rich almonds colour to the prime
For ADORATION; tendrils climb,
  And fruit-trees pledge their gems;
And Ivis, with her gorgeous vest,
Builds for her eggs her cunning nest,
  And bell-flowers bow their stems.

With vinous syrup cedars spout;
From rocks pure honey gushing out,
  Ivis: humming-bird.

30

For ADORATION springs:
All scenes of painting croud the map
Of nature; to the mermaid's pap
  The scaled infant clings.

The spotted ounce and playsome cubs
Run rustling 'mongst the flow'ring shrubs,
  And lizards feed the moss;
For ADORATION beasts embark
While waves upholding halcyon's ark
  No longer roar and toss.

While Israel sits beneath his fig,
With coral root and amber sprig
  The wean'd advent'rer sports;
Where to the palm the jasmin cleaves,
For ADORATION 'mongst the leaves
  The gale his peace reports.

Increasing days their reign exalt,
Nor in the pink and mottled vault
  The opposing spirits tilt;
And, by the coasting reader spied,
The silverlings and crusions glide
  For ADORATION gilt.

For ADORATION rip'ning canes,
And cocoa's purest milk detains
  The western pilgrim's staff;
Where rain in clasping boughs inclos'd,
And vines with oranges dispos'd,
  Embow'r the social laugh.

Now labour his reward receives,
For ADORATION counts his sheaves;
  To peace, her bounteous prince;

ounce: leopard. *crusions*: carp.

31

The nectarine his strong tint imbibes,
And apples of ten thousand tribes,
   And quick peculiar quince.

The wealthy crops of whit'ning rice,
'Mongst thyine woods and groves of spice,
   For ADORATION grow;
And, marshall'd in the fenced land,
The peaches and pomegranates stand,
   Where wild carnations blow.

The laurels with the winter strive;
The crocus burnishes alive
   Upon the snow-clad earth:
For ADORATION myrtles stay
To keep the garden from dismay,
   And bless the sight from dearth.

The pheasant shows his pompous neck;
And ermine, jealous of a speck,
   With fear eludes offence:
The sable, with his glossy pride,
For ADORATION is descried,
   Where frosts the waves condense.

The chearful holly, pensive yew,
And holy thorn, their trim renew;
   The squirrel hoards his nuts:
All creatures batten o'er their stores,
And careful nature all her doors
   For ADORATION shuts.

For ADORATION, David's Psalms
Lift up the heart to deeds of alms;
   And he, who kneels and chants,
Prevails his passions to controul,
Finds meat and med'cine to the soul,
   Which for translation pants.

thyine: sweet.

For ADORATION, beyond match,
The scholar bulfinch aims to catch
    The soft flute's iv'ry touch;
And, careless, on the hazel spray,
The daring redbreast keeps at bay
    The damsel's greedy clutch.

For ADORATION, in the skies,
The Lord's philosopher espies
    The Dog, the Ram, and Rose;
The planet's ring, Orion's sword;
Nor is his greatness less ador'd
    In the vile worm that glows.

For ADORATION on the strings
The western breezes work their wings,
    The captive ear to sooth. –
Hark! 'tis a voice – how still, and small –
That makes the cataracts to fall,
    Or bids the sea be smooth!

For ADORATION, incense comes
From bezoar, and Arabian gums,
    And on the civet's furr:
But as for prayer, or e're it faints,
Far better is the breath of saints
    Than galbanum or myrrh.

For ADORATION from the down
Of dam'sins to th' anana's crown,
    God sends to tempt the taste;
And while the luscious zest invites,
The sense, that in the scene delights,
    Commands desire be chaste.

bezoar: substance found in the stomachs of ruminants. *galbanum*: a resin used in incense. *anana*: pineapple.

For ADORATION, all the paths
Of grace are open, all the baths,
   Of purity refresh;
And all the rays of glory beam
To deck the man of God's esteem,
   Who triumphs o'er the flesh.

For ADORATION, in the dome
Of CHRIST, the sparrow's find an home;
   And on his olives perch:
The swallow also dwells with thee,
O man of God's humility,
   Within his Saviour CHURCH.

Sweet is the dew that falls betimes,
And drops upon the leafy limes;
   Sweet, Hermon's fragrant air:
Sweet is the lilly's silver bell,
And sweet the wakeful tapers smell
   That watch for early pray'r.

Sweet the young nurse, with love intense,
Which smiles o'er sleeping innocence;
   Sweet when the lost arrive:
Sweet the musician's ardour beats,
While his vague mind's in quest of sweets,
   The choicest flow'rs to hive.

Sweeter, in all the strains of love,
The language of thy turtle dove,
   Pair'd to thy swelling chord;
Sweeter, with every grace endu'd,
The glory of thy gratitude,
   Respir'd unto the Lord.

Strong is the horse upon his speed;
Strong in pursuit the rapid glede,

   glede: hawk.

34

Which makes at once his game:
Strong the tall ostrich on the ground;
Strong through the turbulent profound
    Shoots xiphias to his aim.

Strong is the lion – like a coal
His eyeball – like a bastion's mole
    His chest against the foes:
Strong, the gier-eagle on his sail,
Strong against tide, th' enormous whale
    Emerges as he goes.

But stronger still, in earth and air,
And in the sea, the man of pray'r,
    And far beneath the tide;
And in the seat to faith assign'd,
Where ask is have, where seek is find,
    Where knock is open wide.

Beauteous the fleet before the gale;
Beauteous the multitudes in mail,
    Ranked arms and crested heads:
Beauteous the garden's umbrage mild,
Walk, water, meditated wild,
    And all the bloomy beds.

Beauteous the moon full on the lawn;
And beauteous, when the veil's withdrawn,
    The virgin to her spouse:
Beauteous the temple, deck'd and fill'd,
When to the heav'n of heav'ns they build
    Their heart-directed vows.

Beauteous, yea beauteous more than these,
The shepherd king upon his knees,
    For his momentous trust;
With wish of infinite conceit,

    xiphias: swordfish.

35

For man, beast, mute, the small and great,
  And prostrate dust to dust.

Precious the bounteous widow's mite;
And precious, for extream delight,
  The largess from the churl:
Precious the ruby's blushing blaze,
And alba's blest imperial rays,
  And pure cerulean pearl.

Precious the penitential tear;
And precious is the sigh sincere;
  Acceptable to God:
And precious are the winning flow'rs,
In gladsome Israel's feast of bow'rs,
  Bound on the hallow'd sod.

More precious that diviner part
Of David, even the Lord's own heart,
  Great, beautiful, and new:
In all things where it was intent,
In all extreams, in each event,
  Proof – answ'ring true to true.

Glorious the sun in mid career;
Glorious th' assembled fires appear;
  Glorious the comet's train:
Glorious the trumpet and alarm;
Glorious th' almighty stretched-out arm;
  Glorious th' enraptur'd main:

Glorious the northern lights a-stream;
Glorious the song, when God's the theme;
  Glorious the thunder's roar:
Glorious hosannah from the den;
Glorious the catholic amen;
  Glorious the martyr's gore:

alba: alb.

36

Glorious, – more glorious, is the crown
Of Him that brought salvation down,
  By meekness, called thy Son:
Thou at stupendous truth believ'd; –
And now the matchless deed's atchiev'd,
  DETERMINED, DARED, and DONE.

From *Jubilate Agno*

For I will consider my Cat Jeoffry.

For he is the servant of the Living God, duly and daily serving him.

For at the first glance of the glory of God in the East he worships in his way.

For is this done by wreathing his body seven times round with elegant quickness.

For then he leaps up to catch the musk, which is the blessing of God upon his prayer.

For he rolls upon prank to work it in.

For having done duty and received blessing he begins to consider himself.

For this he performs in ten degrees.

For first he looks upon his fore-paws to see if they are clean.

For secondly he kicks up behind to clear away there.

For thirdly he works it upon stretch with the fore-paws extended.

For fourthly he sharpens his paws by wood.

For fifthly he washes himself.

For sixthly he rolls upon wash.

For Seventhly he fleas himself, that he may not be interrupted upon the beat.

For Eighthly he rubs himself against a post.

For Ninthly he looks up for his instructions.

For Tenthly he goes in quest of food.

For having consider'd God and himself he will consider his neighbour.

For if he meets another cat he will kiss her in kindness.

For when he takes his prey he plays with it to give it chance.

For one mouse in seven escapes by his dallying.

For when his day's work is done his business more properly begins.

For keeps the Lord's watch in the night against the adversary.

For he counteracts the powers of darkness by his electrical skin & glaring eyes.

For he counteracts the Devil, who is death, by brisking about the life.

For in his morning orisons he loves the sun and the sun loves him.

For he is of the tribe of Tiger.

For the Cherub Cat is a term of the Angel Tiger.

For he has the subtlety and hissing of a serpent, which in goodness he suppresses.

For he will not do destruction, if he is well-fed, neither will he spit without provocation.

For he purrs in thankfulness, when God tells him he's a good Cat.

For he is an instrument for the children to learn benevolence upon.

For every house is incompleat without him & a blessing is lacking in the spirit.

For the Lord commanded Moses concerning the cats at the departure of the Children of Israel from Egypt.

For every family had one cat at least in the bag.

For the English Cats are the best in Europe.

For he is the cleanest in the use of his fore-paws of any quadrupede.

For the dexterity of his defence is an instance of the love of God to him exceedingly.

For he is the quickest to his mark of any creature.

For he is tenacious of his point.

For he is a mixture of gravity and waggery.

For he knows that God is his Saviour.

For there is nothing sweeter than his peace when at rest.

For there is nothing brisker than his life when in motion.

For he is of the Lord's poor and so indeed is he called by benevolence perpetually – Poor Jeoffry! poor Jeoffry! the rat has bit thy throat.

For I bless the name of the Lord Jesus that Jeoffry is better.

For the divine spirit comes about his body to sustain it in compleat cat.

For his tongue is exceeding pure so that it has in purity what it wants in musick.

For he is docile and can learn certain things.

For he can set up with gravity which is patience upon approbation.

For he can fetch and carry, which is patience in employment.

For he can jump over a stick which is patience upon proof positive.

For he can spraggle upon waggle at the word of command.

For he can jump from an eminence into his master's bosom.

For he can catch the cork and toss it again.

For he is hated by the hypocrite and miser.

For the former is affraid of detection.

For the latter refuses the charge.

For he camels his back to bear the first notion of business.

For he is good to think on, if a man would express himself neatly.

For he made a great figure in Egypt for his signal services.

For he killed the Icneumon-rat very pernicious by land.

For his ears are so acute that they sting again.

For from this proceeds the passing quickness of his attention.

For by stroaking of him I have found out electricity.

For I perceive God's light about him both wax and fire.

For the Electrical fire is the spiritual substance, which God sends from heaven to sustain the bodies both of man and beast.

For God has blessed him in the variety of his movements.

For, tho he cannot fly, he is an excellent clamberer.

For his motions upon the face of the earth are more than
    any other quadrupede.
For he can tread to all the measures upon the musick.
For he can swim for life.
For he can creep.

WILLIAM COWPER

1731–1800

From *The Task*

I was a stricken deer, that left the herd
Long since; with many an arrow deep infix'd
My panting side was charg'd when I withdrew
To seek a tranquil death in distant shades.
There was I found by one who had himself
Been hurt by th' archers. In his side he bore,
And in his hands and feet, the cruel scars.
With gentle force soliciting the darts,
He drew them forth, and heal'd, and bade me live.
Since then, with few associates, in remote
And silent woods I wander, far from those
My former partners of the peopled scene;
With few associates, and not wishing more.
Here much I ruminate, as much I may,
With other views of men and manners now
Than once, and others of a life to come.
I see that all are wand'rers, gone astray
Each in his own delusions; they are lost
In chase of fancied happiness, still woo'd
And never won. Dream after dream ensues;
And still they dream that they shall still succeed,
And still are disappointed. Rings the world
With the vain stir. I sum up half mankind,
And add two thirds of the remaining half,
And find the total of their hopes and fears
Dreams, empty dreams. The million flit as gay
As if created only like the fly,
That spreads his motley wings in th' eye of noon,
To sport their season, and be seen no more.

Lines Written During a Period of Insanity

Hatred and vengeance, my eternal portion,
Scarce can endure delay of execution,
Wait, with impatient readiness, to seize my
                Soul in a moment.

Damn'd below Judas: more abhorr'd than he was,
Who for a few pence sold his holy Master.
Twice betrayed Jesus me, the last delinquent,
                Deems the profanest.

Man disavows, and Deity disowns me:
Hell might afford my miseries a shelter;
Therefore hell keeps her ever hungry mouths all
                Bolted against me.

Hard lot! encompass'd with a thousand dangers;
Weary, faint, trembling with a thousand terrors;
I'm called, if vanquish'd, to receive a sentence
                Worse than Abiram's.

Him the vindictive rod of angry justice
Sent quick and howling to the centre headlong;
I, fed with judgment, in a fleshly tomb, am
                Buried above ground.

To the Nightingale

WHICH THE AUTHOR HEARD SING ON
NEW-YEAR'S DAY, 1792

    Whence is it, that amazed I hear
        From yonder wither'd spray,
    This foremost morn of all the year,
        The melody of May?

And why, since thousands would be proud
  Of such a favour shown,
Am I selected from the crowd,
  To witness it alone?

Sing'st thou, sweet Philomel, to me,
  For that I also long
Have practis'd in the groves like thee,
  Though not like thee in song?

Or sing'st thou rather under force
  Of some divine command,
Commission'd to presage a course
  Of happier days at hand?

Thrice welcome then! for many a long
  And joyless year have I,
As thou today, put forth my song
  Beneath a wintry sky.

But thee no wintry skies can harm,
  Who only need'st to sing,
To make ev'n January charm,
  And ev'ry season Spring.

Yardley Oak

Survivor sole, and hardly such, of all
That once liv'd here thy brethren, at my birth
(Since which I number three-score winters past)
A shatter'd veteran, hollow-trunk'd perhaps
As now, and with excoriate forks deform,
Relicts of ages! Could a mind, imbued
With truth from heav'n, created thing adore,
I might with rev'rence kneel and worship thee.
  It seems idolatry with some excuse

When our forefather Druids in their oaks
Imagin'd sanctity. The conscience yet
Unpurified by an authentic act
Of amnesty, the meed of blood divine,
Lov'd not the light, but gloomy into gloom
Of thickest shades, like Adam after taste
Of fruit proscrib'd, as to a refuge, fled.

   Thou wast a bauble once; a cup and ball,
Which babes might play with; and the thievish jay
Seeking her food, with ease might have purloin'd
The auburn nut that held thee, swallowing down
Thy yet close-folded latitude of boughs
And all thine embryo vastness, at a gulp.
But Fate thy growth decreed: autumnal rains
Beneath thy parent tree mellow'd the soil
Design'd thy cradle, and a skipping deer,
With pointed hoof dibbling the glebe, prepar'd
The soft receptacle in which secure
Thy rudiments should sleep the winter through.

   So Fancy dreams – Disprove it, if ye can,
Ye reas'ners broad awake, whose busy search
Of argument, employ'd too oft amiss,
Sifts half the pleasures of short life away.

   Thou fell'st mature, and in the loamy clod
Swelling, with vegetative force instinct
Didst burst thine egg, as theirs the fabled Twins,
Now stars; two lobes, protruding, pair'd exact:
A leaf succeeded, and another leaf,
And all the elements thy puny growth
Fost'ring propitious, thou becam'st a twig.

   Who liv'd when thou wast such? Oh couldst thou speak,
As in Dodona once thy kindred trees
Oracular, I would not curious ask
The future, best unknown, but at thy mouth
Inquisitive, the less ambiguous past.

   By thee I might correct, erroneous oft,
The clock of history, facts and events

glebe: soil.

Timing more punctual, unrecorded facts
Recov'ring, and misstated setting right –
Desp'rate attempt, till trees shall speak again!
    Time made thee what thou wast – King of the woods;
And Time hath made thee what thou art – a cave
For owls to roost in. Once thy spreading boughs
O'erhung the champain; and the numerous flock
That graz'd it stood beneath that ample cope
Uncrowded, yet safe-shelter'd from the storm.
No flock frequents thee now. Thou hast outliv'd
Thy popularity and art become
(Unless verse rescue thee awhile) a thing
Forgotten, as the foliage of thy youth.
    While thus through all the stages thou hast push'd
Of treeship, first a seedling hid in grass,
Then twig, then sapling, and, as century roll'd
Slow after century, a giant bulk
Of girth enormous, with moss-cushioned root
Upheav'd above the soil, and sides imboss'd
With prominent wens globose, till at the last
The rottenness, which Time is charg'd t' inflict
On other mighty ones, found also thee –
What exhibitions various hath the world
Witness'd of mutability in all
That we account most durable below!
Change is the diet, on which all subsist
Created changeable, and change at last
Destroys them. – Skies uncertain now the heat
Transmitting cloudless, and the solar beam
Now quenching in a boundless sea of clouds, –
Calm and alternate storm, moisture and drought,
Invigorate by turns the springs of life
In all that live, plant, animal, and man,
And in conclusion mar them. Nature's threads,
Fine passing thought, ev'n in her coarsest works,
Delight in agitation, yet sustain
The force that agitates, not unimpaired,
But, worn by frequent impulse, to the cause

Of their best tone their dissolution owe.
  Thought cannot spend itself, comparing still
The great and little of thy lot, thy growth
From almost nullity into a state
Of matchless grandeur, and declension thence
Slow into such magnificent decay.
Time was, when, settling on thy leaf, a fly
Could shake thee to the root – and time has been
When tempests could not. At thy firmest age
Thou hadst within thy bole solid contents
That might have ribb'd the sides or plank'd the deck
Of some flagg'd admiral; and tortuous arms,
The ship-wright's darling treasure, didst present
To the four-quarter'd winds, robust and bold,
Warp'd into tough knee-timber, many a load.
But the axe spar'd thee; in those thriftier days
Oaks fell not, hewn by thousands, to supply
The bottomless demands of contest wag'd
For senatorial honours. Thus to Time
The task was left to whittle thee away
With his sly scythe, whose ever-nibbling edge
Noiseless, an atom and an atom more
Disjoining from the rest, has, unobserv'd,
Achiev'd a labour, which had, far and wide,
(By man perform'd) made all the forest ring.
  Embowell'd now, and of thy ancient self
Possessing naught but the scoop'd rind, that seems
An huge throat calling to the clouds for drink,
Which it would give in riv'lets to thy root,
Thou temptest none, but rather much forbid'st
The feller's toil, which thou couldst ill requite.
Yet is thy root sincere, sound as the rock,
A quarry of stout spurs and knotted fangs,
Which, crooked into a thousand whimsies, clasp
The stubborn soil, and hold thee still erect.
  So stands a kingdom, whose foundations yet
Fail not, in virtue and in wisdom laid,
Though all the superstructure, by the tooth

Pulveriz'd of venality, a shell
Stands now, and semblance only of itself.
    Thine arms have left thee. Winds have rent them off
Long since, and rovers of the forest wild
With bow and shaft have burnt them. Some have left
A splinter'd stump bleach'd to a snowy white;
And some memorial none where once they grew.
Yet life still lingers in thee, and puts forth
Proof not contemptible of what she can,
Even where death predominates. The spring
Thee finds not less alive to her sweet force
Than yonder upstarts of the neighbour wood,
So much thy juniors, who their birth receiv'd
Half a millennium since the date of thine.
    But since, although well qualified by age
To teach, no spirit dwells in thee, nor voice
May be expected from thee, seated here
On thy distorted root, with hearers none
Or prompter, save the scene, I will perform
Myself the oracle, and will discourse
In my own ear such matter as I may.
Thou, like myself, hast stage by stage attain'd
Life's wintry bourn; thou, after many years,
I after few; but few or many prove
A span in retrospect; for I can touch
With my least finger's end my own decease
And with extended thumb my natal hour,
And hadst thou also skill in measurement
As I, the past would seem as short to thee.
Evil and few – said Jacob – at an age
Thrice mine, and few and evil, I may think
The Prediluvian race, whose buxom youth
Endured two centuries, accounted theirs.
'Short-lived as foliage is the race of man.
The wind shakes down the leaves, the budding grove
Soon teems with others, and in spring they grow.
So pass mankind. One generation meets
Its destin'd period, and a new succeeds.'

Such was the tender but undue complaint
Of the Mæonian in old time; for who
Would drawl out centuries in tedious strife
Severe with mental and corporeal ill
And would not rather choose a shorter race
To glory, a few decades here below?
      One man alone, the Father of us all,
Drew not his life from woman; never gaz'd,
With mute unconsciousness of what he saw
On all around him; learn'd not by degrees,
Nor owed articulation to his ear;
But, moulded by his Maker into Man
At once, upstood intelligent, survey'd
All creatures, with precision understood
Their purport, uses, properties, assign'd
To each his name significant, and, fill'd
With love and wisdom, render'd back to heaven
In praise harmonious the first air he drew.
He was excus'd the penalties of dull
Minority. No tutor charg'd his hand
With the thought-tracing quill, or tasked his mind
With problems; History, not wanted yet,
Lean'd on her elbow, watching Time, whose course,
Eventful, should supply her with a theme.

The Castaway

Obscurest night involv'd the sky,
   Th' Atlantic billows roar'd,
When such a destin'd wretch as I,
   Wash'd headlong from on board,
Of friends, of hope, of all bereft,
His floating home for ever left.

No braver chief could Albion boast
   Than he with whom he went,

Nor ever ship left Albion's coast,
  With warmer wishes sent.
He lov'd them both, but both in vain,
Nor him beheld, nor her again.

Not long beneath the whelming brine,
  Expert to swim, he lay;
Nor soon he felt his strength decline,
  Or courage die away;
But wag'd with death a lasting strife,
Supported by despair of life.

He shouted: nor his friends had fail'd
  To check the vessel's course,
But so the furious blast prevail'd,
  That, pitiless perforce,
They left their outcast mate behind,
And scudded still before the wind.

Some succour yet they could afford;
  And, such as storms allow,
The cask, the coop, the floated cord,
  Delay'd not to bestow.
But he (they knew) nor ship, nor shore,
Whate'er they gave, should visit more.

Nor, cruel as it seem'd, could he
  Their haste himself condemn,
Aware that flight, in such a sea,
  Alone could rescue them;
Yet bitter felt it still to die
Deserted, and his friends so nigh.

He long survives, who lives an hour
  In ocean, self-upheld;
And so long he, with unspent pow'r,
  His destiny repell'd;
And ever, as the minutes flew,
Entreated help, or cried – Adieu!

At length, his transient respite past,
  His comrades, who before
Had heard his voice in ev'ry blast,
  Could catch the sound no more.
For then, by toil subdued, he drank
The stifling wave, and then he sank.

No poet wept him: but the page
  Of narrative sincere,
That tells his name, his worth, his age.
  Is wet with Anson's tear.
And tears by bards or heroes shed
Alike immortalize the dead.

I therefore purpose not, or dream,
  Descanting on his fate,
To give the melancholy theme
  A more enduring date:
But misery still delights to trace
Its 'semblance in another's case.

No voice divine the storm allay'd,
  No light propitious shone;
When, snatch'd from all effectual aid,
  We perish'd, each alone:
But I beneath a rougher sea,
And whelm'd in deeper gulphs than he.

JAMES MACPHERSON
1736-1796

From *The Six Bards*

FIRST BARD

Night is dull and dark,
The clouds rest on the hills;
No star with twinkling beam,
No moon looks from the skies.
I hear the blast in the wood,
But distant and dull I hear it.
The stream of the valley murmurs,
Low is its murmur too.
From the tree at the grave of the dead,
The lonely screech-owl groans.
I see a dim form on the plain,
'Tis a ghost! it fades, it flies;
Some dead shall pass this way.
From the lowly hut of the hill
The distant dog is howling;
The stag lies by the mountain-well,
The hind is at his side;
She hears the wind in his horns,
She starts, but lies again.
The roe is in the cleft of the rock:
The heath-cock's head beneath his wing.
No beast, no bird is abroad,
But the owl, and the howling fox;
She on the leafless tree,
He on the cloudy hill.
Dark, panting, trembling, sad,
The traveller has lost his way;
Through shrubs, through thorns he goes,
Beside the gurgling rills;
He fears the rock and the pool,
He fears the ghost of the night.

The old tree groans to the blast;
The falling branch resounds.
The wind drives the clung thorn
　Along the sighing grass;
He shakes amid the night.
Dark, dusky, howling is night,
Cloudy, windy, full of ghosts;
The dead are abroad; my friends
Receive me from the night.

THOMAS CHATTERTON

1752–1770

Song of the Three Minstrels

From Ælla

FIRST MINSTREL

The budding flowerets blushes at the light,
   The mees be sprinkled with the yellow hue;
In daisied mantles is the mountain dight,
   The nesh young cowslip bendeth with the dew;
The trees enleafèd, unto heaven straught,
When gentle winds do blow, to whistling din is brought.

The evening comes, and brings the dew along;
   The ruddy welkin shineth to the eyne;
Around the ale-stake minstrels sing the song,
   Young ivy round the doorpost do entwine;
I lay me on the grass; yet, to my will,
Albeit all is fair, there lacketh something still.

SECOND MINSTREL

So Adam thoughten when, in Paradise,
   All heaven and earth did homage to his mind;
In woman only mannes pleasure lies,
   As instruments of joy were made the kind.
Go, take a wife unto thine arms, and see
Winter, and barren hills, will have a charm for thee.

THIRD MINSTREL

When Autumn bleak and sunburnt do appear,
   With his gold hand gilding the falling leaf,
Bringing up Winter to fulfil the year,
   Bearing upon his back the ripèd sheaf,

mees: meadows. *nesh*: tender. *straught*: stretched.

When all the hills with woody seed is white,
When lightning-fires and lemes do meet from far the sight;

    When the fair apple, red as even sky,
        Do bend the tree unto the fruitful ground.
    When juicy pears, and berries of black dye,
        Do dance in air, and call the eyes around;
Then, be the even foul, or even fair,
Methinks my hartys joy is steyncèd with some care.

SECOND MINSTREL

    Angels be wrought to be of neither kind,
        Angels alone from hot desire be free,
    There is a somewhat ever in the mind,
        That, without woman, cannot stillèd be
No saint in cell, but, having blood and tere,
Do find the sprite to joy on sight woman fair.

    Women be made, not for themselves, but man,
        Bone of his bone, and child of his desire;
From an ynutyle member first began,
        Y-wrought with much of water, little fire;
Therefore they seek the fire of love to heat
The milkiness of kind, and make themselves complete.

    Albeit, without women, men were peers
        To savage kind, and would but live to slay;
But woman oft the sprite of peace so cheers,
        Tochelod in angels' joy they angels be.
Go, take thee quickly to thy bed a wife,
Be banned, or blessèd hie, in proving marriage life.

lemes: gleams. *hartys*: heart's. *steyncèd*: mingled. *tere*: muscle. *tochelod*: endowed.

Minstrel's Song
From *Ælla*

Oh! sing unto my roundelay;
  Oh! drop the briny tear with me;
Dance no more at holiday;
  Like a running river be.
    My love is dead,
    Gone to his death-bed,
    All under the willow-tree.

Black his hair as the winter night,
  White his rode as the summer snow,
Red his face as the morning light;
  Cold he lies in the grave below.
    My love is dead,
    Gone to his death-bed,
    All under the willow-tree.

Sweet his tongue as the throstle's note,
  Quick in dance as thought can be,
Deft his tabour, cudgel stout;
  Oh! he lies by the willow-tree.
    My love is dead,
    Gone to his death-bed,
    All under the willow-tree.

Hark! the raven flaps his wing,
  In the briared dell below;
Hark! the death-owl loud doth sing
  To the night-mares, as they go.
    My love is dead,
    Gone to his death-bed,
    All under the willow-tree.

See! the white moon shines on high,
  Whiter is my true love's shroud,

Whiter than the morning sky,
  Whiter than the evening cloud.
    My love is dead,
    Gone to his death-bed,
    All under the willow-tree.

Here, upon my true love's grave,
  Shall the barren flowers be laid;
Not one holy saint to save
  All the celness of a maid.
    My love is dead,
    Gone to his death-bed,
    All under the willow-tree.

With my hands I'll dente the briars,
  Round his holy corse to gre,
Elfin fairy, light your fires,
  Here my body still shall be.
    My love is dead,
    Gone to his death-bed,
    All under the willow-tree.

Come, with acorn-cup and thorn,
  Drain my hartys blood away;
Life and all its good I scorn,
  Dance by night, or feast by day.
    My love is dead,
    Gone to his death-bed,
    All under the willow-tree.

Water-witches, crowned with reytes,
  Bear me to your lethal tide.
I die! I come! my true love waits; –
  Thus the damsel spake and died.

---

celness: coldness. *dente*: fasten. *gre*: grow. *reytes*: water-flags.

Eclogue the Third

A MAN, A WOMAN, SIR ROGER

Would'st thou know nature in her better part?
 Go, search the huts and bordels of the hind;
If they have any, it is rough-made art,
 In them you see the naked form of kind;
Haveth your mind a liking of a mind?
 Would it know everything, as it might be?
Would it hear phrase of the vulgar from the hind,
 Without wiseacre words and knowledge free?
If so, read this, which I disporting penned,
If naught beside, its rhyme may it commend.

Man. But whither, fair maid, do you go?
  O where do you bend your way?
 I will know whither you go,
  I will not be answered nay.

Woman. To Robin and Nell, all down in the dell,
  To help them at making of hay.

Man. Sir Roger, the parson, have hired me there,
  Come, come, let us trip it away,
 We'll work and we'll sing, and we'll drink of strong
  beer,
 As long as the merry summer's day.

Woman. How hard is my doom to wurch!
  Much is my woe:
 Dame Agnes, who lies in the church
  With birlette gold,
 With gilded aumeres, strong, untold,
 What was she more than me, to be so?

Man. I see Sir Roger from afar,
   Tripping over the lea;
  I ask why the loverd's son
   Is more than me.

bordels: cottages. *wurch*: work. *birlette*: hood. *aumeres*: robes. *loverd's*:
lord's.

Sir Roger. The sultry sun doth hie apace his wain,
  From every beam a seed of life do fall;
Quickly scille up the hay upon the plain,
  Methinks the cocks beginneth to grow tall.
This is alyche our doom; the great, the small,
  Must wither and be dried by deathis dart.
See! the sweet floweret hath no sweet at all;
  It with the rank weed beareth equal part.
The coward, warrior, and the wise be blent,
Alyche to dry away with those they did lament.

Man.   All-a-boon, Sir Priest, all-a-boon!
By your priestship, now say unto me;
Sir Gaufrid the knight, who liveth hard by,
Why should he than me be more great,
In honour, knighthood, and estate?

Sir Roger. Attourne thine eyes around this hayed mee;
  Carefully look around the chaper dell
An answer to thy barganette here see,
  This withered floweret will a lesson tell;
Arist, it blew, it flourished, and did well,
  Looking disdainfully on the neighbour green;
Yet with the deigned green its glory fell,
  Eftsoon it shrank upon the day-burnt plain,
Did not its look, whilèst it there did stand,
To crop it in the bud move some dread hand?
  Such is the way of life; the loverd's ente
   Moveth the robber him therefor to slea;
  If thou hast ease, the shadow of content,
   Believe the truth, there's none more haile
    than thee.
  Thou workest; well, can that a trouble be?
   Sloth more would jade thee than the rough-
    est day.

scille: gather. *alyche*: alike. *all-a-boon*: favour. *chaper*: dry, thirsty. *barganette*: song. *arist*: risen. *deigned*: disdained. *ente*: purse. *slea*: slay. *haile*: happy.

Could'st thou the hidden part of soulès see,
    Thou would'st eftsoon see truth in what I
    say.
But let me hear thy way of life, and then
Hear thou from me the lives of other men.

Man.   I rise with the sun,
          Like him to drive the wain,
        And ere my work is done,
          I sing a song or twain.
      I follow the plough-tail,
      With a long jubb of ale.

        But of the maidens oh!
          It lacketh not to tell;
        Sir Priest might not cry woe,
          Could his bull do as well.
      I dance the best heideignes,
      And foil the wisest feygnes.

        On every saint's high-day
          With the minstrel am I seen,
       All a-footing it away
          With maidens on the green.
      But oh! I wish to be more great
      But oh! I wish to be more great
      In glory, tenure, and estate.

Sir Roger. Hast thou not seen a tree upon a hill,
        Whose unlist branches reachen far to sight?
    When furious tempests do the heaven fill,
        It shaketh dire, in dole and much affright:
    Whilst the dwarf floweret, with humility dight,
        Standeth unhurt, unquashèd by the storm.
        Such is a picte of life; the man of might
        Is tempest-chafed, his woe great as his form;

jubb: bottle. *heideignes*: country dances. *feygnes*: feints. *unlist*: un-
bounded. *picte*: picture.

Thyself, a floweret of a small account,
Wouldst harder feel the wind, as thou didst
    higher mount.

Songe of Seyncte Warburghe

When king Kynghill in his hand
Held the sceptre of this land,
Shining star of Christès light,
The murky mists of pagan night
    'Gan to scatter far and wide.
Then Saint Warburghe he arose,
Doffed his honours and fine clothes;
Preaching his Lord Jesus' name,
To the land of Wessex came,
    Where black Severn rolls his tide.

Strong in faithfulness, he trod
O'er the waters like a god,
Till he gained the distant hecke,
In whose banks his staff did stick,
    Witness to the miracle.
Then he preachèd night and day,
And set many in right way.
This good staff great wonders wrought,
More than guessed by mortal thought,
    Or than mortal tongue can tell.

Then the folk a bridge did make
O'er the stream unto the hecke,
All of wood eke long and wide,
Pride and glory of the tide;
    Which in time did fall away.
Then earl Leof he bespedde
This great river from his bed,

becke: height. *bespedde*: turned away.

60

THOMAS CHATTERTON

Round his castle for to run;
'Twas in truth an ancient one,
    But war and time will all decay.

Now again, with bremie force,
Severn, in his ancient course,
Rolls his rapid stream along,
With a sable swift and strong,
    Moreying many an oaky wood.
We, the men of Bristol town,
Have y-reerd this bridge of stone,
Wishing each that it may last
Till the date of days be past,
    Standing where the other stood.

bremie: furious, strong. *sable*: darkness. *moreying*: rooting up. *y-reerd*:
built.

61

GEORGE CRABBE

1754-1834

From *The World of Dreams*

I sail the sea, I walk the land;
   In all the world am I alone:
Silent I pace the sea-worn sand,
   Silent I view the princely throne;
I listen heartless for the tone
   Of winds and waters, but in vain;
Creation dies without a groan!
   And I without a hope remain!

Unnumber'd riches I behold,
   Glories untasted I survey:
My heart is sick, my bosom cold,
   Friends! neighbours! kindred! where are they?
In the sad, last, long, endless day?
   When I can neither pray nor weep,
Doom'd o'er the sleeping world to stray,
   And not to die, and not to sleep.

Beside the summer sea I stand,
   Where the slow billows swelling shine:
How beautiful this pearly sand,
   That waves, and winds, and years refine:
Be this delicious quiet mine!
   The joy of youth! so sweet before,
When I could thus my frame recline,
   And watch th' entangled weeds ashore.

Yet, I remember not that sea,
   That other shore on yonder side:
Between them narrow bound must be,
   If equal rise the opposing tide –
Lo! lo! they rise – and I abide

The peril of the meeting flood:
Away, away, my footsteps slide –
    I pant upon the clinging mud!

Oh let me now possession take
    Of this – it cannot be a dream.
Yes! now the soul must be awake –
    These pleasures are – they do not seem.
And is it true? Oh joy extreme!
    All whom I loved, and thought them dead,
Far down in Lethe's flowing stream,
    And, with them, life's best pleasures fled:

Yes, many a tear for them I shed –
    Tears that relieve the anxious breast;
And now, by heavenly favour led,
    We meet – and One, the fairest, best,
Among them – ever-welcome guest!
    Within the room, that seem'd destroyed –
This room endear'd, and still possess'd,
    By this dear party still enjoy'd.

Speak to me! speak! that I may know
    I am thus happy! – dearest, speak!
Those smiles that haunt fond memory show!
    Joy makes us doubtful, wavering, weak;
But yet 'tis joy – And all I seek
    Is mine! What glorious day is this!
Now let me bear with spirit meek
    An hour of pure and perfect bliss.

But do ye look indeed as friends?
    Is there no change? Are ye not cold?
Oh! I do dread that Fortune lends
    Fictitious good! – that I behold,
To lose, these treasures, which of old
    Were all my glory, all my pride:
May not these arms that form infold?
    Is all affection asks denied?

Say, what is this? – How are we tried,
    In this sad world! – I know not these –
All strangers, none to me allied –
    Those aspects blood and spirit freeze:
Dear forms, my wandering judgment spare;
    And thou, most dear, these fiends disarm,
Resume thy wonted looks and air,
    And break this melancholy charm.

And are they vanish'd? Is she lost?
    Shall never day that form restore?
Oh! I am all by fears engross'd;
    Sad truth has broken in once more,
And I the brief delight deplore:
    How durst they such resemblance take?
Heavens! with what grace the mask they wore!
    Oh, from what visions I awake!

Once more, once more upon the shore!
    Now back the rolling ocean flows:
The rocky bed now far before
    On the receding water grows –
The treasures and the wealth it owes
    To human misery – all in view;
Fate all on me at once bestows,
    From thousands robbed and murdered too.

But, lo, whatever I can find
    Grows mean and worthless as I view:
They promise, but they cheat the mind,
    As promises are born to do.
How lovely every form and hue,
    Till seized and master'd – Then arise,
For all that admiration drew,
    All that our senses can despise!

Within the basis of a tower,
    I saw a plant – it graced the spot;
There was within nor wind nor shower,
    And this had life that flowers have not.

I drew it forth – Ah, luckless lot!
　　It was the mandrake; and the sound
Of anguish deeply smother'd shot
　　Into my breast with pang profound.

'I would I were a soaring bird,'
　　Said Folly, 'and I then would fly:'
Some mocking Muse or Fairy heard –
　　'You can but fall – suppose you try?
And though you may not mount the sky,
　　You will not grovel in the mire.'
Hail, words of comfort! Now can I
　　Spurn earth, and to the air aspire.

And this, before, might I have done
　　If I had courage – that is all:
'Tis easier now to soar than run;
　　Up! up! – we neither tire nor fall.
Children of dust, be yours to crawl
　　On the vile earth! – while, happier, I
Must listen to an inward call,
　　That bids me mount, that makes me fly.

I tumble from the loftiest tower,
　　Yet evil have I never found;
Supported by some favouring power,
　　I come in safety to the ground.
I rest upon the sea, the sound
　　Of many waters in mine ear,
Yet have no dread of being drowned,
　　But to see my way, and cease to fear.

Awake, there is no living man
　　Who may my fixed spirit shake;
But sleeping, there is one who can
　　And oft does he the trial make:
Against his might resolves I take,
　　And him oppose with high disdain;

But quickly all my powers forsake
  My mind, and I resume my chain.

I know not how, but I am brought
  Into a large and Gothic hall,
Seated with those I never sought –
  Kings, Caliphs, Kaisers, – silent all;
Pale as the dead; enrobed and tall,
  Majestic, frozen, solemn, still;
They wake my fears, my wits appal,
  And with both scorn and terror fill.

Now are they seated at a board
  In that cold grandeur – I am there.
But what can mummied kings afford?
  This is their meagre ghostly fare,
And proves what fleshless things they stare!
  Yes! I am seated with the dead:
How great, and yet how mean they are!
  Yes! I can scorn them while I dread.

They're gone! – and in their room I see
  A fairy being, form and dress
Brilliant as light; nor can there be
  On earth that heavenly loveliness;
Nor words can that sweet look express,
  Or tell what living gems adorn
That wond'rous beauty: who can guess
  Where such celestial charms were born?

Yet, as I wonder and admire,
  The grace is gone, the glory dead:
And now it is but mean attire
  Upon a shrivel'd beldame spread,
Laid loathsome on a pauper's bed,
  Where wretchedness and woe are found,
And the faint putrid odour shed
  By all that's foul and base around!

                                   Stanzas xi–xxxi

66

WILLIAM BLAKE
1757–1827

To the Muses

Whether on Ida's shady brow,
Or in the chambers of the East,
The chambers of the sun, that now
From antient melody have ceas'd;

Whether in Heav'n ye wander fair,
Or the green corners of the earth,
Or the blue regions of the air
Where the melodious winds have birth;

Whether on chrystal rocks ye rove,
Beneath the bosom of the sea
Wand'ring in many a coral grove,
Fair Nine, forsaking Poetry!

How have you left the antient love
That bards of old enjoy'd in you!
The languid strings do scarcely move!
The sound is forc'd, the notes are few!

Introduction to Songs of Innocence

Piping down the valleys wild,
Piping songs of pleasant glee,
On a cloud I saw a child,
And he laughing said to me:

'Pipe a song about a Lamb!'
So I piped with merry chear.
'Piper, pipe that song again;'
So I piped: he wept to hear.

'Drop thy pipe, thy happy pipe,
Sing thy songs of happy chear:'
So I sung the same again
While he wept with joy to hear.

'Piper sit thee down and write
In a book that all may read.'
So he vanish'd from my sight,
And I pluck'd a hollow reed,

And I made a rural pen,
And I stain'd the water clear,
And I wrote my happy songs
Every child may joy to hear.

The Ecchoing Green

The Sun does arise,
And make happy the skies;
The merry bells ring
To welcome the Spring;
The sky-lark and thrush,
The birds of the bush,
Sing louder around
To the bells' chearful sound,
While our sports shall be seen
On the Ecchoing Green.

Old John with white hair,
Does laugh away care,
Sitting under the oak
Among the old folk.
They laugh at our play,
And soon they all say:
'Such, such were the joys
When we all, girls & boys,
In our youth-time were seen
On the Ecchoing Green.'

Till the little ones, weary,
No more can be merry;
The sun does descend,
And our sports have an end.
Round the laps of their mothers
Many sisters and brothers,
Like birds in their nest,
Are ready for rest,
And sport no more seen
On the darkening Green.

Holy Thursday

'Twas on a Holy Thursday, their innocent faces clean,
The children walking two & two, in red & blue & green,
Grey headed beadles walk'd before, with wands as white
  as snow,
Till into the high dome of Paul's they like Thames' waters
  flow.

O what a multitude they seem'd, these flowers of London
  town!
Seated in companies they sit with radiance all their own.
The hum of multitudes was there, but multitudes of lambs,
Thousands of little boys & girls raising their innocent
  hands.

Now like a mighty wind they raise to heaven the voice of
  song,
Or like harmonious thunderings the seats of heaven among.
Beneath them sit the aged men, wise guardians of the poor;
Then cherish pity, lest you drive an angel from your door.

On Another's Sorrow

Can I see another's woe
And not be in sorrow too?
Can I see another's grief
And not seek for kind relief?

Can I see a falling tear
And not feel my sorrow's share?
Can a father see his child
Weep, nor be with sorrow fill'd?

Can a mother sit and hear
An infant groan an infant fear?
No, no! never can it be!
Never, never can it be!

And can he who smiles on all
Hear the wren with sorrows small,
Hear the small bird's grief & care,
Hear the woes that infants bear,

And not sit beside the nest
Pouring pity in their breast;
And not sit the cradle near
Weeping tear on infant's tear;

And not sit both night & day
Wiping all our tears away?
O! no never can it be!
Never, never can it be!

He doth give his joy to all;
He becomes an infant small;
He becomes a man of woe;
He doth feel the sorrow too.

Think not thou canst sigh a sigh
And thy maker is not by;

Think not thou canst weep a tear
And thy maker is not near.

O! he gives to us his joy
That our grief he may destroy;
Till our grief is fled & gone
He doth sit by us and moan.

The School Boy

I love to rise in a summer morn
When the birds sing on every tree;
The distant huntsman winds his horn,
And the sky-lark sings with me.
O! what sweet company.

But to go to school in a summer morn,
O! it drives all joy away;
Under a cruel eye outworn,
The little ones spend the day
In sighing and dismay.

Ah! then at times I drooping sit,
And spend many an anxious hour,
Nor in my book can I take delight,
Nor sit in learning's bower,
Worn thro' with the dreary shower.

How can the bird that is born for joy
Sit in a cage and sing?
How can a child when fears annoy,
But droop his tender wing,
And forget his youthful spring?

O! father & mother, if buds are nip'd
And blossoms blown away,
And if the tender plants are strip'd
Of their joy in the springing day,
By sorrow and care's dismay,

How shall the summer arise in joy,
Or the summer fruits appear?
Or how shall we gather what griefs destroy,
Or bless the mellowing year
When the blasts of winter appear?

Introduction to Songs of Experience

Hear the voice of the Bard!
Who Present, Past & Future sees;
Whose ears have heard
The Holy Word
That walk'd among the ancient trees,

Calling the lapsed Soul,
And weeping in the evening dew;
That might controll
The starry pole,
And fallen, fallen light renew!

'O Earth, O Earth return!
Arise from out the dewy grass;
Night is worn,
And the morn
Rises from the slumberous mass.

'Turn away no more;
Why wilt thou turn away?
The starry floor
The wat'ry shore
Is giv'n thee till the break of day.'

The Clod & the Pebble

'Love seeketh not Itself to please
Nor for itself hath any care,
But for another gives its ease
And builds a Heaven in Hell's despair.'

So sung a little Clod of Clay
Trodden with the cattle's feet,
But a Pebble of the brook
Warbled out these metres meet:

'Love seeketh only Self to please,
To bind another to Its delight,
Joys in another's loss of ease,
And builds a Hell in Heaven's despite.'

Holy Thursday

Is this a holy thing to see
In a rich and fruitful land,
Babes reduc'd to misery,
Fed with cold and usurous hand?

Is that trembling cry a song?
Can it be a song of joy?
And so many children poor?
It is a land of poverty!

And their sun does never shine,
And their fields are bleak & bare,
And their ways are fill'd with thorns:
It is eternal winter there.

For where-e'er the sun does shine,
And where-e'er the rain does fall,
Babe can never hunger there,
Nor poverty the mind appall.

The Sick Rose

O Rose, thou art sick!
The invisible worm
That flies in the night,
In the howling storm,

Has found out thy bed
Of crimson joy:
And his dark secret love
Does thy life destroy.

The Tyger

Tyger! Tyger! burning bright
In the forests of the night,
What immortal hand or eye
Could frame thy fearful symmetry?

In what distant deeps or skies
Burnt the fire of thine eyes?
On what wings dare he aspire?
What the hand dare seize the fire?

And what shoulder, & what art,
Could twist the sinews of thy heart?
And when thy heart began to beat,
What dread hand? & what dread feet?

What the hammer? what the chain?
In what furnace was thy brain?
What the anvil? what dread grasp
Dare its deadly terrors clasp?

When the stars threw down their spears
And water'd heaven with their tears,
Did he smile his work to see?
Did he who made the Lamb make thee?

Tyger! Tyger! burning bright
In the forests of the night,
What immortal hand or eye
Dare frame thy fearful symmetry?

London

I wander thro' each charter'd street
Near where the charter'd Thames does flow,
And mark in every face I meet
Marks of weakness, marks of woe.

In every cry of every Man,
In every Infant's cry of fear,
In every voice, in every ban,
The mind-forg'd manacles I hear.

How the Chimney-sweeper's cry
Every black'ning Church appalls,
And the hapless Soldier's sigh
Runs in blood down Palace walls.

But most thro' midnight streets I hear
How the youthful Harlot's curse
Blasts the new born Infant's tear,
And blights with plagues the Marriage hearse.

Infant Sorrow

My mother groan'd! my father wept,
Into the dangerous world I leapt:
Helpless, naked, piping loud:
Like a fiend hid in a cloud.

Struggling in my father's hands,
Striving against my swadling bands,
Bound and weary I thought best
To sulk upon my mother's breast.

A Little Boy Lost

'Nought loves another as itself,
Nor venerates another so,
Nor is it possible to Thought
A greater than itself to know:

'And Father, how can I love you
Or any of my brothers more?
I love you like the little bird
That picks up crumbs around the door.'

The Priest sat by and heard the child,
In trembling zeal he seiz'd his hair:
He led him by his little coat,
And all admir'd the Priestly care.

And standing on the altar high,
'Lo, what a fiend is here!' said he,
'One who sets reason up for judge
Of our most holy Mystery.'

The weeping child could not be heard,
The weeping parents wept in vain;
They strip'd him to his little shirt,
And bound him in an iron chain;

And burn'd him in a holy place,
Where many had been burn'd before:
The weeping parents wept in vain.
Are such things done on Albion's shore?

'I asked a thief'

I asked a thief to steal me a peach:
He turned up his eyes.
I asked a lithe lady to lie her down:
Holy & meek, she cries –

As soon as I went
An angel came.
He wink'd at the thief
And smil'd at the dame.

And without one word said
Had a peach from the tree,
And still as a maid
Enjoy'd the lady.

'My Spectre around me night & day'

My Spectre around me night & day
Like a Wild beast guards my way.
My Emanation far within
Weeps incessantly for my Sin.

A Fathomless & boundless Deep
There we wander, there we weep;
On the hungry craving wind
My Spectre follows thee behind.

He scents thy footsteps in the snow
Wheresoever thou dost go
Thro' the wintry hail & rain.
When wilt thou return again?

Dost thou not in Pride & scorn
Fill with tempests all my morn,
And with jealousies & fears
Fill my pleasant nights with tears?

Seven of my sweet loves thy knife
Has bereaved of their life.
Their marble tombs I built with tears
And with cold & shuddering fears.

Seven more loves weep night & day
Round the tombs where my loves lay,
And seven more loves attend each night
Around my couch with torches bright.

And seven more Loves in my bed
Crown with wine my mournful head,
Pitying & forgiving all
Thy transgressions, great & small.

When wilt thou return & view
My loves, & them to life renew?
When wilt thou return & live?
When wilt thou pity as I forgive?

'Never, Never I return:
Still for Victory I burn.
Living, thee alone I'll have
And when dead I'll be thy Grave.

'Thro' the Heav'n & Earth & Hell
Thou shalt never never quell;
I will fly & thou pursue,
Night & Morn the flight renew.'

Till I turn from Female Love,
And root up the Infernal Grove,
I shall never worthy be
To Step into Eternity.

And to end thy cruel mocks,
Annihilate thee on the rocks,
And another form create
To be subservient to my Fate.

Let us agree to give up Love,
And root up the infernal grove;
Then we shall return & see
The worlds of happy Eternity.

& Throughout all Eternity
I forgive you, you forgive me.
As our dear Redeemer said:
'This the Wine & this the Bread.'

Several Questions Answered

What is it men in women do require?
The lineaments of Gratified Desire.
What is it women do in men require?
The lineaments of Gratified Desire.

The look of love alarms
Because 'tis fill'd with fire;
But the look of soft deceit
Shall Win the lover's hire.

Soft Deceit & Idleness,
These are Beauty's sweetest dress.

He who binds to himself a joy
Doth the winged life destroy;
But he who kisses the joy as it flies
Lives in Eternity's sunrise.

Two Epigrams

I

Her whole Life is an Epigram, smack, smooth, & neatly
    pen'd,
Platted quite neat to catch applause with a sliding noose at
    the end.

II

When a Man has Married a Wife he finds out whether
Her Knees & Elbows are only glued together.

'When Klopstock England defied'

When Klopstock England defied,
Up rose terrible Blake in his pride;
For old Nobodaddy aloft
Farted & belch'd & cough'd;
Then swore a great oath that made heaven quake,
And call'd aloud to English Blake.
Blake was giving his body ease
At Lambeth beneath the poplar trees.
From his seat then started he,
And turned himself round three times three.
The Moon at that sight blush'd scarlet red,
The stars threw down their cups & fled,
And all the devils that were in hell
Answered with a ninefold yell.
Klopstock felt the intripled turn,
And all his bowels began to churn,
And his bowels turned round three times three,
And lock'd his soul with a ninefold key,
That from his body it ne'er could be parted
Till to the last trumpet it was farted.
Then again old Nobodaddy swore
He ne'er had seen such a thing before,
Since Noah was shut in the ark,
Since Eve first chose her hellfire spark,
Since 'twas the fashion to go naked,
Since the old anything was created,
And so feeling, he beg'd me to turn again
And ease poor Klopstock's ninefold pain.

. . . . .

If Blake could do this when he rose up from shite,
What might he not do if he sat down to write?

Morning

To find the Western path
Right thro' the Gates of Wrath
I urge my way;
Sweet Mercy leads me on:
With soft repentant moan
I see the break of day.

The war of swords & spears
Melted by dewy tears
Exhales on high;
The Sun is freed from fears
And with soft grateful tears
Ascends the sky.

The Mental Traveller

I travel'd thro' a Land of Men,
A Land of Men & Women too,
And heard & saw such dreadful things
As cold Earth wanderers never knew.

For there the Babe is born in joy
That was begotten in dire woe;
Just as we Reap in joy the fruit
Which we in bitter tears did sow.

And if the Babe is born a Boy
He's given to a Woman Old
Who nails him down upon a rock,
Catches his shrieks in cups of gold.

She binds iron thorns around his head,
She pierces both his hands & feet,
She cuts his heart out at his side
To make it feel both cold & heat.

Her fingers number every Nerve,
Just as a Miser counts his gold;
She lives upon his shrieks & cries,
And She grows young as he grows old.

Till he becomes a bleeding youth
And She becomes a Virgin bright;
Then he rends up his Manacles
And binds her down for his delight.

He plants himself in all her Nerves,
Just as a Husbandman his mould;
And She becomes his dwelling place
And Garden fruitful seventy fold.

An aged Shadow, soon he fades,
Wand'ring round an Earthly Cot,
Full filled all with gems & gold
Which he by industry had got.

And these are the gems of the Human Soul,
The rubies & pearls of a lovesick eye,
The countless gold of the akeing heart,
The martyr's groan & the lover's sigh.

They are his meat, they are his drink;
He feeds the Beggar & the Poor
And the wayfaring Traveller:
For ever open is his door.

His grief is their eternal joy;
They make the roofs & walls to ring;
Till from the fire on the hearth
A little Female Babe does spring.

And She is all of solid fire
And gems & gold, that none his hand
Dares stretch to touch her Baby form,
Or wrap her in his swaddling-band.

But She comes to the Man she loves,
If young or old, or rich or poor;
They soon drive out the aged Host,
A Beggar at another's door,

He wanders weeping far away,
Untill some other take him in;
Oft blind & age-bent, sore distrest,
Untill he can a Maiden win.

And to allay his freezing Age,
The Poor Man takes her in his arms;
The Cottage fades before his sight,
The Garden & its lovely Charms.

The Guests are scatter'd thro' the land,
For the Eye altering alters all;
The Senses roll themselves in fear
And the flat Earth becomes a Ball;

The Stars, Sun, Moon, all shrink away,
A desart vast without a bound,
And nothing left to eat or drink,
And a dark desart all around.

The honey of her Infant lips,
The bread & wine of her sweet smile,
The wild game of her roving Eye,
Does him to Infancy beguile:

For as he eats & drinks he grows
Younger & younger every day;
And on the desart wild they both
Wander in terror & dismay.

Like the wild Stag she flees away,
Her fear plants many a thicket wild;
While he pursues her night & day,
By various arts of Love beguil'd;

By various arts of Love & Hate,
Till the wide desart planted o'er
With Labyrinths of wayward Love,
Where roams the Lion, Wolf & Boar;

Till he becomes a wayward Babe,
And she a weeping Woman Old.
Then many a Lover wanders here;
The Sun & Stars are nearer roll'd.

The trees bring forth sweet Extacy
To all who in the desart roam,
Till many a City there is Built,
And many a pleasant Shepherd's home.

But when they find the frowning Babe,
Terror strikes thro' the region wide:
They cry, 'The Babe! the Babe is Born!'
And flee away on Every side.

For who dare touch the frowning form,
His arm is wither'd to its root;
Lions, Boars, Wolves, all howling flee,
And every Tree does shed its fruit.

And none can touch that frowning form,
Except it be a Woman Old;
She nails him down upon the Rock,
And all is done as I have told.

Auguries of Innocence

To see a World in a Grain of Sand
And a Heaven in a Wild Flower,
Hold Infinity in the palm of your hand
And Eternity in an hour.

A Robin Red breast in a Cage
Puts all Heaven in a Rage.
A Dove house fill'd with Doves & Pigeons
Shudders Hell thro' all its regions.
A Dog starv'd at his Master's Gate
Predicts the ruin of the State.
A Horse misus'd upon the Road
Calls to Heaven for Human blood.
Each outcry of the hunted Hare
A fibre from the Brain does tear.
A Skylark wounded in the wing,
A Cherubim does cease to sing.
The Game Cock clip'd & arm'd for fight
Does the Rising Sun affright.
Every Wolf's & Lion's howl
Raises from Hell a Human Soul.
The wild Deer wand'ring here & there
Keeps the Human Soul from Care.
The Lamb misus'd breeds Public strife
And yet forgives the Butcher's Knife.
The Bat that flits at close of Eve
Has left the Brain that won't Believe.
The Owl that calls upon the Night
Speaks the Unbeliever's fright.
He who shall hurt the little Wren
Shall never be belov'd by Men.
He who the Ox to wrath has mov'd
Shall never be by Woman lov'd.
The wanton Boy that kills the Fly
Shall feel the Spider's enmity.
He who torments the Chafer's sprite
Weaves a Bower in endless Night.
The Catterpiller on the Leaf
Repeats to thee thy Mother's grief.
Kill not the Moth nor Butterfly
For the Last Judgment draweth nigh.
He who shall train the Horse to war
Shall never pass the Polar Bar.

The Beggar's Dog & Widow's Cat,
Feed them, & thou wilt grow fat.
The Gnat that sings his Summer's song
Poison gets from Slander's tongue.
The poison of the Snake & Newt
Is the sweat of Envy's Foot.
The Poison of the Honey Bee
Is the Artist's Jealousy.
The Prince's Robes & Beggar's Rags
Are Toadstools on the Miser's Bags.
A truth that's told with bad intent
Beats all the Lies you can invent.
It is right it should be so;
Man was made for Joy & Woe,
And when this we rightly know
Thro' the World we safely go.
Joy & Woe are woven fine,
A Clothing for the Soul divine;
Under every grief & pine
Runs a joy with silken twine.
The Babe is more than swadling Bands;
Throughout all these Human Lands
Tools were made, & Born were hands,
Every Farmer Understands.
Every Tear from Every Eye
Becomes a Babe in Eternity;
This is caught by Females bright
And return'd to its own delight.
The Bleat, the Bark, Bellow & Roar
Are Waves that Beat on Heaven's Shore.
The Babe that weeps the Rod beneath
Writes Revenge in realms of Death.
The Beggar's Rags, fluttering in Air,
Does to Rags the Heavens tear.
The Soldier arm'd with Sword & Gun
Palsied strikes the Summer's Sun.
The poor Man's Farthing is worth more
Than all the Gold on Afric's Shore.

One Mite wrung from the Lab'rer's hands
Shall buy & sell the Miser's Lands:
Or, if protected from on high,
Does that whole Nation sell & buy.
He who mocks the Infant's Faith
Shall be mock'd in Age & Death.
He who shall teach the Child to Doubt
The rotting Grave shall ne'er get out.
He who respects the Infant's faith
Triumphs over Hell & Death.
The Child's Toys & the Old Man's Reasons
Are the Fruits of the Two seasons.
The Questioner who sits so sly
Shall never know how to Reply.
He who replies to words of Doubt
Doth put the Light of Knowledge out.
The Strongest Poison ever known
Came from Caesar's Laurel Crown.
Nought can deform the Human Race
Like to the Armour's iron brace.
When Gold & Gems adorn the Plow
To peaceful Arts shall Envy Bow.
A Riddle or the Cricket's Cry
Is to Doubt a fit Reply.
The Emmet's Inch & Eagle's Mile
Make Lame Philosophy to smile.
He who Doubts from what he sees
Will ne'er Believe, do what you Please.
If the Sun & Moon should doubt,
They'd immediately Go out.
To be in a Passion you Good may do,
But no Good if a Passion is in you.
The Whore & Gambler, by the State
Licenc'd, build that Nation's Fate.
The Harlot's cry from Street to Street
Shall weave Old England's winding Sheet.
The Winner's Shout, the Loser's Curse,
Dance before dead England's Hearse.

Every Night & every Morn
Some to Misery are Born.
Every Morn & every Night
Some are Born to sweet delight.
Some are Born to sweet delight,
Some are Born to Endless Night.
We are led to Believe a Lie
When we see not Thro' the Eye
Which was Born in a Night, to perish in a Night,
When the Soul Slept in Beams of Light.
God Appears & God is Light
To those poor Souls who dwell in Night,
But does a Human Form Display
To those who Dwell in Realms of Day.

William Bond

I wonder whether the Girls are mad,
And I wonder whether they mean to kill,
And I wonder if William Bond will die,
For assuredly he is very ill.

He went to Church in a May morning,
Attended by Fairies, one, two, & three;
But the Angels of Providence drove them away,
And he return'd home in Misery.

He went not out to the Field nor Fold,
He went not out to the Village nor Town,
But he came home in a black, black cloud,
And he took to his Bed, & there lay down.

And an Angel of Providence at his Feet,
And an Angel of Providence at his Head,
And in the midst a Black, Black Cloud,
And in the midst the Sick Man on his Bed.

And on his Right hand was Mary Green,
And on his Left hand was his Sister Jane,
And their tears fell thro' the black, black Cloud
To drive away the sick man's pain.

'O William, if thou dost another Love,
Dost another Love better than poor Mary,
Go & take that other to be thy Wife,
And Mary Green shall her Servant be.'

'Yes, Mary I do another Love,
Another I Love far better than thee,
And Another I will have for my Wife;
Then what have I to do with thee?

'For thou art Melancholy Pale,
And on thy Head is the cold Moon's Shine,
But she is ruddy & bright as day,
And the sun beams dazzle from her eyne.'

Mary trembled & Mary chill'd
And Mary fell down on the right hand floor,
That William Bond & his Sister Jane
Scarce could recover Mary more.

When Mary woke & found her Laid
On the Right hand of her William dear,
On the Right hand of his loved Bed,
And saw her William Bond so near,

The Fairies that fled from William Bond
Danced around her Shining Head;
They danced over the Pillow white,
And the Angels of Providence left the Bed.

I thought Love liv'd in the hot sun shine,
But O he lives in the Moony light!
I thought to find Love in the heat of day,
But sweet Love is the Comforter of Night.

Seek Love in the Pity of others' Woe,
In the gentle relief of another's care,
In the darkness of night & the winter's snow,
In the naked & outcast, Seek Love there!

To the Jews

From *Jerusalem*

The fields from Islington to Marybone,
To Primrose Hill and Saint John's Wood,
   Were builded over with pillars of gold,
And there Jerusalem's pillars stood.

Her Little-ones ran on the fields,
The Lamb of God among them seen,
   And fair Jerusalem, his Bride,
Among the little meadows green.

Pancrass & Kentish-town repose
Among her golden pillars high,
   Among her golden arches which
Shine upon the starry sky.

The Jew's-harp-house & the Green Man,
The Ponds where Boys to bathe delight,
   The fields of Cows by Willan's farm,
Shine in Jerusalem's pleasant sight.

She walks upon our meadows green,
The Lamb of God walks by her side,
   And every English Child is seen
Children of Jesus & his Bride.

Forgiving trespasses and sins
Lest Babylon with cruel Og
   With Moral & Self-righteous Law
Should Crucify in Satan's Synagogue!

What are those golden Builders doing
Near mournful ever-weeping Paddington,
   Standing above that mighty Ruin
Where Satan the first victory won,

   Where Albion slept beneath the Fatal Tree,
And the Druids' golden Knife
   Rioted in human gore,
In Offerings of Human Life?

   They groan'd aloud on London Stone,
They groan'd aloud on Tyburn's Brook,
   Albion gave his deadly groan,
And all the Atlantic Mountains shook.

   Albion's Spectre from his Loins
Tore forth in all the pomp of War:
   Satan his name: in flames of fire
He stretch'd his Druid Pillars far.

   Jerusalem fell from Lambeth's Vale
Down thro' Poplar & Old Bow,
   Thro' Malden & acros the Sea,
In War & howling, death & woe.

   The Rhine was red with human blood,
The Danube roll'd a purple tide,
   On the Euphrates Satan stood,
And over Asia stretch'd his pride.

   He wither'd up sweet Zion's Hill
From every Nation of the Earth;
   He wither'd up Jerusalem's Gates,
And in a dark Land gave her birth.

   He wither'd up the Human Form
By laws of sacrifice for sin,
   . Till it became a Mortal Worm,
But O! translucent all within.

The Divine Vision still was seen,
Still was the Human Form Divine,
    Weeping in weak & mortal clay,
O Jesus, still the Form was thine.

And thine the Human Face & thine
The Human Hands & Feet & Breath
    Entering thro' the Gates of Birth
And passing thro' the Gates of Death.

And O thou Lamb of God, whom I
Slew in my dark self-righteous pride,
    Art thou return'd to Albion's Land?
And is Jerusalem thy Bride?

Come to my arms & never more
Depart, but dwell for ever here:
    Create my Spirit to thy Love:
Subdue my Spectre to thy Fear.

Spectre of Albion! warlike Fiend!
In clouds of blood & ruin roll'd,
    I here reclaim thee as my own,
My Selfhood! Satan! arm'd in gold.

Is this thy soft Family-Love,
Thy cruel Patriarchal pride,
    Planting thy Family alone,
Destroying all the World beside?

A man's worst enemies are those
Of his own house & family;
    And he who makes his law a curse
By his own law shall surely die.

In my Exchanges every Land
Shall walk, & mine in every Land,
    Mutual shall build Jerusalem,
Both heart in heart & hand in hand.

To The Accuser who is
The God of This World

Truly, My Satan, thou art but a Dunce,
And dost not know the Garment from the Man.
Every Harlot was a Virgin once,
Nor can'st thou ever change Kate into Nan.

Tho' thou art Worship'd by the Names Divine
Of Jesus & Jehovah, thou art still
The Son of Morn in weary Night's decline,
The lost Traveller's Dream under the Hill.

ROBERT BURNS
1759–1796

Tam o' Shanter

When chapman billies leave the street,
And drouthy neebors, neebors meet,
As market-days are wearing late,
An' folk begin to tak the gate;
While we sit bousing at the nappy,
An' getting fou and unco happy,
We think na on the lang Scots miles,
The mosses, waters, slaps, and styles,
That lie between us and our hame,
Whare sits our sulky sullen dame,
Gathering her brows like gathering storm,
Nursing her wrath to keep it warm.

This truth fand honest Tam o' Shanter,
As he frae Ayr ae night did canter,
(Auld Ayr wham ne'er a town surpasses,
For honest men and bonny lasses.)

O Tam! hadst thou but been sae wise,
As ta'en they ain wife Kate's advice!
She tauld thee weel thou was a skellum,
A blethering, blustering, drunken blellum;
That frae November till October,
Ae market-day thou was nae sober;
That ilka melder, wi' the miller,
Thou sat as lang as thou had siller;
That ev'ry naig was ca'd a shoe on,
The smith and thee gat roaring fou on;
That at the Lord's house, ev'n on Sunday,
Thou drank wi' Kirkton Jean till Monday.
She prophesy'd that late or soon,
Thou would be found deep drown'd in Doon;

chapman billies: packmen. *drouthy*: thirsty. *gate*: way. *nappy*: ale.
mosses: bogs. *slaps*: gaps, passes. *ta'en*: to have taken. *skellum*: rascal.
blellum: babbler. *melder*: meal-grinding. *naig*: nag. *ca'd a shoe on*: shod.

Or catch'd wi' warlocks in the mirk,
By Alloway's auld haunted kirk.

Ah, gentle dames! it gars me greet,
To think how mony counsels sweet,
How mony lengthen'd sage advices,
The husband frae the wife despises!

But to our tale: Ae market night,
Tam had got planted unco right;
Fast by an ingle, bleezing finely,
Wi' reaming swats, that drank divinely;
And at his elbow, Souter Johnny,
His ancient, trusty, drouthy crony;
Tam lo'ed him like a vera brither;
They had been fou for weeks thegither.
The night drave on wi' sangs and clatter;
And ay the ale was growing better:
The landlady and Tam grew gracious,
Wi' favours, secret, sweet, and precious:
The Souter tauld his queerest stories;
The landlord's laugh was ready chorus:
The storm without might rair and rustle,
Tam did na mind the storm a whistle.

Care, mad to see a man sae happy,
E'en drown'd himself amang the nappy.
As bees flee hame wi' lades o' treasure,
The minutes wing'd their way wi' pleasure:
Kings may be blest, but Tam was glorious,
O'er a' the ills o' life victorious!

But pleasures are like poppies spread,
You seize the flow'r, its bloom is shed;
Or like the snow falls in the river,
A moment white – then melts for ever;
Or like the borealis race,
That flit ere you can point their place;
Or like the rainbow's lovely form
Evanishing amid the storm. –

mirk: dark. *greet*: weep. *reaming swats*: frothing ale. *Souter*: cobbler.

Nae man can tether time or tide;
The hour approaches Tam maun ride;
That hour, o' night's black arch the key-stane,
That dreary hour he mounts his beast in;
And sic a night he taks the road in,
As ne'er poor sinner was abroad in.
   The wind blew as 'twad blawn its last;
The rattling show'rs rose on the blast;
The speedy gleams the darkness swallow'd;
Loud, deep, and lang, the thunder bellow'd:
That night, a child might understand,
The Deil had business on his hand.
   Weel mounted on his gray mare, Meg,
A better never lifted leg,
Tam skelpit on thro' dub and mire,
Despising wind, and rain, and fire;
Whiles holding fast his gude blue bonnet;
Whiles crooning o'er some auld Scots sonnet;
Whiles glow'ring round wi' prudent cares,
Lest bogles catch him unawares:
Kirk-Alloway was drawing nigh,
Whare ghaists and houlets nightly cry. –
   By this time he was cross the ford,
Whare in the snaw, the chapman smoor'd;
And past the birks and meikle stane,
Whare drunken Charlie brak's neck-bane;
And thro' the whins, and by the cairn,
Whare hunters fand the murder'd bairn;
And near the thorn, aboon the well,
Whare Mungo's mither hang'd hersel. –
Before him Doon pours all his floods;
The doubling storm roars thro' the woods;
The lightnings flash from pole to pole;
Near and more near the thunders roll:
When, glimmering thro' the groaning trees,
Kirk-Alloway seem'd in a bleeze;

skelpit: hurried. *dub*: puddle. *houlets*: owlets. *smoor'd*: smothered.

Thro' ilka bore the beams were glancing;
And loud resounded mirth and dancing. –
    Inspiring bold John Barleycorn!
What dangers thou canst make us scorn!
Wi' tippeny, we fear nae evil;
Wi' usquabae we'll face the devil! –
The swats sae ream'd in Tammie's noddle,
Fair play, he car'd na deils a boddle.
But Maggie stood right fair astonish'd,
Till, by the heel and hand admonish'd,
She ventur'd forward on the light;
And, vow! Tam saw an unco sight!
Warlocks and witches in a dance;
Nae cotillion brent new frae France,
But hornpipes, jigs, strathspeys, and reels,
Put life and mettle in their heels.
A winnock-bunker in the east,
There sat aud Nick, in shape o' beast;
A towzie tyke, black, grim, and large,
To gie them music was his charge:
He screw'd the pipes and gart them skirl,
Till roof and rafters a' did dirl. –
Coffins stood round, like open presses,
That shaw'd the dead in their last dresses;
And by some devilish cantraip slight
Each in its cauld hand held a light. –
By which heroic Tam was able
To note upon the haly table,
A murderer's banes in gibbet airns;
Twa span-lang, wee, unchristen'd bairns;
A thief, new-cutted frae a rape,
Wi' his last gasp his gab did gape;
Five tomahawks, wi' blude red-rusted;
Five scymitars, wi' murder crusted;

tippeny: twopenny ale. *usquabae*: whisky. *na deils a boddle*: not a
farthing for devils. *brent*: brand. *winnock-bunker*: window-seat. *towzie*:
dishevelled, shaggy. *dirl*: vibrate. *cantraip*: magic. *airns*: irons. *rape*:
rope.

A garter, which a babe had strangled;
A knife, a father's throat had mangled,
Whom his ain son o' life bereft,
The grey hairs yet stack to the heft;
Wi' mair o' horrible and awefu',
Which ev'n to name wad be unlawfu'.

  As Tammie glowr'd, amaz'd, and curious,
The mirth and fun grew fast and furious:
The piper loud and louder blew;
The dancers quick and quicker flew;
They reel'd, they set, they cross'd, they cleekit,
Till ilka carlin swat and reekit,
And coost her duddies to the wark,
And linket at it in her sark!
Now Tam, O Tam! had thae been queans,
A' plump and strapping in their teens,
Their sarks, instead o' creeshie flannen,
Been snaw-white seventeen hunder linnen!
Thir breeks o' mine, my only pair,
That ance were plush, o' gude blue hair,
I wad hae gi'en them off my hurdies,
For ae blink o' the bonie burdies!

  But wither'd beldams, auld and droll,
Rigwoodie hags wad spean a foal,
Lowping and flinging on a crummock,
I wonder didna turn thy stomach.

  But Tam kend what was what fu' brawlie,
There was ae winsome wench and wawlie,
That night enlisted in the core,
(Lang after kend on Carrick shore;
For mony a beast to dead she shot,
And perish'd mony a bony boat,
And shook baith meikle corn and bear,
And kept the country-side in fear.)

---

cleekit: joined arms. *coost her duddies*: cast off her clothes. *linket*: went quickly. *creeshie flannen*: greasy flannel. *thir*: these. *hurdies*: buttocks. *burdies*: girls. *rigwoodie*: wretched(?). *spean*: wean. *crummock*: crooked staff. *brawlie*: well. *wawlie*: comely. *core*: corps. *bear*: barley.

Her cutty sark, o' Paisley harn,
That while a lassie she had worn,
In longitude tho' sorely scanty,
It was her best, and she was vauntie. –
Ah! little kend thy reverend grannie,
That sark she coft for her wee Nannie,
Wi' twa pund Scots, ('twas a' her riches),
Wad ever grac'd a dance of witches!

But here my Muse her wing maun cour;
Sic flights are far beyond her pow'r;
To sing how Nannie lap and flang,
(A souple jade she was, and strang),
And how Tam stood, like ane bewitch'd,
And thought his very een enrich'd;
Even Satan glowr'd, and fidg'd fu' fain,
And hotch'd and blew wi' might and main:
Till first ae caper, syne anither,
Tam tint his reason a' thegither,
And roars out, 'Weel done, Cutty-sark!'
And in an instant all was dark:
And scarcely had he Maggie rallied,
When out the hellish legion sallied.

As bees bizz out wi' angry fyke,
When plundering herds assail their byke;
As open pussie's mortal foes,
When, pop! she starts before their nose;
As eager runs the market-crowd,
When 'Catch the thief!' resounds aloud;
So Maggie runs, the witches follow,
Wi' mony an eldritch skreech and hollow.

Ah, Tam! Ah, Tam! thou'll get thy fairin!
In hell they'll roast thee like a herrin!
In vain thy Kate awaits thy comin!
Kate soon will be a woefu' woman!
Now, do thy speedy utmost, Meg,

cutty: short. _harn_: coarse cloth. _coft_: bought. _fidg'd_: fidgeted. _hotch'd_:
jerked. _tint_: lost. _fyke_: fuss. _herds_: shepherd-boys. _byke_: hive. _pussie's_:
the hare's. _fairin_: present from a fair.

And win the key-stane of the brig;
There at them thou thy tail may toss,
A running stream they dare na cross.
But ere the key-stane she could make,
The fient a tail she had to shake!
For Nannie, far before the rest,
Hard upon noble Maggie prest,
And flew at Tam wi' furious ettle;
But little wist she Maggie's mettle –
Ae spring brought off her master hale,
But left behind her ain gray tail:
The carlin claught her by the rump,
And left poor Maggie scarce a stump.

   Now, wha this tale o' truth shall read,
Ilk man and mother's son, take heed:
Whene'er to drink you are inclin'd,
Or cutty sarks run in your mind,
Think, ye may buy the joys o'er dear,
Remember Tam o' Shanter's mare.

Holy Willie's Prayer

O Thou, wha in the heavens dost dwell,
Wha, as it pleases best thysel',
Sends ane to heaven, and ten to hell,
     A' for thy glory,
And no for ony guid or ill
     They've done afore thee!

I bless and praise thy matchless might,
Whan thousands thou hast left in night,
That I am here afore thy sight,
     For gifts and grace,
A burnin' and a shinin' light
     To a' this place.

ent: devil. *ettle*: purpose. *hale*: whole. *claught*: clutched.

What was I, or my generation,
That I should get sic exaltation,
I wha deserve sic just damnation
      For broken laws,
Five thousand years 'fore my creation,
        Through Adam's cause!

When frae my mither's womb I fell,
Thou might hae plungèd me in hell,
To gnash my gums, to weep and wail,
      In burnin' lake,
Whare damnèd devils roar and yell,
      Chain'd to a stake.

Yet I am here, a chosen sample,
To show thy grace is great and ample;
I'm here a pillar in thy temple,
      Strong as a rock,
A guide, a buckler, and example,
      To a' thy flock.

O Lord! thou kens what zeal I bear,
When drinkers drink, and swearers swear,
And singin' there, and dancin' here,
      Wi' great an' sma';
For I am keepit by the fear
      Free frae them a'.

But yet, Lord! confess I must,
At times I'm fash'd wi' fleshly lust;
And sometimes, too, wi' warldly trust
      Vile self gets in:
But thou remembers we are dust,
      Defiled in sin.

O Lord! yestreen, thou kens, wi' Meg –
Thy pardon I sincerely beg,
Oh! may't ne'er be a livin' plague,
      To my dishonour,

And I'll ne'er lift a lawless leg
        Again upon her.

Besides, I farther maun avow,
Wi' Leezie's lass, three times I trow;
But, Lord! that Friday I was fou,
        When I cam near her,
Or, else, thou kens, thy servant true
        Wad ne'er hae steer'd her.

Maybe thou lets this fleshly thorn
Beset thy servant e'en and morn,
Lest he owre high and proud should turn,
        'Cause he's sae gifted;
If sae, thy han' maun e'en be borne,
        Until thou lift it.

Lord, bless thy chosen in this place,
For here thou hast a chosen race;
But God confound their stubborn face,
        And blast their name,
Wha bring thy elders to disgrace
        And public shame.

Lord! mind Gaw'n Hamilton's deserts;
He drinks, and swears, and plays at cartes,
Yet has sae mony takin' arts,
        Wi' grit and sma',
Frae God's ain priests the people's hearts
        He steals awa'.

And when we chasten'd him therefor,
Thou kens how he bred sic a splore,
As set the warld in a roar
        O' laughin' at us:
Curse thou his basket and his store,
        Kail and potatoes.

fou: drunk. *cartes*: cards. *splore*: riot.

Lord, hear my earnest cry and prayer,
Against that Presbyt'ry of Ayr;
Thy strong right hand, Lord, make it bare,
      Upo' their heads,
Lord, weigh it down, and dinna spare,
      For their misdeeds.

O Lord my God! that glib-tongued Aiken
My very heart and saul are quakin',
To think how I sat sweatin', shakin',
      And piss'd wi' dread,
While he, wi' hingin' lip an' snakin',
      Held up his head.

Lord, in the day of vengeance try him,
Lord, visit them wha did employ him,
And pass not in thy mercy by 'em,
      Nor hear their prayer;
But for thy people's sake destroy 'em,
      And dinna spare.

But, Lord, remember me and mine
Wi' mercies temporal and divine,
That I for gear and grace may shine,
      Excell'd by nane,
And a' the glory shall be thine,
      Amen! Amen!

It was a' for our Rightfu' King

It was a' for our rightfu' king
  We left fair Scotland's strand;
It was a' for our rightfu' king,
  We e'er saw Irish land, my dear,
  We e'er saw Irish land.

Now a' is done that men can do,
    And a' is done in vain:
My Love and Native Land fareweel,
    For I maun cross the main, my dear,
      For I maun cross the main.

He turn'd him right and round about,
    Upon the Irish shore,
And gae his bridle reins a shake,
    With, adieu for evermore, my dear,
      With, adieu for evermore!

The soger frae the wars returns,
    The sailor frae the main,
But I hae parted frae my Love,
    Never to meet again, my dear,
      Never to meet again.

When day is gane, and night is come,
    And a' folk bound to sleep;
I think on him that's far awa,
    The lee-lang night, and weep, my dear,
      The lee-lang night and weep.

Ye Flowery Banks

Ye flowery banks o' bonie Doon,
    How can ye blume sae fair?
How can ye chant, ye little birds,
    And I sae fu' o' care?

Thou'll break my heart, thou bonie bird,
    That sings upon the bough:
Thou minds me o' the happy days
    When my fause Luve was true.

Thou'll break my heart, thou bonie bird,
   That sings beside thy mate:
For sae I sat, and sae I sang,
   And wist na o' my fate.

Aft hae I rov'd by bonie Doon
   To see the woodbine twine,
And ilka bird sang o' its luve,
   And sae did I o' mine.

Wi' lightsome heart I pu'd a rose
   Frae aff its thorny tree,
And my fause luver staw my rose,
   But left the thorn wi' me.

O, wert thou in the cauld blast

O, wert thou in the cauld blast,
   On yonder lea, on yonder lea,
My plaidie to the angry airt,
   I'd shelter thee, I'd shelter thee.
Or did Misfortune's bitter storms
   Around thee blaw, around thee blaw,
Thy bield should be my bosom,
   To share it a', to share it a'.

Or were I in the wildest waste,
   Sae black and bare, sae black and bare,
The desert were a Paradise,
   If thou wert there, if thou wert there.
Or were I monarch o' the globe,
   Wi' thee to reign, wi' thee to reign,
The brightest jewel in my crown
   Wad be my queen, wad be my queen.

bield: shelter.

ROBERT BLOOMFIELD
1766–1823

From *The Farmer's Boy*

Yet never fam'd was he, nor foremost found
To break the seal of sleep; his sleep was sound:
But when at day-break summon'd from his bed,
Light as the lark that carol'd o'er his head. –
His sandy way deep-worn by hasty showers,
O'er arch'd with oaks that form'd fantastic bow'rs,
Waving aloft their tow'ring branches proud,
In borrow'd tinges from the eastern cloud,
Gave inspiration, pure as ever flow'd,
And genuine transport in his bosom glow'd.
His own shrill matin join'd the various notes
Of Nature's music, from a thousand throats:
The blackbird strove with emulation sweet,
And echo answer'd from her close retreat;
The sporting white-throat on some twig's end borne,
Pour'd hymns to freedom and the rising morn;
Stopt in her song perchance the starting thrush
Shook a white shower from the black-thorn bush,
Where dew-drops thick as early blossoms hung,
And trembled as the minstrel sweetly sung.

WILLIAM WORDSWORTH
1770–1850

*Remembrance of Collins**

COMPOSED UPON THE THAMES
NEAR RICHMOND

Glide gently, thus for ever glide,
O Thames! that other bards may see
As lovely visions by thy side
As now, fair river! come to me.
O glide, fair stream! for ever so,
Thy quiet soul on all bestowing,
Till all our minds for ever flow
As thy deep waters now are flowing.

Vain thought! – Yet be as now thou art,
That in thy waters may be seen
The image of a poet's heart,
How bright, how solemn, how serene!
Such as did once the Poet bless,
Who murmuring here a later ditty,
Could find no refuge from distress
But in the milder grief of pity.

Now let us, as we float along,
For *him* suspend the dashing oar;
And pray that never child of song
May know that Poet's sorrows more.
How calm! how still! the only sound,
The dripping of the oar suspended!
– The evening darkness gathers round
By virtue's holiest Powers attended.

* See William Collins: *Ode on the Death of Thomson*, p. 18.

From *The Borderers*

Action is transitory – a step, a blow,
The motion of a muscle – this way or that –
'Tis done, and in the after-vacancy
We wonder at ourselves like men betrayed:
Suffering is permanent, obscure and dark,
And shares the nature of infinity.

Lines Written in Early Spring

I heard a thousand blended notes,
While in a grove I sate reclined,
In that sweet mood when pleasant thoughts
Bring sad thoughts to the mind.

To her fair works did Nature link
The human soul that through me ran;
And much it grieved my heart to think
What man has made of man.

Through primrose tufts, in that green bower,
The periwinkle trailed its wreaths;
And 'tis my faith that every flower
Enjoys the air it breathes.

The birds around me hopped and played,
Their thoughts I cannot measure: –
But the least motion which they made,
It seemed a thrill of pleasure.

The budding twigs spread out their fan,
To catch the breezy air;
And I must think, do all I can,
That there was pleasure there.

If this belief from heaven be sent,
If such be Nature's holy plan,
Have I not reason to lament
What man has made of man!

Lines

COMPOSED A FEW MILES ABOVE TINTERN ABBEY,
ON REVISITING THE BANKS OF THE WYE DURING
A TOUR
JULY 13, 1798

Five years have past; five summers, with the length
Of five long winters! and again I hear
These waters, rolling from their mountain-springs
With a soft inland murmur. – Once again
Do I behold these steep and lofty cliffs,
That on a wild secluded scene impress
Thoughts of more deep seclusion; and connect
The landscape with the quiet of the sky.
The day is come when I again repose
Here, under this dark sycamore, and view
These plots of cottage-ground, these orchard-tufts,
Which at this season, with their unripe fruits,
Are clad in one green hue, and lose themselves
'Mid groves and copses. Once again I see
These hedge-rows, hardly hedge-rows, little lines
Of sportive wood run wild: these pastoral farms,
Green to the very door; and wreaths of smoke
Sent up, in silence, from among the trees!
With some uncertain notice, as might seem
Of vagrant dwellers in the houseless woods,
Or of some Hermit's cave, where by his fire
The Hermit sits alone.

                These beauteous forms,
Through a long absence, have not been to me

As is a landscape to a blind man's eye:
But oft, in lonely rooms, and 'mid the din
Of towns and cities, I have owed to them
In hours of weariness, sensations sweet,
Felt in the blood, and felt along the heart;
And passing even into my purer mind,
With tranquil restoration: — feelings too
Of unremembered pleasure: such, perhaps,
As have no slight or trivial influence
On that best portion of a good man's life,
His little, nameless, unremembered, acts
Of kindness and of love. Nor less, I trust,
To them I may have owed another gift,
Of aspect more sublime; that blessed mood,
In which the burthen of the mystery,
In which the heavy and the weary weight
Of all this unintelligible world
Is lightened: — that serene and blessed mood,
In which the affections gently lead us on, —
Until, the breath of this corporeal frame
And even the motion of our human blood
Almost suspended, we are laid asleep
In body, and become a living soul:
While with an eye made quiet by the power
Of harmony, and the deep power of joy,
We see into the life of things.
                                        If this
Be but a vain belief, yet, oh! how oft —
In darkness and amid the many shapes
Of joyless daylight; when the fretful stir
Unprofitable, and the fever of the world,
Have hung upon the beatings of my heart —
How oft, in spirit, have I turned to thee,
O sylvan Wye! thou wanderer thro' the woods,
How often has my spirit turned to thee!

And now, with gleams of half-extinguished thought,
With many recognitions dim and faint,

And somewhat of a sad perplexity,
The picture of the mind revives again:
While here I stand, not only with the sense
Of present pleasure, but with pleasing thoughts
That in this moment there is life and food
For future years. And so I dare to hope,
Though changed, no doubt, from what I was when first
I came among these hills; when like a roe
I bounded o'er the mountains, by the sides
Of the deep rivers, and the lonely streams,
Wherever nature led: more like a man
Flying from something that he dreads, than one
Who sought the thing he loved. For nature then
(The coarser pleasures of my boyish days,
And their glad animal movements all gone by)
To me was all in all. – I cannot paint
What then I was. The sounding cataract
Haunted me like a passion: the tall rock,
The mountain, and the deep and gloomy wood,
Their colours and their forms, were then to me
An appetite; a feeling and a love,
That had no need of a remoter charm,
By thought supplied, nor any interest
Unborrowed from the eye. – That time is past,
And all its aching joys are now no more,
And all its dizzy raptures. Not for this
Faint I, nor mourn nor murmur; other gifts
Have followed; for such loss, I would believe,
Abundant recompence. For I have learned
To look on nature, not as in the hour
Of thoughtless youth; but hearing oftentimes
The still, sad music of humanity,
Nor harsh nor grating, though of ample power
To chasten and subdue. And I have felt
A presence that disturbs me with the joy
Of elevated thoughts; a sense sublime
Of something far more deeply interfused,
Whose dwelling is the light of setting suns,

And the round ocean and the living air,
And the blue sky, and in the mind of man:
A motion and a spirit, that impels
All thinking things, all objects of all thought,
And rolls through all things. Therefore am I still
A lover of the meadows and the woods,
And mountains; and of all that we behold
From this green earth; of all the mighty world
Of eye, and ear, – both what they half create,
And what perceive; well pleased to recognise
In nature and the language of the sense,
The anchor of my purest thoughts, the nurse,
The guide, the guardian of my heart, and soul
Of all my moral being.
                                  Nor perchance,
If I were not thus taught, should I the more
Suffer my genial spirits to decay:
For thou art with me here upon the banks
Of this fair river; thou my dearest Friend,
My dear, dear Friend; and in thy voice I catch
The language of my former heart, and read
My former pleasures in the shooting lights
Of thy wild eyes. Oh! yet a little while
May I behold in thee what I was once,
My dear, dear Sister! and this prayer I make,
Knowing that Nature never did betray
The heart that loved her; 'tis her privilege,
Through all the years of this our life, to lead
From joy to joy: for she can so inform
The mind that is within us, so impress
With quietness and beauty, and so feed
With lofty thoughts, that neither evil tongues,
Rash judgments, nor the sneers of selfish men,
Nor greetings where no kindness is, nor all
The dreary intercourse of daily life,
Shall e'er prevail against us, or disturb
Our cheerful faith, that all which we behold
Is full of blessings. Therefore let the moon

Shine on thee in thy solitary walk;
And let the misty mountain winds be free
To blow against thee: and, in after years,
When these wild ecstasies shall be matured
Into a sober pleasure; when thy mind
Shall be a mansion for all lovely forms,
Thy memory be as a dwelling place
For all sweet sounds and harmonies; oh! then,
If solitude, or fear, or pain, or grief,
Should be thy portion, with what healing thoughts
Of tender joy wilt thou remember me,
And these my exhortations! Nor, perchance –
If I should be where I no more can hear
Thy voice, nor catch from thy wild eyes these gleams
Of past existence – wilt thou then forget
That on the banks of this delightful stream
We stood together; and that I, so long
A worshipper of Nature, hither came
Unwearied in that service: rather say
With warmer love – oh! with far deeper zeal
Of holier love. Nor wilt thou then forget,
That after many wanderings, many years
Of absence, these steep woods and lofty cliffs,
And this green pastoral landscape, were to me
More dear, both for themselves and for thy sake!

From *The Prelude* (1805 version)

(i)

Wisdom and Spirit of the universe!
Thou Soul that art the Eternity of Thought!
That giv'st to forms and images a breath
And everlasting motion! not in vain,
By day or star-light thus from my first dawn
Of Childhood didst Thou intertwine for me
The passions that build up our human Soul,

Not with the mean and vulgar works of Man,
But with high objects, with enduring things,
With life and nature, purifying thus
The elements of feeling and of thought,
And sanctifying, by such discipline,
Both pain and fear, until we recognize
A grandeur in the beatings of the heart.

Nor was this fellowship vouchsaf'd to me
With stinted kindness. In November days,
When vapours, rolling down the valleys, made
A lonely scene more lonesome; among woods
At noon, and 'mid the calm of summer nights,
When, by the margin of the trembling Lake,
Beneath the gloomy hills I homeward went
In solitude, such intercourse was mine;
'Twas mine among the fields both day and night,
And by the waters all the summer long.

And in the frosty season, when the sun
Was set, and visible for many a mile
The cottage windows through the twilight blaz'd,
I heeded not the summons: – happy time
It was, indeed, for all of us; to me
It was a time of rapture: clear and loud
The village clock toll'd six; I wheel'd about,
Proud and exulting, like an untired horse,
That cares not for its home. – All shod with steel,
We hiss'd along the polish'd ice, in games
Confederate, imitative of the chace
And woodland pleasures, the resounding horn,
The Pack loud bellowing, and the hunted hare.
So through the darkness and the cold we flew,
And not a voice was idle; with the din,
Meanwhile, the precipices rang aloud,
The leafless trees, and every icy crag
Tinkled like iron, while the distant hills
Into the tumult sent an alien sound

Of melancholy, not unnoticed, while the stars,
Eastward, were sparkling clear, and in the west
The orange sky of evening died away.

Not seldom from the uproar I retired
Into a silent bay, or sportively
Glanced sideway, leaving the tumultuous throng,
To cut across the image of a star
That gleam'd upon the ice: and oftentimes
When we had given our bodies to the wind,
And all the shadowy banks, on either side,
Came sweeping through the darkness, spinning still
The rapid line of motion; then at once
Have I, reclining back upon my heels,
Stopp'd short, yet still the solitary Cliffs
Wheeled by me, even as if the earth had roll'd
With visible motion her diurnal round;
Behind me did they stretch in solemn train
Feebler and feebler, and I stood and watch'd
Till all was tranquil as a dreamless sleep.

Book I, lines 428–489

(ii)

A thought is with me sometimes, and I say,
Should earth by inward throes be wrench'd throughout,
Or fire be sent from far to wither all
Her pleasant habitations and dry up
Old Ocean in his bed left sing'd and bare,
Yet would the living Presence still subsist
Victorious; and composure would ensue,
And kindlings like morning; presage sure,
Though slow, perhaps, of a returning day.
But all the meditations of mankind,
Yea, all the adamantine holds of truth,
By reason built, or passion, which itself
Is highest reason in a soul sublime;
The consecrated works of Bard and Sage,

Sensuous or intellectual, wrought by men,
Twin labourers and heirs of the same hopes,
Where would they be? Oh! why hath not the mind
Some element to stamp her image on
In nature somewhat nearer to her own?
Why, gifted with such powers to send abroad
Her spirit, must it lodge in shrines so frail?

One day, when in the hearing of a Friend,
I had given utterance to thoughts like these,
He answer'd with a smile that, in plain truth
'Twas going far to seek disquietude;
But on the front of his reproof, confess'd
That he, at sundry seasons, had himself
Yielded to kindred hauntings. And forthwith
Added, that once upon a summer's noon,
While he was sitting in a rocky cave
By the sea-side, perusing, as it chanced,
The famous History of the Errant Knight
Recorded by Cervantes, these same thoughts
Came to him; and to height unusual rose
While listlessly he sate, and having closed
The Book, had turned his eyes towards the Sea.
On Poetry and geometric Truth,
The knowledge that endures upon these two,
And their high privilege of lasting life,
Exempt from all internal injury,
He mused: upon these chiefly: and at length,
His senses yielding to the sultry air,
Sleep seiz'd him, and he pass'd into a dream.
He saw before him an Arabian Waste,
A Desart; and he fancied that himself
Was sitting there in the wide wilderness,
Alone, upon the sands. Distress of mind
Was growing in him when, behold! at once
To his great joy a Man was at his side,
Upon a dromedary, mounted high.
He seem'd an Arab of the Bedouin Tribes,

A Lance he bore, and underneath one arm
A Stone; and, in the opposite hand, a Shell
Of a surpassing brightness. Much rejoic'd
The dreaming Man that he should have a Guide
To lead him through the Desart; and he thought,
While questioning himself what this strange freight
Which the Newcomer carried through the Waste
Could mean, the Arab told him that the Stone,
To give it in the language of the Dream,
Was Euclid's Elements; 'and this,' said he,
'This other,' pointing to the Shell, 'this Book
Is something of more worth.' And, at the word,
The Stranger, said my Friend continuing,
Stretch'd forth the Shell towards me, with command
That I should hold it to my ear; I did so,
And heard that instant in an unknown Tongue,
Which yet I understood, articulate sounds,
A loud prophetic blast of harmony,
An Ode, in passion utter'd, which foretold
Destruction to the Children of the Earth,
By deluge now at hand. No sooner ceas'd
The Song, but with calm look, the Arab said
That all was true; that it was even so
As had been spoken; and that he himself
Was going then to bury those two Books:
The one that held acquaintance with the stars
And wedded man to man by purest bond
Of nature, undisturbed by space or time;
Th' other that was a God, yea many Gods,
Had voices more than all the winds, and was
A joy, a consolation, and a hope.
My friend continued, 'strange as it may seem,
I wonder'd not, although I plainly saw
The one to be a Stone, th' other a Shell,
Nor doubted once but that they both were Books,
Having a perfect faith in all that pass'd.
A wish was now ingender'd in my fear
To cleave unto this Man, and I begg'd leave

To share his errand with him. On he pass'd
Not heeding me; I follow'd, and took note
That he look'd often backward with wild look,
Grasping his twofold treasure to his side.
– Upon a Dromedary, Lance in rest,
He rode, I keeping pace with him, and now
I fancied that he was the very Knight
Whose Tale Cervantes tells, yet not the Knight,
But was an Arab of the Desart, too;
Of these was neither, and was both at once.
His countenance, meanwhile, grew more disturb'd,
And, looking backwards when he look'd, I saw
A glittering light, and ask'd him whence it came.
'It is,' said he, 'the waters of the deep
Gathering upon us,' quickening then his pace
He left me: I call'd after him aloud;
He heeded not: but with his twofold charge
Beneath his arm, before me full in view
I saw him riding o'er the Desart Sands,
With the fleet waters of the drowning world
In chase of him, whereat I wak'd in terror,
And saw the Sea before me; and the Book,
In which I had been reading, at my side.

Book V, lines 28–139

(iii)

The immeasurable height
Of woods decaying, never to be decay'd,
The stationary blasts of water-falls,
And every where along the hollow rent
Winds thwarting winds, bewilder'd and forlorn,
The torrents shooting from the clear blue sky,
The rocks that mutter'd close upon our ears,
Black drizzling crags that spake by the way-side
As if a voice were in them, the sick sight
And giddy prospect of the raving stream,
The unfetter'd clouds, and region of the Heavens,

Tumult and peace, the darkness and the light
Were all like workings of one mind, the features
Of the same face, blossoms upon one tree,
Characters of the great Apocalypse,
The types and symbols of Eternity,
Of first and last, and midst, and without end.

Book VI, lines 556–572

A Poet's Epitaph

Art thou a Statist in the van
Of public conflicts trained and bred?
– First learn to love one living man;
Then may'st thou think upon the dead.

A Lawyer art thou? – draw not nigh!
Go, carry to some fitter place
The keenness of that practised eye,
The hardness of that sallow face.

Art thou a Man of purple cheer?
A rosy Man, right plump to see?
Approach; yet, Doctor, not too near,
This grave no cushion is for thee.

Or art thou one of gallant pride.
A Soldier and no man of chaff!
Welcome! – but lay thy sword aside,
And lean upon a peasant's staff.

Physician art thou? one, all eyes,
Philosopher! a fingering slave,
One that would peep and botanize
Upon his mother's grave?

Wrapt closely in thy sensual fleece,
O turn aside, – and take, I pray,
That he below may rest in peace,
Thy ever-dwindling soul, away!

Statist: statesman. *Doctor*: i.e., Doctor of Divinity.

A Moralist perchance appears;
Led, Heaven knows how! to this poor sod:
And he has neither eyes nor ears;
Himself his world, and his own God;

One to whose smooth-rubbed soul can cling
Nor form, nor feeling, great or small;
A reasoning, self-sufficing thing,
An intellectual All-in-all!

Shut close the door; press down the latch;
Sleep in thy intellectual crust;
Nor lose ten tickings of thy watch
Near this unprofitable dust.

But who is He, with modest looks,
And clad in homely russet brown?
He murmurs near the running brooks
A music sweeter than their own.

He is retired as noontide dew,
Or fountain in a noon-day grove;
And you must love him, ere to you
He will seem worthy of your love.

The outward shows of sky and earth,
Of hill and valley, he has viewed;
And impulses of deeper birth
Have come to him in solitude.

In common things that round us lie
Some random truths he can impart, —
The harvest of a quiet eye
That broods and sleeps on his own heart.

But he is weak; both Man and Boy,
Hath been an idler in the land;
Contented if he might enjoy
The things which others understand.

– Come hither in thy hour of strength;
Come, weak as is a breaking wave!
Here stretch thy body at full length;
Or build thy house upon this grave.

Resolution and Independence

There was a roaring in the wind all night;
The rain came heavily and fell in floods;
But now the sun is rising calm and bright;
The birds are singing in the distant woods;
Over his own sweet voice the Stock-dove broods;
The Jay makes answer as the Magpie chatters;
And all the air is filled with pleasant noise of waters.

All things that love the sun are out of doors;
The sky rejoices in the morning's birth;
The grass is bright with rain-drops; – on the moors
The hare is running races in her mirth;
And with her feet she from the plashy earth
Raises a mist, that, glittering in the sun,
Runs with her all the way, wherever she doth run.

I was a Traveller then upon the moor;
I saw the hare that raced about with joy;
I heard the woods and distant waters roar;
Or heard them not, as happy as a boy:
The pleasant season did my heart employ:
My old remembrances went from me wholly;
And all the ways of men, so vain and melancholy.

But, as it sometimes chanceth, from the might
Of joy in minds that can no further go,
As high as we have mounted in delight
In our dejection do we sink as low;
To me that morning did it happen so;
And fears and fancies thick upon me came;
Dim sadness – and blind thoughts, I knew not, nor could
    name.

I heard the sky-lark warbling in the sky;
And I bethought me of the playful hare:
Even such a happy Child of earth am I;
Even as these blissful creatures do I fare;
Far from the world I walk, and from all care;
But there may come another day to me –
Solitude, pain of heart, distress, and poverty.

My whole life I have lived in pleasant thought,
As if life's business were a summer mood;
As if all needful things would come unsought
To genial faith, still rich in genial good;
But how can He expect that others should
Build for him, sow for him, and at his call
Love him, who for himself will take no heed at all?

I thought of Chatterton, the marvellous Boy,
The sleepless Soul that perished in his pride;
Of Him who walked in glory and in joy
Following his plough, along the mountain-side:
By our own spirits are we deified:
We Poets in our youth begin in gladness;
But thereof come in the end despondency and madness.

Now, whether it were by peculiar grace,
A leading from above, a something given,
Yet it befel, that, in this lonely place,
When I with these untoward thoughts had striven,
Beside a pool bare to the eye of heaven
I saw a Man before me unawares:
The oldest man he seemed that ever wore grey hairs.

As a huge stone is sometimes seen to lie
Couched on the bald top of an eminence;
Wonder to all who do the same espy,
By what means it could thither come, and whence;
So that it seems a thing endued with sense:
Like a sea-beast crawled forth, that on a shelf
Of rock or sand reposeth, there to sun itself;

Such seemed this Man, not all alive nor dead,
Nor all asleep – in his extreme old age:
His body was bent double, feet and head
Coming together in life's pilgrimage;
As if some dire constraint of pain, or rage
Of sickness felt by him in times long past,
A more than human weight upon his frame had cast.

Himself he propped, limbs, body, and pale face,
Upon a long grey staff of shaven wood:
And, still as I drew near with gentle pace,
Upon the margin of that moorish flood
Motionless as a cloud the old Man stood,
That heareth not the loud winds when they call;
And moveth all together, if it move at all.

At length, himself unsettling, he the pond
Stirred with his staff, and fixedly did look
Upon the muddy water, which he conned,
As if he had been reading in a book:
And now a stranger's privilege I took;
And, drawing to his side, to him did say,
'This morning gives us promise of a glorious day.'

A gentle answer did the old Man make,
In courteous speech which forth he slowly drew:
And him with further words I thus bespake,
'What occupation do you there pursue?
This is a lonesome place for one like you.'
Ere he replied, a flash of mild surprise
Broke from the sable orbs of his yet-vivid eyes.

His words came feebly, from a feeble chest,
But each in solemn order followed each,
With something of a lofty utterance drest –
Choice word and measured phrase, above the reach
Of ordinary men; a stately speech;
Such as grave Livers do in Scotland use,
Religious men, who give to God and man their dues.

He told, that to these waters he had come
To gather leeches, being old and poor:
Employment hazardous and wearisome!
And he had many hardships to endure:
From pond to pond he roamed, from moor to moor;
Housing, with God's good help, by choice or chance;
And in this way he gained an honest maintenance.

The old Man still stood talking by my side;
But now his voice to me was like a stream
Scarce heard; nor word from word could I divide;
And the whole body of the Man did seem
Like one whom I had met with in a dream;
Or like a man from some far region sent,
To give me human strength, by apt admonishment.

My former thoughts returned: the fear that kills;
And hope that is unwilling to be fed;
Cold, pain and labour, and all fleshly ills;
And mighty Poets in their misery dead.
– Perplexed, and longing to be comforted,
My question eagerly did I renew,
'How is it that you live, and what is it you do?'

He with a smile did then his words repeat;
And said, that, gathering leeches, far and wide
He travelled; stirring thus about his feet
The waters of the pools where they abide.
'Once I could meet with them on every side;
But they have dwindled long by slow decay;
Yet still I persevere, and find them where I may.'

While he was talking thus, the lonely place,
The old Man's shape, and speech – all troubled me:
In my mind's eye I seemed to see him pace
About the weary moors continually,
Wandering about alone and silently.
While I these thoughts within myself pursued,
He, having made a pause, the same discourse renewed.

And soon with this he other matter blended,
Cheerfully uttered, with demeanour kind,
But stately in the main; and when he ended,
I could have laughed myself to scorn to find
In that decrepit Man so firm a mind.
'God', said I, 'be my help and stay secure;
I'll think of the Leech-gatherer on the lonely moor!'

To Toussaint L'Ouverture

Toussaint, the most unhappy man of men!
Whether the whistling Rustic tend his plough
Within thy hearing, or thy head be now
Pillowed in some deep dungeon's earless den; –
O miserable Chieftain! where and when
Wilt thou find patience? Yet die not; do thou
Wear rather in thy bonds a cheerful brow:
Though fallen thyself, never to rise again,
Live, and take comfort. Thou hast left behind
Powers that will work for thee; air, earth, and skies;
There's not a breathing of the common wind
That will forget thee; thou hast great allies;
Thy friends are exultations, agonies,
And love, and man's unconquerable mind.

The Green Linnet

Beneath these fruit-tree boughs that shed
Their snow-white blossoms on my head,
With brightest sunshine round me spread
    Of spring's unclouded weather,
In this sequestered nook how sweet
To sit upon my orchard-seat!
And birds and flowers once more to greet,
    My last year's friends together.

One have I marked, the happiest guest
In all this covert of the blest:
Hail to Thee, far above the rest
    In joy of voice and pinion!
Thou, Linnet! in thy green array,
Presiding Spirit here to-day,
Dost lead the revels of the May;
    And this is thy dominion.

While birds, and butterflies, and flowers,
Make all one band of paramours,
Thou, ranging up and down the bowers,
    Art sole in thy employment:
A Life, a Presence like the Air,
Scattering thy gladness without care,
Too blest with any one to pair;
    Thyself thy own enjoyment.

Amid yon tuft of hazel trees,
That twinkle to the gusty breeze,
Behold him perched in ecstasies,
    Yet seeming still to hover;
There! where the flutter of his wings
Upon his back and body flings
Shadows and sunny glimmerings,
    That cover him all over.

My dazzled sight he oft deceives,
A Brother of the dancing leaves;
Then flits, and from the cottage-eaves
    Pours forth his song in gushes;
As if by that exulting strain
He mocked and treated with disdain
The voiceless Form he chose to feign,
    While fluttering in the bushes.

To the Cuckoo

O blithe New-comer! I have heard,
I hear thee and rejoice.
O Cuckoo! shall I call thee Bird,
Or but a wandering Voice?

While I am lying on the grass
Thy twofold shout I hear,
From hill to hill it seems to pass,
At once far off, and near.

Though babbling only to the Vale,
Of sunshine and of flowers,
Thou bringest unto me a tale
Of visionary hours.

Thrice welcome, darling of the Spring!
Even yet thou art to me
No bird, but an invisible thing,
A voice, a mystery;

The same whom in my school-boy days
I listened to; that Cry
Which made me look a thousand ways
In bush, and tree, and sky.

To seek thee did I often rove
Through woods and on the green;
And thou wert still a hope, a love;
Still longed for, never seen.

And I can listen to thee yet;
Can lie upon the plain
And listen, till I do beget
That golden time again.

O blessèd Bird! the earth we pace
Again appears to be
An unsubstantial, faery place;
That is fit home for Thee!

The Affliction of Margaret

Where art thou, my beloved Son,
Where art thou, worse to me than dead?
Oh find me, prosperous or undone!
Or, if the grave be now thy bed,
Why am I ignorant of the same
That I may rest; and neither blame
Nor sorrow may attend thy name?

Seven years, alas! to have received
No tidings of an only child;
To have despaired, have hoped, believed,
And been for evermore beguiled;
Sometimes with thoughts of very bliss!
I catch at them, and then I miss;
Was ever darkness like to this?

He was among the prime in worth,
An object beauteous to behold;
Well born, well bred; I sent him forth
Ingenuous, innocent, and bold:
If things ensued that wanted grace,
As hath been said, they were not base;
And never blush was on my face.

Ah! little doth the young-one dream,
When full of play and childish cares,
What power is in his wildest scream,
Heard by his mother unawares!
He knows it not, he cannot guess:
Years to a mother bring distress;
But do not make her love the less.

Neglect me! no, I suffered long
From that ill thought; and, being blind,
Said, 'Pride shall help me in my wrong:
Kind mother have I been, as kind
As ever breathed:' and that is true;
I've wet my path with tears like dew,
Weeping for him when no one knew.

My Son, if thou be humbled, poor,
Hopeless of honour and of gain,
Oh! do not dread thy mother's door;
Think not of me with grief and pain:
I now can see with better eyes;
And wordly grandeur I despise,
And fortune with her gifts and lies.

Alas! the fowls of heaven have wings,
And blasts of heaven will aid their flight;
They mount – how short a voyage brings
The wanderers back to their delight!
Chains tie us down by land and sea;
And wishes, vain as mine, may be
All that is left to comfort thee.

Perhaps some dungeon hears thee groan,
Maimed, mangled by inhuman men;
Or thou upon a desert thrown
Inheritest the lion's den;
Or hast been summoned to the deep,
Thou, thou and all thy mates, to keep
An incommunicable sleep.

I look for ghosts; but none will force
Their way to me: 'tis falsely said
That there was ever intercourse
Between the living and the dead;
For, surely, then I should have sight
Of him I wait for day and night,
With love and longings infinite.

My apprehensions come in crowds;
I dread the rustling of the grass;
The very shadows of the clouds
Have power to shake me as they pass:
I question things and do not find
One that will answer to my mind;
And all the world appears unkind.

Beyond participation lie
My troubles, and beyond relief:
If any chance to heave a sigh,
They pity me, and not my grief.
Then come to me, my Son, or send
Some tidings that my woes may end;
I have no other earthly friend!

The Small Celandine

There is a Flower, the lesser Celandine,
That shrinks, like many more, from cold and rain;
And, the first moment that the sun may shine,
Bright as the sun himself, 'tis out again!

When hailstones have been falling, swarm on swarm,
Or blasts the green field and the trees distrest,
Oft have I seen it muffled up from harm,
In close self-shelter, like a Thing at rest.

But lately, one rough day, this Flower I passed
And recognised it, though an altered form,
Now standing forth an offering to the blast,
And buffeted at will by rain and storm.

I stopped, and said with inly-muttered voice,
'It doth not love the shower, nor seek the cold:
This neither is its courage nor its choice,
But its necessity in being old.

The sunshine may not cheer it, nor the dew;
It cannot help itself in its decay;
Stiff in its members, withered, changed of hue.'
And, in my spleen, I smiled that it was grey.

To be a Prodigal's Favourite – then, worse truth,
A Miser's Pensioner – behold our lot!
O Man, that from thy fair and shining youth
Age might but take the things Youth needed not!

Fidelity*

A barking sound the Shepherd hears,
A cry as of a dog or fox;
He halts – and searches with his eyes
Among the scattered rocks:
And now at distance can discern
A stirring in a brake of fern;
And instantly a dog is seen,
Glancing through that covert green.

The Dog is not of mountain breed;
Its motions, too, are wild and shy;
With something, as the Shepherd thinks,
Unusual in its cry:
Nor is there any one in sight
All round, in hollow or on height;
Nor shout, nor whistle strikes his ear;
What is the creature doing here?

It was a cove, a huge recess,
That keeps, till June, December's snow;
A lofty precipice in front,
A silent tarn below!

* See Sir Walter Scott: *Helvellyn*, p. 146. The two poems were
inspired by the same incident.

Far in the bosom of Helvellyn,
Remote from public road or dwelling,
Pathway, or cultivated land;
From trace of human foot or hand.

There sometimes doth a leaping fish
Send through the tarn a lonely cheer;
The crags repeat the raven's croak,
In symphony austere;
Thither the rainbow comes – the cloud –
And mists that spread the flying shroud;
And sunbeams; and the sounding blast,
That, if it could, would hurry past;
But that enormous barrier holds it fast.

Not free from boding thoughts, a while
The Shepherd stood; then makes his way
O'er rocks and stones, following the Dog
As quickly as he may;
Nor far had gone before he found
A human skeleton on the ground;
The appalled Discoverer with a sigh
Looks round, to learn the history.

From those abrupt and perilous rocks
The Man had fallen, that place of fear!
At length upon the Shepherd's mind
It breaks, and all is clear:
He instantly recalled the name,
And who he was, and whence he came;
Remembered, too, the very day
On which the Traveller passed this way.

But hear a wonder, for whose sake
This lamentable tale I tell!
A lasting monument of words
This wonder merits well.
The Dog, which still was hovering nigh,

Repeating the same timid cry,
This Dog, had been through three months' space
A dweller in that savage place.

Yes, proof was plain that, since the day
When this ill-fated Traveller died,
The Dog had watched about the spot,
Or by his master's side:
How nourished here through such long time
He knows, who gave that love sublime;
And gave that strength of feeling, great
Above all human estimate!

Ode

INTIMATIONS OF IMMORTALITY FROM
RECOLLECTIONS OF EARLY CHILDHOOD

> The Child is Father of the Man;
> And I could wish my days to be
> Bound each to each by natural piety.

There was a time when meadow, grove, and stream,
The earth, and every common sight,
        To me did seem
        Apparelled in celestial light,
The glory and the freshness of a dream.
It is not now as it hath been of yore;—
        Turn whereso'er I may,
            By night or day,
The things which I have seen I now can see no more.

        The Rainbow comes and goes,
        And lovely is the Rose,
        The Moon doth with delight
Look round her when the heavens are bare,

Waters on a starry night
Are beautiful and fair;
The sunshine is a glorious birth;
But yet I know, where'er I go,
That there hath past away a glory from the earth.

Now, while the birds thus sing a joyous song,
And while the young lambs bound
As to the tabor's sound,
To me alone there came a thought of grief:
A timely utterance gave that thought relief,
And I again am strong:
The cataracts blow their trumpets from the steep;
No more shall grief of mine the season wrong;
I hear the Echoes through the mountains throng,
The Winds come to me from the fields of sleep,
And all the earth is gay;
Land and sea
Give themselves up to jollity,
And with the heart of May
Doth every Beast keep holiday; –
Thou child of Joy,
Shout round me, let me hear thy shouts, thou happy
Shepherd-boy!

Ye blessed Creatures, I have heard the call
Ye to each other make; I see
The heavens laugh with you in your jubilee;
My heart is at your festival,
My head hath its coronal,
The fulness of your bliss, I feel – I feel it all.
Oh evil day! if I were sullen
While Earth herself is adorning,
This sweet May-morning,
And the Children are culling
On every side,
In a thousand valleys far and wide,
Fresh flowers; while the sun shines warm,

And the Babe leaps up on his Mother's arm: —
      I hear, I hear, with joy I hear!
      — But there's a Tree, of many, one,
A single Field which I have looked upon,
Both of them speak of something that is gone:
         The Pansy at my feet
         Doth the same tale repeat:
Whither is fled the visionary gleam?
Where is it now, the glory and the dream?

Our birth is but a sleep and a forgetting:
The Soul that rises with us, our life's Star,
      Hath had elsewhere its setting,
         And cometh from afar:
      Not in entire forgetfulness,
      And not in utter nakedness,
But trailing clouds of glory do we come
         From God, who is our home:
Heaven lies about us in our infancy!
Shades of the prison-house begin to close
         Upon the growing Boy,
But He beholds the light, and whence it flows,
         He sees it in his joy;
The Youth, who daily farther from the east
         Must travel, still is Nature's Priest,
         And by the vision splendid
         Is on his way attended;
At length the Man perceives it die away,
And fade into the light of common day.

Earth fills her lap with pleasures of her own;
Yearnings she hath in her own natural kind,
And, even with something of a Mother's mind,
         And no unworthy aim,
         The homely Nurse doth all she can
To make her Foster-child, her Inmate Man,
         Forget the glories he hath known,
And that imperial palace whence he came.

Behold the Child among his new-born blisses,
A six years' Darling of a pigmy size!
See, where 'mid work of his own hand he lies,
Fretted by sallies of his mother's kisses,
With light upon him from his father's eyes!
See, at his feet, some little plan or chart,
Some fragment from his dream of human life,
Shaped by himself with newly-learned art;
    A wedding or a festival,
    A mourning or a funeral:
        And this hath now his heart,
        And unto this he frames his song:
        Then will he fit his tongue
To dialogues of business, love, or strife;
        But it will not be long
        Ere this be thrown aside,
        And with new joy and pride
The little Actor cons another part;
Filling from time to time his 'humorous stage'
With all the Persons, down to palsied Age,
That Life brings with her in her equipage;
        As if his whole vocation
        Were endless imitation.

Thou, whose exterior semblance doth belie
        Thy Soul's immensity;
Thou best Philosopher, who yet dost keep
Thy heritage, thou Eye among the blind,
That, deaf and silent, read'st the eternal deep,
Haunted for ever by the eternal mind, –
        Mighty Prophet! Seer blest!
        On whom those truths do rest,
Which we are toiling all our lives to find,
In darkness lost, the darkness of the grave;
Thou, over whom thy Immortality
Broods like the Day, a Master o'er a Slave,
A Presence which is not to be put by;
Thou little Child, yet glorious in the might

Of heaven-born freedom on thy being's height,
Why with such earnest pains dost thou provoke
The years to bring the inevitable yoke,
Thus blindly with thy blessedness at strife?
Full soon thy Soul shall have her earthly freight,
And custom lie upon thee with a weight,
Heavy as frost, and deep almost as life!

     O joy! that in our embers
     In something that doth live,
     That nature yet remembers
     What was so fugitive!
The thought of our past years in me doth breed
Perpetual benediction: not indeed
For that which is most worthy to be blest;
Delight and liberty, the simple creed
Of Childhood, whether busy or at rest,
With new-fledged hope still fluttering in his breast: –
     Not for these I raise
     The song of thanks and praise;
   But for those obstinate questionings
   Of sense and outward things,
   Fallings from us, vanishings;
   Blank misgivings of a Creature
Moving about in worlds not realised,
High instincts before which our mortal Nature
Did tremble like a guilty Thing surprised:
     But for those first affections,
     Those shadowy recollections,
    Which, be they what they may,
Are yet the fountain light of all our day,
Are yet a master light of all our seeing;
   Uphold us, cherish, and have power to make
Our noisy years seem moments in the being
Of the eternal Silence: truths that wake,
     To perish never;
Which neither listlessness, nor mad endeavour,
     Nor Man nor Boy,

Nor all that is at enmity with joy,
Can utterly abolish or destroy!
      Hence in a season of calm weather
      Though inland far we be,
Our souls have sight of that immortal sea
    Which brought us hither,
      Can in a moment travel thither,
And see the Children sport upon the shore,
And hear the mighty waters rolling evermore.

Then sing, ye Birds, sing, sing a joyous song!
      And let the young Lambs bound
      As to the tabor's sound!
We in thought will join your throng,
      Ye that pipe and ye that play,
      Ye that through your hearts to-day
      Feel the gladness of the May!
What though the radiance which was once so bright
Be now for ever taken from my sight,
    Though nothing can bring back the hour
Of splendour in the grass, of glory in the flower;
      We will grieve not, rather find
      Strength in what remains behind;
      In the primal sympathy
      Which having been must ever be;
      In the soothing thoughts that spring
      Out of human suffering;
      In the faith that looks through death,
In years that bring the philosophic mind.

And O, ye Fountains, Meadows, Hills, and Groves,
Forebode not any severing of our loves!
Yet in my heart of hearts I feel your might;
I only have relinquished one delight
To live beneath your more habitual sway.
I love the Brooks which down their channels fret,
Even more than when I tripped lightly as they;

The innocent brightness of a new-born Day
           Is lovely yet;
The Clouds that gather round the setting sun
Do take a sober colouring from an eye
That hath kept watch o'er man's mortality;
Another race hath been, and other palms are won.
Thanks to the human heart by which we live,
Thanks to its tenderness, its joys, and fears,
To me the meanest flower that blows can give
Thoughts that do often lie too deep for tears.

Elegiac Stanzas

**SUGGESTED BY A PICTURE OF PEELE CASTLE, IN
A STORM, PAINTED BY SIR GEORGE BEAUMONT**

I was thy neighbour once, thou rugged Pile!
Four summer weeks I dwelt in sight of thee:
I saw thee every day; and all the while
Thy Form was sleeping on a glassy sea.

So pure the sky, so quiet was the air!
So like, so very like, was day to day!
Whene'er I looked, thy Image still was there;
It trembled, but it never passed away.

How perfect was the calm! it seemed no sleep;
No mood, which season takes away, or brings:
I could have fancied that the mighty Deep
Was even the gentlest of all gentle Things.

Ah! THEN, if mine had been the Painter's hand,
To express what then I saw; and add the gleam,
The light that never was, on sea or land,
The consecration, and the Poet's dream;

139

I would have planted thee, thou hoary Pile
Amid a world how different from this!
Beside a sea that could not cease to smile;
On tranquil land, beneath a sky of bliss.

Thou shouldst have seemed a treasure-house divine
Of peaceful years; a chronicle of heaven; —
Of all the sunbeams that did ever shine
The very sweetest had to thee been given.

A Picture had it been of lasting ease,
Elysian quiet, without toil or strife;
No motion but the moving tide, a breeze,
Or merely silent Nature's breathing life.

Such, in the fond illusion of my heart,
Such Picture would I at that time have made:
And seen the soul of truth in every part,
A stedfast peace that might not be betrayed.

So once it would have been, — 'tis so no more;
I have submitted to a new control:
A power is gone, which nothing can restore;
A deep distress hath humanised my Soul.

Not for a moment could I now behold
A smiling sea, and be what I have been:
The feeling of my loss will ne'er be old;
This, which I know, I speak with mind serene.

Then, Beaumont, Friend! who would have been the Friend,
If he had lived, of Him whom I deplore,
This work of thine I blame not, but commend;
This sea in anger, and that dismal shore.

O 'tis a passionate Work! — yet wise and well,
Well chosen is the spirit that is here;
That Hulk which labours in the deadly swell,
This rueful sky, this pageantry of fear!

And this huge Castle, standing here sublime,
I love to see the look with which it braves,
Cased in the unfeeling armour of old time,
The lightning, the fierce wind, and trampling waves.

Farewell, farewell the heart that lives alone,
Housed in a dream, at distance from the Kind!
Such happiness, wherever it be known,
Is to be pitied; for 'tis surely blind.

But welcome fortitude, and patient cheer,
And frequent sights of what is to be borne!
Such sights, or worse, as are before me here. –
Not without hope we suffer and we mourn.

'Surprised by joy'

Surprised by joy – impatient as the Wind
I turned to share the transport – Oh! with whom
But Thee, deep buried in the silent tomb,
That spot which no vicissitude can find?
Love, faithful love, recalled thee to my mind –
But how could I forget thee? Through what power,
Even for the least division of an hour,
Have I been so beguiled as to be blind
To my most grievous loss? – That thought's return
Was the worst pang that sorrow ever bore,
Save one, one only, when I stood forlorn,
Knowing my heart's best treasure was no more;
That neither present time, nor years unborn
Could to my sight that heavenly face restore.

After-Thought

I thought of Thee, my partner and my guide,
As being past away. – Vain sympathies!
For, backward, Duddon! as I cast my eyes,
I see what was, and is, and will abide;
Still glides the Stream, and shall for ever glide;
The Form remains, the Function never dies;
While we, the brave, the mighty, and the wise,
We Men, who in our morn of youth defied
The elements, must vanish; – be it so!
Enough, if something from our hands have power
To live, and act, and serve the future hour;
And if, as toward the silent tomb we go,
Through love, through hope, and faith's transcendent
    dower,
We feel that we are greater than we know.

Mutability

From low to high doth dissolution climb,
And sink from high to low, along a scale
Of awful notes, whose concord shall not fail;
A musical but melancholy chime,
Which they can hear who meddle not with crime,
Nor avarice, nor over-anxious care.
Truth fails not; but her outward forms that bear
The longest date do melt like frosty rime,
That in the morning whitened hill and plain
And is no more; drop like the tower sublime
Of yesterday, which royally did wear
His crown of weeds, but could not even sustain
Some casual shout that broke the silent air,
Or the unimaginable touch of Time.

Inside of King's College Chapel, Cambridge

Tax not the royal Saint with vain expense,
With ill-matched aims the Architect who planned –
Albeit labouring for a scanty band
Of white robed Scholars only – this immense
And glorious Work of fine intelligence!
Give all thou canst; high Heaven rejects the lore
Of nicely-calculated less or more;
So deemed the man who fashioned for the sense
These lofty pillars, spread that branching roof
Self-poised, and scooped into ten thousand cells,
Where light and shade repose, where music dwells
Lingering – and wandering on as loth to die;
Like thoughts whose very sweetness yieldeth proof
That they were born for immortality.

Extempore Effusion upon the Death of James Hogg

When first, descending from the moorlands,
I saw the Stream of Yarrow glide
Along a bare and open valley,
The Ettrick Shepherd was my guide.

When last along its banks I wandered,
Through groves that had begun to shed
Their golden leaves upon the pathways,
My steps the Border-minstrel led.

The mighty Minstrel breathes no longer,
'Mid mouldering ruins low he lies;
And death upon the braes of Yarrow,
Has closed the Shepherd-poet's eyes:

Nor has the rolling year twice measured,
From sign to sign, its stedfast course,
Since every mortal power of Coleridge
Was frozen at its marvellous source;

The rapt One, of the godlike forehead,
The heaven-eyed creature sleeps in earth:
And Lamb, the frolic and the gentle,
Has vanished from his lonely hearth.

Like clouds that rake the mountain-summits,
Or waves that own no curbing hand,
How fast has brother followed brother,
From sunshine to the sunless land!

Yet I, whose lids from infant slumber
Were earlier raised, remain to hear
A timid voice, that asks in whispers,
'Who next will drop and disappear?'

Our haughty life is crowned with darkness,
Like London with its own black wreath,
On which with thee, O Crabbe! forth-looking,
I gazed from Hampstead's breezy heath.

As if but yesterday departed,
Thou too art gone before; but why,
O'er ripe fruit, seasonably gathered,
Should frail survivors heave a sigh?

Mourn rather for that holy Spirit,
Sweet as the spring, as ocean deep;
For Her who, ere her summer faded,
Has sunk into a breathless sleep.

No more of old romantic sorrows,
For slaughtered Youth or love-lorn Maid!
With sharper grief is Yarrow smitten,
And Ettrick mourns with her their Poet dead.

'Near Anio's stream
I spied a gentle Dove'

Near Anio's stream I spied a gentle Dove
Perched on an olive branch, and heard her cooing
'Mid new-born blossoms that soft airs were wooing,
While all things present told of joy and love.
But restless Fancy left that olive grove
To hail the exploratory Bird renewing
Hope for the few, who, at the world's undoing,
On the great flood were spared to live and move.
O bounteous Heaven! signs true as dove and bough
Brought to the ark are coming evermore,
Given though we seek them not, but, while we plough
This sea of life without a visible shore,
Do neither promise ask nor grace implore
In what alone is ours, the living Now.

Composed at Rydal on May Morning, 1838

If with old love of you, dear Hills! I share
New love of many a rival image brought
From far, forgive the wanderings of my thought:
Nor art thou wronged, sweet May! when I compare
Thy present birth-morn with thy last, so fair,
So rich to me in favours. For my lot
Then was, within the famed Egerian Grot
To sit and muse, fanned by its dewy air
Mingling with thy soft breath! That morning too,
Warblers I heard their joy unbosoming
Amid the sunny, shadowy, Coloseum;
Heard them, unchecked by aught of saddening hue,
For victories there won by flower-crowned Spring,
Chant in full choir their innocent Te Deum.

SIR WALTER SCOTT

1771–1832

Helvellyn*

In the spring of 1805, a young gentleman of talents, and of a most amiable disposition, perished by losing his way on the mountain Helvellyn. His remains were not discovered till three months afterwards, when they were found guarded by a faithful terrier-bitch, his constant attendant during frequent solitary rambles through the wilds of Cumberland and Westmorland.

I climb'd the dark brow of the mighty Helvellyn,
 Lakes and mountains beneath me gleam'd misty and
 wide;
All was still, save by fits, when the eagle was yelling,
 And starting around me the echoes replied.
On the right, Striden-edge round the Red-tarn was
 bending,
And Catchedicam its left verge was defending,
One huge nameless rock in the front was ascending,
 When I mark'd the sad spot where the wanderer had
 died.

Dark green was that spot 'mid the brown mountain-
 heather,
 Where the Pilgrim of Nature lay stretch'd in decay,
Like the corpse of an outcast abandon'd to weather,
 Till the mountain winds wasted the tenantless clay.
Nor yet quite deserted, though lonely extended,
For, faithful in death, his mute favourite attended,
The much-loved remains of her master defended,
 And chased the hill-fox and the raven away.

How long didst thou think that his silence was slumber?
 When the wind waved his garment, how oft didst thou
 start?

* See William Wordsworth: *Fidelity*, p. 131.

146

SIR WALTER SCOTT

How many long days and long weeks didst thou number,
  Ere he faded before thee, the friend of thy heart?
And, oh, was it meet, that – no requiem read o'er him –
No mother to weep, and no friend to deplore him,
And thou, little guardian, alone stretch'd before him –
  Unhonour'd the Pilgrim from life should depart?

When a Prince to the fate of the Peasant has yielded,
  The tapestry waves dark round the dim-lighted hall;
With scutcheons of silver the coffin is shielded,
  And pages stand mute by the canopied pall:
Through the courts, at deep midnight, the torches are
    gleaming;
In the proudly-arch'd chapel the banners are beaming,
Far adown the long aisle sacred music is streaming,
  Lamenting a Chief of the people should fall.

But meeter for thee, gentle lover of nature,
  To lay down thy head like the meek mountain lamb,
When, wilder'd, he drops from some cliff huge in stature,
  And draws his last sob by the side of his dam.
And more stately thy couch by this desert lake lying,
Thy obsequies sung by the gray plover flying,
With one faithful friend but to witness thy dying,
  In the arms of Helvellyn and Catchedicam.

Boat Song

From *The Lady of The Lake*

'Hail to the Chief who in triumph advances!
  Honour'd and bless'd be the evergreen Pine!
Long may the tree, in his banner that glances,
  Flourish the shelter and grace of our line!
    Heaven send it happy dew,
    Earth lend it sap anew,

147

Gaily to burgeon, and broadly to grow,
 While every Highland glen
 Sends our shout back agen,
Roderigh Vich Alpine dhu, ho! ieroe!

'Ours is no sapling, chance-sown by the fountain,
 Blooming at Beltane, in winter to fade;
When the whirlwind has stripped every leaf on the moun-
  tain,
 The more shall Clan-Alpine exult in her shade.
  Moored in the rifted rock,
  Proof to the tempest's shock,
Firmer he roots him the ruder it blow;
  Menteith and Breadalbane, then,
  Echo his praise agen,
Roderigh Vich Alpine dhu, ho! ieroe!

'Proudly our pibroch has thrill'd in Glen Fruin,
 And Bannochar's groans to our slogan replied;
Glen Luss and Ross-dhu, they are smoking in ruin,
 And the best of Loch Lomond lie dead on her side.
  Widow and Saxon maid
  Long shall lament our raid,
Think of Clan-Alpine with fear and with woe;
  Lennox and Leven-glen
  Shake when they hear agen,
Roderigh Vich Alpine dhu, ho! ieroe!

'Row, vassals, row for the pride of the Highlands!
 Stretch to your oars for the evergreen pine!
O! that the rose-bud that graces yon islands
 Were wreathed in a garland around him to twine!
  O that some seedling gem,
  Worthy such noble stem,
Honour'd and bless'd in their shadow might grow!
  Loud should Clan-Alpine then
  Ring from her deepmost glen,
Roderigh Vich Alpine dhu, ho! ieroe!'

Pibroch of Donuil Dhu

Pibroch of Donuil Dhu,
   Pibroch of Donuil,
Wake thy wild voice anew,
   Summon Clan-Conuil.
Come away, come away,
   Hark to the summons!
Come in your war array,
   Gentles and commons.

Come from deep glen, and
   From mountain so rocky,
The war-pipe and pennon
   Are at Inverlochy.
Come every hill-plaid, and
   True heart that wears one,
Come every steel blade, and
   Strong hand that bears one.

Leave untended the herd,
   The flock without shelter;
Leave the corpse uninterr'd,
   The bride at the altar;
Leave the deer, leave the steer,
   Leave nets and barges:
Come with your fighting gear,
   Broadswords and targes.

Come as the winds come, when
   Forests are rended,
Come as the waves come, when
   Navies are stranded:
Faster come, faster come,
   Faster and faster,
Chief, vassal, page and groom,
   Tenant and master.

Fast they come, fast they come;
   See how they gather!
Wide waves the eagle plume,
   Blended with heather.
Cast your plaids, draw your blades,
   Forwards, each man, set!
Pibroch of Donuil Dhu,
   Knell for the onset!

The Song of the Tempest

Stern eagle of the far north-west,
Thou that bearest in thy grasp the thunderbolt,
Thou whose rushing pinions stir ocean to madness,
Thou the destroyer of herds, thou the scatterer of navies,
Amidst the scream of thy rage,
Amidst the rushing of thy onward wings,
Though thy scream be loud as the cry of a perishing nation,
Though the rushing of thy wings be like the roar of ten
    thousand waves,
Yet hear, in thine ire and thy haste,
Hear thou the voice of the Reim-kennar.

Thou hast met the pine-trees of Drontheim,
Their dark-green heads lie prostrate beside their up-rooted
    stems;
Thou hast met the rider of the ocean,
The tall, the strong bark of the fearless rover,
And she has struck to thee the topsail
That she had not veil'd to a royal armada.
Thou hast met the tower that bears its crest among the
    clouds,
The battled massive tower of the Jarl of former days,
And the cope-stone of the turret
Is lying upon its hospitable hearth;
But thou too shalt stoop, proud compeller of clouds,
When thou hearest the voice of the Reim-kennar.

SIR WALTER SCOTT

There are verses that can stop the stag in the forest,
Ay, and when the dark-colour'd dog is opening on his
    track;
There are verses can make the wild hawk pause on the wing,
Like the falcon that wears the hood and the jesses,
And who knows the shrill whistle of the fowler.
Thou who canst mock at the scream of the drowning
    mariner,
And the crash of the ravaged forest,
And the groan of the overwhelmed crowds,
When the church hath fallen in the moment of prayer;
There are sounds which thou also must list,
When they are chanted by the voice of the Reim-kennar.

Enough of woe has thou wrought on the ocean.
The widows wring their hands on the beach;
Enough of woe hast thou wrought on the land,
The husbandman folds his arms in despair;
Cease thou the waving of thy pinions,
Let the ocean repose in her dark strength;
Cease thou the flashing of thine eye,
Let the thunderbolt sleep in the armoury of Odin;
Be thou still at my bidding, viewless racer of the north-
    western heaven, –
Sleep thou at the voice of Norna the Reim-kennar.

Eagle of the far north-western waters,
Thou hast heard the voice of the Reim-kennar,
Thou hast closed thy wide sails at her bidding,
And folded them in peace by thy side.
My blessing be on thy retiring path;
When thou stoopest from thy place on high,
Soft be thy slumbers in the caverns of the unknown ocean,
Rest till destiny shall again awaken thee;
Eagle of the north-west, thou hast heard the voice of the
    Reim-kennar.

The Dreary Change

The sun upon the Weirdlaw Hill,
  In Ettrick's vale, is sinking sweet;
The westland wind is hush and still,
  The lake lies sleeping at my feet.
Yet not the landscape to mine eye
  Bears those bright hues that once it bore;
Though evening, with her richest dye,
  Flames o'er the hills of Ettrick's shore.

With listless look along the plain,
  I see Tweed's silver current glide,
And coldly mark the holy fane
  Of Melrose rise in ruin'd pride.
The quiet lake, the balmy air,
  The hill, the stream, the tower, the tree, —
Are they still such as once they were?
  Or is the dreary change in me?

Alas, the warp'd and broken board,
  How can it bear the painter's dye!
The harp of strain'd and tuneless chord,
  How to the minstrel's skill reply!
To aching eyes each landscape lowers,
  To feverish pulse each gale blows chill;
And Araby's or Eden's bowers
  Were barren as this moorland hill.

SAMUEL TAYLOR COLERIDGE
1772–1834

This Lime-Tree Bower my Prison

In the June of 1797, some long-expected friends* paid a visit
to the author's cottage; and on the morning of their arrival, he
met with an accident, which disabled him from walking during
the whole time of their stay. One evening, when they had left
him for a few hours, he composed the following lines in the
garden-bower.

Well, they are gone, and here must I remain,
This lime-tree bower my prison! I have lost
Beauties and feelings, such as would have been
Most sweet to my remembrance even when age
Had dimmed mine eyes to blindness! They, meanwhile,
Friends, whom I never more may meet again,
On springy heath, along the hill-top edge,
Wander in gladness, and wind down, perchance,
To that still roaring dell, of which I told;
The roaring dell, o'erwooded, narrow, deep,
And only speckled by the mid-day sun;
Where its slim trunk the ash from rock to rock
Flings arching like a bridge; – that branchless ash,
Unsunned and damp, whose few poor yellow leaves
Ne'er tremble in the gale, yet tremble still,
Fanned by the water-fall! and there my friends
Behold the dark green file of long lank weeds,
That all at once (a most fantastic sight!)
Still nod and drip beneath the dripping edge
Of the blue clay-stone.

                                    Now, my friends emerge
Beneath the wide wide Heaven – and view again
The many-steepled tract magnificent

* Charles Lamb, William and Dorothy Wordsworth.

Of hilly fields and meadows, and the sea,
With some fair bark, perhaps, whose sails light up
'The slip of smooth clear blue betwixt two Isles
Of purple shadow! Yes! they wander on
In gladness all; but thou, methinks, most glad,
My gentle-hearted Charles! for thou hast pined
And hungered after Nature, many a year,
In the great City pent, winning thy way
With sad yet patient soul, through evil and pain
And strange calamity! Ah! slowly sink
Behind the western ridge, thou glorious sun!
Shine in the slant beams of the sinking orb,
Ye purple heath-flowers! richlier burn, ye clouds!
Live in the yellow light, ye distant groves!
And kindle, thou blue ocean! So my Friend
Struck with deep joy may stand, as I have stood,
Silent with swimming sense; yea, gazing round
On the wide landscape, gaze till all doth seem
Less gross than bodily; and of such hues
As veil the Almighty Spirit, when yet he makes
Spirits perceive his presence.
                                        A delight
Comes sudden on my heart, and I am glad
As I myself were there! Nor in this bower,
This little lime-tree bower, have I not marked
Much that has soothed me. Pale beneath the blaze
Hung the transparent foliage; and I watched
Some broad and sunny leaf, and loved to see
The shadow of the leaf and stem above
Dappling its sunshine! And that walnut-tree
Was richly tinged, and a deep radiance lay
Full on the ancient ivy, which usurps
Those fronting elms, and now, with blackest mass
Makes their dark branches gleam a lighter hue
Through the late twilight: and though now the bat
Wheels silent by, and not a swallow twitters,
Yet still the solitary humble bee
Sings in the bean-flower! Henceforth I shall know

That Nature ne'er deserts the wise and pure;
No plot so narrow, be but Nature there,
No waste so vacant, but may well employ
Each faculty of sense, and keep the heart
Awake to Love and Beauty! and sometimes
'Tis well to be bereft of promised good,
That we may lift the Soul, and contemplate
With lively joy the joys we cannot share.
My gentle-hearted Charles! when the last rook
Beat its straight path along the dusky air
Homewards, I blest it! deeming, its black wing
(Now a dim speck, now vanishing in light)
Had crossed the mighty orb's dilated glory,
While thou stood'st gazing; or when all was still,
Flew creeking o'er thy head, and had a charm
For thee, my gentle-hearted Charles, to whom
No sound is dissonant which tells of Life.

The Rime of the Ancient Mariner

PART I

It is an ancient Mariner,
And he stoppeth one of three.
'By thy long grey beard and glittering eye,
Now wherefore stopp'st thou me?

An ancient Mariner meeteth three gallants bidden to a wedding-feast, and detaineth one.

'The Bridegroom's doors are opened wide,
And I am next of kin;
The guests are met, the feast is set:
May'st hear the merry din.'

He holds him with his skinny hand,
'There was a ship,' quoth he.
'Hold off! unhand me, grey-beard loon!'
Eftsoons his hand dropt he.

The wedding guest is spell-bound by the eye of the old sea-faring man, and constrained to hear his tale.

He holds him with his glittering eye –
The Wedding-Guest stood still,
And listens like a three years' child:
The Mariner hath his will.

The Wedding-Guest sat on a stone:
He cannot choose but hear;
And thus spake on that ancient man,
The bright-eyed Mariner.

The ship was cheered, the harbour cleared,
Merrily did we drop
Below the kirk, below the hill,
Below the light house top.

The Mariner tells how the ship sailed southward with a good wind and fair weather, till it reached the Line.

The Sun came up upon the left,
Out of the sea came he!
And he shone bright, and on the right
Went down into the sea.

Higher and higher every day,
Till over the mast at noon –
The Wedding-Guest here beat his breast,
For he heard the loud bassoon.

The wedding guest heareth the bridal music; but the Mariner continueth his tale.

The bride hath paced into the hall,
Red as a rose is she;
Nodding their heads before her goes
The merry minstrelsy.

The Wedding-Guest he beat his breast,
Yet he cannot choose but hear;
And thus spake on that ancient man,
The bright-eyed Mariner.

The ship drawn by a storm toward the south pole.

And now the Storm-blast came, and he
Was tyrannous and strong:
He struck with his o'ertaking wings,
And chased us south along.

With sloping masts and dipping prow,
As who pursued with yell and blow
Still treads the shadow of his foe,
And forward bends his head,
The ship drove fast, loud roared the blast,
And southward aye we fled.

And now there came both mist and snow,
And it grew wondrous cold:
And ice, mast-high, came floating by,
As green as emerald.

And through the drifts the snowy clifts
Did send a dismal sheen:
Nor shapes of men nor beasts we ken –
The ice was all between.

The land of ice, and of fearful sounds where no living thing was to be seen.

The ice was here, the ice was there,
The ice was all around:
It cracked and growled, and roared and howled
Like noises in a swound!

At length did cross an Albatross,
Thorough the fog it came;
As if it had been a Christian soul,
We hailed it in God's name.

Till a great sea-bird, called the Albatross, came through the snow-fog, and was received with great joy and hospitality.

It ate the food it ne'er had eat,
And round and round it flew.
The ice did split with a thunder-fit;
The helmsman steered us through!

And lo! the Albatross proveth a bird of good omen, and followeth the ship as it returned northward through fog and floating ice.

And a good south wind sprung up behind;
The Albatross did follow,
And every day, for food or play,
Came to the mariners' hollo!

157

In mist or cloud, on mast or shroud,
It perched for vespers nine;
Whiles all the night, through fog-smoke white,
Glimmered the white moon-shine.

The ancient
Mariner
inhospitably
killeth the
pious bird of
good omen.

'God save thee, ancient Mariner!
From the fiends, that plague thee thus! –
Why look'st thou so?' – With my cross-bow
I shot the Albatross.

PART II

The Sun now rose upon the right:
Out of the sea came he,
Still hid in mist, and on the left
Went down into the sea.

And the good south wind still blew behind,
But no sweet bird did follow,
Nor any day for food or play
Came to the mariners' hollo!

His shipmates
cry out against
the ancient
Mariner, for
killing the bird
of good luck.

And I had done a hellish thing,
And it would work 'em woe:
For all averred, I had killed the bird
That made the breeze to blow.
Ah wretch! said they, the bird to slay,
That made the breeze to blow!

But when the
fog cleared
off, they justify
the same, and
thus make
themselves
accomplices in
the crime.

Nor dim nor red, like God's own head,
The glorious Sun uprist:
Then all averred, I had killed the bird
That brought the fog and mist.
'Twas right, said they, such birds to slay,
That bring the fog and mist.

The fair
breeze continues;
the ship enters
the Pacific
Ocean, and sails
northward,
even till it
reaches the Line.

The fair breeze blew, the white foam flew,
The furrow followed free;
We were the first that ever burst
Into that silent sea.

Down dropt the breeze, the sails dropt down, *The ship hath*
'Twas sad as sad could be; *been suddenly*
And we did speak only to break *becalmed.*
The silence of the sea!

All in a hot and copper sky,
The bloody Sun, at noon,
Right up above the mast did stand,
No bigger than the Moon.

Day after day, day after day,
We stuck, nor breath nor motion;
As idle as a painted ship
Upon a painted ocean.

Water, water, every where, *And the*
And all the boards did shrink; *Albatross begins*
Water, water, every where, *to be avenged.*
Nor any drop to drink.

The very deep did rot: O Christ!
That ever this should be!
Yea, slimy things did crawl with legs
Upon the slimy sea.

About, about, in reel and rout
The death-fires danced at night;
The water, like a witch's oils,
Burnt green, and blue and white.

And some in dreams assured were *A spirit had followed*
Of the spirit that plagued us so; *them; one of the invisible*
Nine fathom deep he had followed us *inhabitants of this planet,*
From the land of mist and snow. *neither departed souls*
nor angels; concerning
whom the learned Jew,
Josephus, and the
Platonic Constanti-
And every tongue, through utter drought, *nopolitan, Michael*
Was withered at the root; *Psellus, may be consulted.*
We could not speak, no more than if *They are very numerous,*
We had been choked with soot. *and there is no climate*
or element without one
or more.

The shipmates, in their sore distress would fain throw the whole guilt on the ancient Mariner, in sign whereof they hang the dead sea-bird round his neck.

Ah! well a-day! what evil looks
Had I from old and young!
Instead of the cross, the Albatross
About my neck was hung.

PART III

There passed a weary time. Each throat
Was parched, and glazed each eye.
A weary time! a weary time!

The ancient Mariner beholdeth a sign in the element afar off.

How glazed each weary eye,
When looking westward, I beheld
A something in the sky.

At first it seemed a little speck,
And then it seemed a mist;
It moved and moved, and took at last
A certain shape, I wist.

A speck, a mist, a shape, I wist!
And still it neared and neared:
As if it dodged a water-sprite,
It plunged and tacked and veered.

At its nearer approach, it seemeth him to be a ship; and at a dear ransom he freeth his speech from the bonds of thirst.

With throats unslaked, with black lips baked,
We could nor laugh nor wail;
Through utter drought all dumb we stood!
I bit my arm, I sucked the blood,
And cried, A sail! a sail!

A flash of joy;

With throats unslaked, with black lips baked,
Agape they heard me call:
Gramercy! they for joy did grin,
And all at once their breath drew in,
As they were drinking all.

And horror follows. For can it be a ship that comes onward without wind or tide?

See! see! (I cried) she tacks no more!
Hither to work us weal;
Without a breeze, without a tide,
She steadies with upright keel!

160

The western wave was all a-flame.
The day was well nigh done!
Almost upon the western wave
Rested the broad bright Sun;
When that strange shape drove suddenly
Betwixt us and the Sun.

And straight the Sun was flecked with bars,
(Heaven's Mother send us grace!)
As if through a dungeon-grate he peered
With broad and burning face.

It seemeth him but the skeleton of a ship.

Alas! (thought I, and my heart beat loud)
How fast she nears and nears!
Are those her sails that glance in the Sun,
Like restless gossameres?

Are those her ribs through which the Sun
Did peer, as through a grate?
And is that Woman all her crew?
Is that a Death? and are there two?
Is Death that woman's mate?

And its ribs are seen as bars on the face of the setting Sun. The Spectre-woman and her Deathmate, and no other on board the skeleton-ship.

Her lips were red, her looks were free,
Her locks were yellow as gold:
Her skin was as white as leprosy,
The Night-mare Life-in-Death was she,
Who thicks man's blood with cold.

Like vessel, like crew!

The naked hulk alongside came,
And the twain were casting dice;
'The game is done! I've won, I've won!'
Quoth she, and whistles thrice.

Death and Life-in-death have diced for the ship's crew, and she (the latter) winneth the ancient Mariner.

The Sun's rim dips; the stars rush out:
At one stride comes the dark;
With far-heard whisper, o'er the sea,
Off shot the spectre-bark.

No twilight within the courts of the sun.

At the rising of the Moon,

We listened and looked sideways up!
Fear at my heart, as at a cup,
My life-blood seemed to sip!
The stars were dim, and thick the night,
The steersman's face by his lamp gleamed white;
From the sails the dew did drip –
Till clomb above the eastern bar
The hornèd Moon, with one bright star
Within the nether tip.

One after another,

One after one, by the star-dogged Moon,
Too quick for groan or sigh,
Each turned his face with a ghastly pang,
And cursed me with his eye.

His shipmates drop down dead.

Four times fifty living men,
(And I heard nor sigh nor groan)
With heavy thump, a lifeless lump,
They dropped down one by one.

But Life-in-Death begins her work on the ancient Mariner.

The souls did from their bodies fly, –
They fled to bliss or woe!
And every soul, it passed me by,
Like the whizz of my cross-bow!

PART IV

The wedding guest feareth that a Spirit is talking to him.

'I fear thee, ancient Mariner!
I fear thy skinny hand!
And thou art long, and lank, and brown,
As is the ribbed sea-sand.

But the ancient Mariner assureth him of his bodily life, and proceedeth to relate his horrible penance.

I fear thee and thy glittering eye,
And thy skinny hand, so brown.' –
Fear not, fear not, thou Wedding-Guest!
This body dropt not down.

Alone, alone, all, all alone,
Alone on a wide wide sea!
And never a saint took pity on
My soul in agony.

The many men, so beautiful!
And they all dead did lie:
And a thousand thousand slimy things
Lived on; and so did I.

He despiseth
the creatures
of the calm,

I looked upon the rotting sea,
And drew my eyes away;
I looked upon the rotting deck,
And there the dead men lay.

And envieth
that they
should live,
and so many
lie dead.

I looked to heaven, and tried to pray;
But or ever a prayer had gusht,
A wicked whisper came, and made
My heart as dry as dust.

I closed my lids, and kept them close,
And the balls like pulses beat;
For the sky and the sea, and the sea and the sky
Lay like a load on my weary eye,
And the dead were at my feet.

The cold sweat melted from their limbs,
Nor rot nor reek did they:
The look with which they looked on me
Had never passed away.

But the curse
liveth for him
in the eye of
the dead men.

An orphan's curse would drag to hell
A spirit from on high;
But oh! more horrible than that
Is the curse in a dead man's eye!
Seven days, seven nights, I saw that curse,
And yet I could not die.

The moving Moon went up the sky,
And no where did abide:
Softly she was going up,
And a star or two beside —

In his loneliness and fixedness he yearneth to-
wards the journeying Moon, and the stars that
still sojourn, yet still move onward; and every
where the blue sky belongs to them, and is their
appointed rest, and their native country and
their own natural homes, which they enter un-
announced, as lords that are certainly expected
and yet there is a silent joy at their arrival.

Her beams bemocked the sultry main,
Like April hoar-frost spread;
But where the ship's huge shadow lay,
The charmèd water burnt alway
A still and awful red.

By the light
of the Moon
he beholdeth
God's creatures
of the great
calm.

Beyond the shadow of the ship,
I watched the water-snakes:
They moved in tracks of shining white,
And when they reared, the elfish light
Fell off in hoary flakes.

Within the shadow of the ship
I watched their rich attire:
Blue, glossy green, and velvet black,
They coiled and swam; and every track
Was a flash of golden fire.

Their beauty
and their
happiness.

O happy living things! no tongue
Their beauty might declare:
A spring of love gushed from my heart,
And I blessed them unaware:

He blesseth
them in his
heart.

Sure my kind saint took pity on me,
And I blessed them unaware.

The spell
begins to
break.

The selfsame moment I could pray:
And from my neck so free
The Albatross fell off, and sank
Like lead into the sea.

PART V

Oh sleep! it is a gentle thing,
Beloved from pole to pole!
To Mary Queen the praise be given!
She sent the gentle sleep from Heaven,
That slid into my soul.

The silly buckets on the deck,
That had so long remained,
I dreamt that they were filled with dew;
And when I awoke, it rained.

*By grace of the
holy Mother,
the ancient
Mariner is
refreshed with
rain.*

My lips were wet, my throat was cold,
My garments all were dank;
Sure I had drunken in my dreams,
And still my body drank.

I moved, and could not feel my limbs:
I was so light – almost
I thought that I had died in sleep,
And was a blessèd ghost.

And soon I heard a roaring wind:
It did not come anear;
But with its sound it shook the sails,
That were so thin and sere.

*He heareth
sounds and
seeth strange
sights and
commotions in
the sky and the
element.*

The upper air burst into life!
And a hundred fire-flags sheen,
To and fro they were hurried about!
And to and fro, and in and out,
The wan stars danced between.

And the coming wind did roar more loud,
And the sails did sigh like sedge;
And the rain poured down from one black cloud;
The Moon was at its edge.

The thick black cloud was cleft, and still
The Moon was at its side:
Like waters shot from some high crag,
The lightning fell with never a jag,
A river steep and wide.

The bodies of the ship's crew are inspired, and the ship moves on;

The loud wind never reached the ship,
Yet now the ship moved on!
Beneath the lightning and the moon
The dead men gave a groan.

They groaned, they stirred, they all uprose,
Nor spake, nor moved their eyes;
It had been strange, even in a dream,
To have seen those dead men rise.

The helmsman steered, the ship moved on;
Yet never a breeze up blew;
The mariners all 'gan work the ropes,
Where they were wont to do;
They raised their limbs like lifeless tools –
We were a ghastly crew.

The body of my brother's son
Stood by me, knee to knee:
The body and I pulled at one rope,
But he said nought to me.

But not by the souls of the men, nor by demons of earth or middle air, but by a blessed troop of angelic spirits, sent down by the invocation of the guardian saint.

'I fear thee, ancient Mariner!'
Be calm, thou Wedding-Guest!
'Twas not those souls that fled in pain,
Which to their corses came again,
But a troop of spirits blest:

For when it dawned – they dropped their arms,
And clustered round the mast;
Sweet sounds rose slowly through their mouths,
And from their bodies passed.

Around, around, flew each sweet sound,
Then darted to the Sun;
Slowly the sounds came back again,
Now mixed, now one by one.

Sometimes a-dropping from the sky
I heard the sky-lark sing;
Sometimes all little birds that are,
How they seemed to fill the sea and air
With their sweet jargoning!

And now 'twas like all instruments,
Now like a lonely flute;
And now it is an angel's song,
That makes the heavens be mute.

It ceased; yet still the sails made on
A pleasant noise till noon,
A noise like of a hidden brook
In the leafy month of June,
That to the sleeping woods all night
Singeth a quiet tune.

Till noon we quietly sailed on,
Yet never a breeze did breathe:
Slowly and smoothly went the ship,
Moved onward from beneath.

Under the keel nine fathom deep,
From the land of mist and snow,
The spirit slid; and it was he
That made the ship to go.
The sails at noon left off their tune,
And the ship stood still also.

The lonesome Spirit from the south pole carries on the ship as far as the Line, in obedience to the angelic troop, but still requireth vengeance.

The Sun, right up above the mast,
Had fixed her to the ocean:
But in a minute she 'gan stir,
With a short uneasy motion –
Backwards and forwards half her length
With a short uneasy motion.

Then like a pawing horse let go,
She made a sudden bound:
It flung the blood into my head,
And I fell down in a swound.

*The Polar
Spirit's fellow
demons, the
invisible
inhabitants of
the element,
take part in his
wrong; and two
of them relate,
one to the other,
that penance
long and heavy
for the ancient
Mariner hath
been accorded
to the Polar
Spirit, who
returneth
southward.*

How long in that same fit I lay,
I have not to declare;
But ere my living life returned,
I heard, and in my soul discerned
Two voices in the air.

'Is it he?' quoth one, 'Is this the man?
By him who died on cross,
With his cruel bow he laid full low
The harmless Albatross.

'The spirit who bideth by himself
In the land of mist and snow,
He loved the bird that loved the man
Who shot him with his bow.'

The other was a softer voice,
As soft as honey-dew:
Quoth he, 'The man hath penance done,
And penance more will do.'

PART VI
First Voice

But tell me, tell me! speak again,
Thy soft response renewing –
What makes that ship drive on so fast?
What is the ocean doing?

Second Voice

Still as a slave before his lord,
The ocean hath no blast;
His great bright eye most silently
Up to the Moon is cast –

If he may know which way to go;
For she guides him smooth or grim.
See, brother, see! how graciously
She looketh down on him.

*The Mariner
hath been cast
into a trance;
for the angelic
power causeth
the vessel to
drive northward
faster than
human life
could endure.*

First Voice

But why drives on that ship so fast,
Without or wave or wind?

Second Voice

The air is cut away before,
And closes from behind.

Fly, brother, fly! more high, more high!
Or we shall be belated:
For slow and slow that ship will go,
When the Mariner's trance is abated.

I woke, and were sailing on
As in a gentle weather:
'Twas night, calm night, the Moon was high;
The dead men stood together.

*The super-
natural motion
is retarded;
the Mariner
awakes, and his
penance begins
anew.*

All stood together on the deck,
For a charnel-dungeon fitter:
All fixed on me their stony eyes,
That in the Moon did glitter.

The pang, the curse, with which they died,
Had never passed away:
I could not draw my eyes from theirs,
Nor turn them up to pray.

And now this spell was snapt: once more
I viewed the ocean green,
And looked far forth, yet little saw
Of what had else been seen —

*The curse is
finally expiated.*

169

Like one, that on a lonesome road
Doth walk in fear and dread,
And having once turned round walks on,
And turns no more his head;
Because he knows, a frightful fiend
Doth close behind him tread.

But soon there breathed a wind on me,
Nor sound nor motion made:
Its path was not upon the sea,
In ripple or in shade.

It raised my hair, it fanned my cheek
Like a meadow-gale of spring –
It mingled strangely with my fears,
Yet it felt like a welcoming.

Swiftly, swiftly flew the ship,
Yet she sailed softly too:
Sweetly, sweetly blew the breeze –
On me alone it blew.

And the ancient
Mariner be-
holdeth his
native country.

Oh! dream of joy! is this indeed
The light-house top I see?
Is this the hill? is this the kirk?
Is this mine own countree?

We drifted o'er the harbour-bar,
And I with sobs did pray –
O let me be awake, my God!
Or let me sleep alway.

The harbour-bay was clear as glass,
So smoothly it was strewn!
And on the bay the moonlight lay,
And the shadow of the Moon.

170

The rock shone bright, the kirk no less,
That stands above the rock:
The moonlight steeped in silentness
The steady weathercock.

And the bay was white with silent light,
Till rising from the same,
Full many shapes, that shadows were,
In crimson colours came.

*The angelic
spirits leave
the dead
bodies.*

A little distance from the prow
Those crimson shadows were:
I turned my eyes upon the deck –
Oh, Christ! what saw I there!

*And appear
in their own
forms of light.*

Each corse lay flat, lifeless and flat,
And, by the holy rood!
A man all light, a seraph-man,
On every corse there stood.

This seraph-band, each waved his hand:
It was a heavenly sight!
They stood as signals to the land,
Each one a lovely light;

This seraph-band, each waved his hand,
No voice did they impart –
No voice; but oh! the silence sank
Like music on my heart.

But soon I heard the dash of oars,
I heard the Pilot's cheer;
My head was turned perforce away,
And I saw a boat appear.

The Pilot and the Pilot's boy,
I heard them coming fast:
Dear Lord in Heaven! it was a joy
The dead men could not blast.

I saw a third – I heard his voice:
It is the Hermit good!
He singeth loud his godly hymns
That he makes in the wood.
He'll shrieve my soul, he'll wash away
The Albatross's blood.

PART VII

The Hermit
of the wood,

This Hermit good lives in that wood
Which slopes down to the sea.
How loudly his sweet voice he rears!
He loves to talk with marineres
That come from a far countree.

He kneels at morn, and noon, and eve –
He hath a cushion plump:
It is the moss that wholly hides
The rotted old oak-stump.

The skiff-boat neared: I heard them talk,
'Why, this is strange, I trow!
Where are those lights so many and fair,
That signal made but now?'

Approacheth
the ship with
wonder.

'Strange, by my faith!' the Hermit said –
'And they answered not our cheer!
The planks looked warped! and see those sails,
How thin they are and sere!
I never saw aught like to them,
Unless perchance it were

Brown skeletons of leaves that lag
My forest-brook along;
When the ivy-tod is heavy with snow,
And the owlet whoops to the wolf below,
That eats the she-wolf's young.'

'Dear Lord! it hath a fiendish look –
(The Pilot made reply)
I am a-feared' – 'Push on, push on!'
Said the Hermit cheerily.

The boat came closer to the ship,
But I nor spake nor stirred;
The boat came close beneath the ship,
And straight a sound was heard.

Under the water it rumbled on,
Still louder and more dread:
It reached the ship, it split the bay;
The ship went down like lead.

*The ship
suddenly
sinketh.*

Stunned by that loud and dreadful sound,
Which sky and ocean smote,
Like one that hath been seven days drowned
My body lay afloat;
But swift as dreams, myself I found
Within the Pilot's boat.

*The ancient
Mariner is
saved in the
Pilot's boat.*

Upon the whirl, where sank the ship,
The boat spun round and round;
And all was still, save that the hill
Was telling of the sound.

I moved my lips – the Pilot shrieked
And fell down in a fit;
The holy Hermit raised his eyes,
And prayed where he did sit.

I took the oars: the Pilot's boy,
Who now doth crazy go,
Laughed loud and long, and all the while
His eyes went to and fro.
'Ha! ha!' quoth he, 'full plain I see,
The Devil knows how to row.'

And now, all in my own countree,
I stood on the firm land!
The Hermit stepped forth from the boat,
And scarcely he could stand.

The ancient
Mariner
earnestly
entreateth
the Hermit
to shrieve him;
and the penance
of life falls on
him.

'O shrieve me, shrieve me, holy man!'
The Hermit crossed his brow.
'Say quick,' quoth he, 'I bid thee say –
What manner of man art thou?'

Forthwith this frame of mine was wrenched
With a woful agony,
Which forced me to begin my tale;
And then it left me free.

And ever and
anon throughout
his future life
an agony
constraineth
him to travel
from land to
land.

Since then, at an uncertain hour,
That agony returns:
And till my ghastly tale is told,
This heart within me burns.

I pass, like night, from land to land;
I have strange power of speech;
That moment that his face I see,
I know the man that must hear me:
To him my tale I teach.

What loud uproar bursts from that door!
The wedding-guests are there:
But in the garden-bower the bride
And bride-maids singing are:
And hark the little vesper bell,
Which biddeth me to prayer!

O Wedding-Guest! this soul hath been
Alone on a wide wide sea:
So lonely 'twas, that God himself
Scarce seemed there to be.

O sweeter than the marriage-feast,
'Tis sweeter far to me,
To walk together to the kirk
With a goodly company! –

To walk together to the kirk,
And all together pray,
While each to his great Father bends,
Old men, and babes, and loving friends,
And youths and maidens gay!

Farewell, farewell! but this I tell
To thee, thou Wedding-Guest!
He prayeth well, who loveth well
Both man and bird and beast.

*And to teach,
by his own
example, love
and reverence
to all things
that God made
and loveth.*

He prayeth best, who loveth best
All things both great and small;
For the dear God who loveth us,
He made and loveth all.

The Mariner, whose eye is bright,
Whose beard with age is hoar,
Is gone: and now the Wedding-Guest
Turned from the bridegroom's door.

He went like one that hath been stunned
And is of sense forlorn:
A sadder and a wiser man,
He rose the morrow morn.

Frost at Midnight

The frost performs its secret ministry,
Unhelped by any wind. The owlet's cry
Came loud – and hark, again! loud as before.
The inmates of my cottage, all at rest,

Have left me to that solitude, which suits
Abstruser musings: save that at my side
My cradled infant slumbers peacefully.
'Tis calm indeed! so calm, that it disturbs
And vexes meditation with its strange
And extreme silentness. Sea, hill, and wood,
This populous village! Sea, and hill, and wood,
With all the numberless goings on of life,
Inaudible as dreams! the thin blue flame
Lies on my low burnt fire, and quivers not;
Only that film, which fluttered on the grate,
Still flutters there, the sole unquiet thing.
Methinks, its motion in this hush of nature
Gives it dim sympathies with me who live,
Making it a companionable form,
Whose puny flaps and freaks the idling Spirit
By its own moods interprets, every where
Echo or mirror seeking of itself,
And makes a toy of Thought.

                                    But O! how oft,
How oft, at school, with most believing mind,
Presageful, have I gazed upon the bars,
To watch that fluttering stranger! and as oft
With unclosed lids, already had I dreamt
Of my sweet birth-place, and the old church-tower,
Whose bells, the poor man's only music, rang
From morn to evening, all the hot Fair-day,
So sweetly, that they stirred and haunted me
With a wild pleasure, falling on mine ear
Most like articulate sounds of things to come!
So gazed I, till the soothing things I dreamt
Lulled me to sleep, and sleep prolonged my dreams!
And so I brooded all the following morn,
Awed by the stern preceptor's face, mine eye
Fixed with mock study on my swimming book:
Save if the door half opened, and I snatched
A hasty glance, and still my heart leaped up,
For still I hoped to see the stranger's face,

Townsman, or aunt, or sister more beloved,
My play-mate when we both were clothed alike!

Dear Babe, that sleepest cradled by my side,
Whose gentle breathings, heard in this deep calm,
Fill up the interspersed vacancies
And momentary pauses of the thought!
My babe so beautiful! it thrills my heart
With tender gladness, thus to look at thee,
And think that thou shalt learn far other lore
And in far other scenes! For I was reared
In the great city, pent 'mid cloisters dim,
And saw nought lovely but the sky and stars.
But thou, my babe! shalt wander like a breeze
By lakes and sandy shores, beneath the crags
Of ancient mountain, and beneath the clouds,
Which image in their bulk both lakes and shores
And mountain crags: so shalt thou see and hear
The lovely shapes and sound intelligible
Of that eternal language, which thy God
Utters, who from eternity doth teach
Himself in all, and all things in himself.
Great universal Teacher! he shall mould
Thy spirit, and by giving make it ask.

Therefore all seasons shall be sweet to thee,
Whether the summer clothe the general earth
With greenness, or the redbreast sit and sing
Betwixt the tufts of snow on the bare branch
Of mossy apple-tree, while the night thatch
Smokes in the sun-thaw; whether the eve-drops fall
Heard only in the trances of the blast,
Or if the secret ministry of frost
Shall hang them up in silent icicles,
Quietly shining to the quiet Moon.

The Nightingale

A CONVERSATION POEM. APRIL 1798

No cloud, no relique of the sunken day
Distinguishes the West, no long thin slip
Of sullen light, no obscure trembling hues.
Come, we will rest on this old mossy bridge!
You see the glimmer of the stream beneath,
But hear no murmuring: it flows silently,
O'er its soft bed of verdure. All is still,
A balmy night! and though the stars be dim,
Yet let us think upon the vernal showers
That gladden the green earth, and we shall find
A pleasure in the dimness of the stars.
And hark! the Nightingale begins its song,
'Most musical, most melancholy' bird!
A melancholy bird! Oh! idle thought!
In nature there is nothing melancholy.
But some night-wandering man whose heart was pierced
With the remembrance of a grievous wrong,
Or slow distemper, or neglected love,
(And so, poor wretch! filled all things with himself,
And made all gentle sounds tell back the tale
Of his own sorrow) he, and such as he,
First named these notes a melancholy strain
And many a poet echoes the conceit;
Poet who hath been building up the rhyme
When he had better far have stretched his limbs
Beside a brook in mossy forest-dell,
By sun or moon-light, to the influxes
Of shapes and sounds and shifting elements
Surrendering his whole spirit, of his song
And of his fame forgetful! so his fame
Should share in Nature's immortality,
A venerable thing! and so his song
Should make all Nature lovelier, and itself
Be loved like Nature! But 'twill not be so;

And youths and maidens most poetical,
Who lost the deepening twilights of the spring
In ball-rooms and hot theatres, they still
Full of meek sympathy must heave their sighs
O'er Philomela's pity-pleading strains.

My Friend, and thou, our Sister! we have learnt
A different lore: we may not thus profane
Nature's sweet voices, always full of love
And joyance! 'Tis the merry Nightingale
That crowds, and hurries, and precipitates
With fast thick warble his delicious notes,
As he were fearful that an April night
Would be too short for him to utter forth
His love-chant, and disburthen his full soul
Of all its music!

              And I know a grove
Of large extent, hard by a castle huge,
Which the great lord inhabits not; and so
This grove is wild with tangling underwood,
And the trim walks are broken up, and grass,
Thin grass and king-cups grow within the paths.
But never elsewhere in one place I knew
So many nightingales; and far and near,
In wood and thicket, over the wide grove,
They answer and provoke each other's song,
With skirmish and capricious passagings,
And murmurs musical and swift jug jug,
And one low piping sound more sweet than all –
Stirring the air with such a harmony,
That should you close your eyes, you might almost
Forget it was not day! On moon-lit bushes,
Whose dewy leaflets are but half disclosed,
You may perchance behold them on the twigs,
Their bright, bright eyes, their eyes both bright and full,
Glistening, while many a glow-worm in the shade
Lights up her love-torch.

                        A most gentle Maid,
Who dwelleth in her hospitable home
Hard by the castle, and at latest eve
(Even like a Lady vowed and dedicate
To something more than Nature in the grove)
Glides through the pathways; she knows all their notes,
That gentle Maid! and oft a moment's space,
What time the moon was lost behind a cloud,
Hath heard a pause of silence; till the moon
Emerging, hath awakened earth and sky
With one sensation, and these wakeful birds
Have all burst forth in choral minstrelsy,
As if some sudden gale had swept at once
A hundred airy harps! And she hath watched
Many a nightingale perched giddily
On blossomy twig still swinging from the breeze,
And to that motion tune his wanton song
Like tipsy joy that reels with tossing head.

    Farewell, O Warbler! till to-morrow eve,
And you, my friends! farewell, a short farewell!
We have been loitering long and pleasantly,
And now for our dear homes. – That strain again!
Full fain it would delay me! My dear babe,
Who, capable of no articulate sound,
Mars all things with his imitative lisp,
How he would place his hand beside his ear,
His little hand, the small forefinger up,
And bid us listen! And I deem it wise
To make him Nature's play-mate. He knows well
The evening-star; and once, when he awoke
In most distressful mood (some inward pain
Had made up that strange thing, an infant's dream. –)
I hurried with him to our orchard-plot,
And he beheld the moon, and hushed at once,
Suspends his sobs, and laughs most silently,
While his fair eyes, that swam with undropped tears,
Did glitter in the yellow moon-beam! Well! –

It is a father's tale: But if that Heaven
Should give me life, his childhood shall grow up
Familiar with these songs, that with the night
He may associate joy. – Once more, farewell,
Sweet Nightingale! Once more, my friends! farewell.

Dejection

A LETTER*

Well! if the Bard was weatherwise, who made
The grand old Ballad of Sir Patrick Spence,
This Night, so tranquil now, will not go hence
Unrous'd by winds, that ply a busier trade
Than that, which moulds yon clouds in lazy flakes,
Or the dull sobbing Draft, that drones and rakes
Upon the Strings of this Eolian Lute,
Which better far were mute.
For, lo! the New Moon, winter-bright!
And overspread with phantom Light
(With swimming phantom Light o'erspread
But rimm'd and circled with a silver Thread)
I see the Old Moon in her Lap, foretelling
The coming-on of Rain and squally Blast –
O! Sara! that the Gust ev'n now were swelling,
And the slant Night-shower driving loud and fast!

A Grief without a pang, void, dark and drear,
A stifling, drowsy, unimpassion'd Grief
That finds no natural outlet, no Relief
In word, or sigh, or tear –
This, Sara! well thou know'st,
Is that sore Evil, which I dread the most,

* Written at Keswick, and addressed to Sara Hutchinson, Words-
worth's sister-in-law, who was staying with the Wordsworths at
Grasmere. In this letter Wordsworth, his wife, and his sister are
referred to as 'William', 'Mary', and 'Dorothy'.

And oft'nest suffer! In this heartless Mood,
To other thoughts by yonder Throstle woo'd,
That pipes within the Larch tree, not unseen,
(The Larch, which pushes out in tassels green
It's bundled Leafits) woo'd to mild Delights
By all the tender Sounds and gentle Sights
Of this sweet Primrose-month – and *vainly* woo'd
O dearest Sara! in this heartless Mood
All this long Eve, so balmy and serene,
Have I been gazing on the western Sky
And its peculiar Tint of Yellow Green –
And still I gaze – and with how blank an eye!
And those thin Clouds above, in flakes and bars,
That give away their Motion to the Stars;
Those Stars, that glide behind them, or between,
Now sparkling, now bedimm'd, but always seen;
Yon crescent Moon, as fix'd as if it grew
In it's own cloudless, starless Lake of Blue –
A boat becalm'd! dear William's Sky Canoe!
– I see them all, so excellently fair!
I see, not feel, how beautiful they are.

My genial Spirits fail –
And what can these avail
To lift the smoth'ring Weight from off my Breast?
It were a vain Endeavour,
Tho' I should gaze for ever
On that Green Light that lingers in the West!
I may not hope from outward Forms to win
The Passion and the Life, whose Fountains are within!

These lifeless Shapes, around, below, above,
    O what can they impart?
When even the gentle Thought, that thou, my Love!
Art gazing, now, like me,
And see'st the Heaven, I see –
Sweet Thought it is – yet feebly stirs my Heart!
Feebly! O feebly! – Yet
(I well remember it)

In my first Dawn of Youth that Fancy stole
With many secret Yearnings on my Soul.
At eve, sky-gazing in 'ecstatic fit'
(Alas! for cloister'd in a city School
The Sky was all, I knew, of Beautiful)
At the barr'd window often did I sit,
And oft upon the leaded School-roof lay,
And to myself would say –
There does not live the Man so stripp'd of good affections
As not to love to see a Maiden's quiet Eyes
Uprais'd, and linking on sweet Dreams by dim Connections
To Moon, or Evening Star, or glorious western Skies –
While yet a Boy, this Thought would so pursue me,
That often it became a kind of Vision to me!

Sweet Thought! and dear of old
To Hearts of finer Mould!
Ten thousand times by Friends and Lovers blest!
I spake with rash Despair,
And ere I was aware,
The Weight was somewhat lifted from my Breast!
O Sara! in the weather-fended Wood,
Thy lov'd haunt! where the Stock-doves coo at Noon
I guess, that thou hast stood
And watch'd yon Crescent, and it's ghost-like Moon.
And yet, far rather in my present Mood
I would, that thou'dst been sitting all this while
Upon the sod-built Seat of Camomile –
And tho' thy Robin may have ceas'd to sing,
Yet needs for *my* sake must thou love to hear
The Bee-hive murmuring near,
That ever-busy and most quiet Thing
Which I have heard at Midnight murmuring.

I feel my spirit moved.
And whereso'er thou be,
O Sister! O Beloved!
Those dear mild Eyes, that see

Even now the Heaven, *I* see –
There is a Prayer in them! It is for *me* –
And I, dear Sara, *I* am blessing *thee*!

It was as calm as this, that happy night
When Mary, thou, and I together were,
The low decaying Fire our only Light,
And listen'd to the Stillness of the Air!
O that affectionate and blameless Maid,
Dear Mary! on her Lap my head she lay'd –
Her Hand was on my Brow,
Even as my own is now;
And on my Cheek I felt the eye-lash play.
Such joy I had, that I may truly say,
My spirit was awe-stricken with the Excess
And trance-like Depth of it's brief Happiness.

Ah fair Remembrances, that so revive
The Heart, and fill it with a living Power,
Where were they, Sara? – or did I not strive
To win them to me? – on the fretting Hour
Then when I wrote thee that complaining Scroll,
Which even to bodily Sickness bruis'd thy Soul!
And yet thou blam'st thyself alone! And yet
Forbidd'st me all Regret!
And must I not regret, that I distress'd
Thee, best belov'd, who lovest me the best?
My better mind had fled, I know not whither,
For O! was this an absent Friend's Employ
To send from far both Pain and Sorrow thither
Where still his Blessings should have call'd down Joy!
I read thy guileless Letter o'er again –
I hear thee of thy blameless Self complain –
And only this I learn – and this, alas! I know –
That thou art weak and pale with Sickness, Grief, and Pain –
And *I*, – *I* made thee so!

O for my own sake I regret perforce
Whatever turns thee, Sara! from the course

Of calm Well-being and a Heart at rest!
When thou, and with thee those, whom thou lov'st best,
Shall dwell together in one happy Home,
One House, the dear *abiding* Home of All,
I too will crown me with a Coronal –
Nor shall this Heart in idle Wishes roam
    Morbidly soft!
No! let me trust, that I shall wear away
In no inglorious Toils the manly Day,
And only now and then, and not too oft,
Some dear and memorable Eve will bless
Dreaming of all your Loves and Quietness.
Be happy, and I need thee not in sight.
Peace in thy Heart, and Quiet in thy Dwelling,
Health in thy Limbs, and in thine eyes the Light
Of Love and Hope and honorable Feeling –
Where e'er I am, I shall be well content!
Not near thee, haply shall be more content!
To all things I prefer the Permanent.
And better seems it, for a Heart, like mine,
Always to *know*, than sometimes to behold,
    Their Happiness and thine –
For Change doth trouble me with pangs untold!
To see thee, hear thee, feel thee – then to part
    Oh! it weighs down the heart!
To *visit* those, I love, as I love thee,
Mary, and William, and dear Dorothy,
It is but a temptation to repine –
The transientness is Poison in the Wine,
Eats out the pith of Joy, makes all Joy hollow,
All Pleasure a dim Dream of Pain to follow!
My own peculiar Lot, my house-hold Life
It is, and will remain, Indifference or Strife.
While *Ye* are *well* and *happy*, 'twould but wrong you
If I should fondly yearn to be among you –
Wherefore, O wherefore! should I wish to be
A wither'd branch upon a blossoming Tree?

But (let me say it! for I vainly strive
To beat away the Thought), but if thou pin'd
Whate'er the Cause, in body or in mind,
I were the miserablest Man alive.
To know it and be absent! Thy Delights
Far off, or near, alike I may partake –
But O! to mourn for thee, and to forsake
All power, all hope, of giving comfort to thee –
To know that thou art weak and worn with pain,
And not to hear thee, Sara! not to view thee –
  Not sit beside thy Bed,
  Not press thy aching Head,
  Not bring thee Health again –
  At least to hope, to try –
By this Voice, which thou lov'st, and by this earnest Eye –
Nay, wherefore did I let it haunt my Mind
The dark distressful Dream!
I turn from it, and listen to the Wind
Which long has rav'd unnotic'd! What a Scream
Of agony, by Torture lengthen'd out
That Lute sent forth! O thou wild Storm without!
Jagg'd Rock, or mountain Pond, or blasted Tree,
Or Pine-Grove, whither Woodman never clomb,
Or lonely House, long held the Witches' Home,
Methinks were fitter Instruments for Thee,
Mad Lutanist! that in this month of Showers,
Of dark brown Gardens and of peeping Flowers,
Mak'st Devil's Yule with worse than wintry Song
The Blossoms, Buds, and timorous Leaves among!
Thou Actor, perfect in all tragic Sounds!
Thou mighty Poet, even to frenzy bold!
What tell'st thou now about?
'Tis of the Rushing of an Host in Rout
And many groans for men with smarting Wounds –
At once they groan with smart, and shudder with the cold!
'Tis hush'd! there is a Trance of deepest Silence,
Again! but all that Sound, as of a rushing Crowd,
And Groans and tremulous Shudderings, all are over.

And it has other Sounds, and all less deep, less loud!
A Tale of less Affright,
And tempered with Delight,
As William's self had made the tender Lay –
'Tis of a little Child
Upon a heathy Wild,
Not far from home, but it has lost it's way –
And now moans low in utter grief and fear –
And now screams loud, and hopes to make it's Mother
   hear!

'Tis Midnight! and small Thoughts have I of Sleep.
Full seldom may my Friend such Vigils keep –
O breathe She softly in her gentle Sleep!
Cover her, gentle sleep! with wings of Healing.
And be this Tempest but a Mountain Birth!
May all the Stars hang bright above her Dwelling,
Silent, as though they *watch'd* the sleeping Earth!
Healthful and light, my Darling! may'st thou rise
With clear and chearful Eyes –
And of the same good Tidings to me send!
For oh! beloved Friend!
I am not the buoyant Thing I was of yore
When like an own Child, I to Joy belong'd:
For others mourning oft, myself oft sorely wrong'd,
Yet bearing all things then, as if I nothing bore!

Yes, dearest Sara, yes!
There *was* a time when tho' my path was rough,
The Joy within me dallied with Distress;
And all Misfortunes were but as the Stuff
Whence Fancy made me Dreams of Happiness;
For Hope grew round me, like the climbing Vine,
And Leaves and Fruitage, not my own, seem'd mine!
But now Ill Tidings bow me down to earth,
Nor care I that they rob me of my Mirth –
But Oh! each Visitation

Suspends what nature gave me at my Birth,
My shaping spirit of Imagination!

I speak not now of those habitual Ills
That wear out Life, when two unequal Minds
Meet in one House and two discordant Wills –
   This leaves me, where it finds,
Past Cure, and past Complaint, – a fate austere
Too fix'd and hopeless to partake of Fear!
But thou, dear Sara! (dear indeed thou art,
My Comforter, a Heart within my Heart!)
Thou, and the Few, we love, tho' few ye be,
Make up a World of Hopes and Fears for me.
And if Affliction, or distemp'ring Pain,
Or wayward Chance befall you, I complain
Not that I mourn – O Friends, most dear! most true!
   Methinks to weep with you
Were better far than to rejoice alone –
But that my coarse domestic Life has known
No Habits of heart-nursing Sympathy,
No Griefs but such as dull and deaden me,
No mutual mild Enjoyments of it's own,
No Hopes of its own Vintage, None O! none –
Whence when I mourn'd for you, my Heart might borrow
Fair forms and living Motions for it's Sorrow.
For not to think of what I needs must feel,
But to be still and patient all I can;
And haply by abstruse Research to steal
From my own Nature, all the Natural man –
This was my sole Resource, my wisest plan!
And that, which suits a part, infects the whole,
And now is almost grown the Temper of my Soul.

My little Children are a Joy, a Love,
   A good Gift from above!
But what is Bliss, that still calls up a Woe,
   And makes it doubly keen
Compelling me to *feel*, as well as *know*,

What a most blessed Lot mine might have been.
Those little Angel Children (woe is me!)
There have been hours when feeling how they bind
And pluck out the Wing-feathers of my Mind,
Turning my Error to Necessity,
I have half-wish'd they never had been born!
That seldom! but sad Thoughts they always bring,
And like the Poet's Philomel, I sing
My Love-song, with my breast against a Thorn.

With no unthankful Spirit I confess,
This clinging Grief, too, in it's turn, awakes
That Love, and Father's Joy; but O! it makes
The Love the greater, and the Joy far less.
These Mountains too, these Vales, these Woods, these
    Lakes,
Scenes full of Beauty and of Loftiness
Where all my Life I fondly hop'd to live —
I were sunk low indeed, did they *no* solace give;
But oft I seem to feel, and evermore I fear,
They are not to me now the Things, which once they were.

O Sara! we receive but what we give,
And in *our* life alone does Nature live
Our's is her Wedding Garment, our's her Shroud —
And would we aught behold of higher Worth
Than that inanimate cold World allow'd
To that poor loveless ever anxious Crowd,
Ah! from the Soul itself must issue forth
A Light, a Glory, and a luminous Cloud
Enveloping the Earth!
And from the Soul itself must there be sent
A sweet and potent Voice, of it's own Birth,
Of all sweet Sounds, the Life and Element.
O pure of Heart! thou need'st not ask of me
What this strong music in the Soul may be,
What and wherein it doth exist,
This Light, this Glory, this fair luminous Mist,
This beautiful and beauty-making Power!

Joy, innocent Sara! Joy, that ne'er was given
Save to the pure, and in their purest Hour,
Joy, Sara! is the Spirit and the Power,
That wedding Nature to us gives in Dower
    A new Earth and new Heaven,
Undreamt of by the Sensual and the Proud!
Joy is that strong Voice, Joy that luminous Cloud –
    We, we ourselves rejoice!
And thence flows all that charms or ear or sight,
All melodies, the Echoes of that Voice,
All Colors a Suffusion of that Light.
Sister and Friend of my devoutest Choice
Thou being innocent and full of love,
And nested with the Darlings of thy Love,
And feeling in thy Soul, Heart, Lips, and Arms
Even what the conjugal and mother Dove,
That borrows genial Warmth from those she warms,
Feels in the thrill'd wings, blessedly outspread –
Thou free'd awhile from Cares and human Dread
By the Immenseness of the Good and Fair
    Which thou seest everywhere –
Thus, thus, should'st thou rejoice!
To thee would all things live from Pole to Pole;
Their Life the Eddying of thy living Soul –
O dear! O Innocent! O full of Love!
A very Friend! A sister of my Choice –
O dear, as Light and Impulse from above,
Thus may'st thou ever, evermore rejoice!

To William Wordsworth

COMPOSED ON THE NIGHT AFTER HIS RECITA-
TION OF A POEM ON THE GROWTH OF AN
INDIVIDUAL MIND

    Friend of the wise! and teacher of the good!
    Into my heart have I received that lay
    More than historic, that prophetic lay

Wherein (high theme by thee first sung aright)
Of the foundations and the building up
Of a Human Spirit thou hast dared to tell
What may be told, to the understanding mind
Revealable; and what within the mind
By vital breathings secret as the soul
Of vernal growth, oft quickens in the heart
Thoughts all too deep for words! –

                Theme hard as high!
Of smiles spontaneous, and mysterious fears,
(The first-born they of Reason and twin-birth)
Of tides obedient to external force,
And currents self-determined, as might seem,
Or by some inner power; of moments awful,
Now in thy inner life, and now abroad,
When power streamed from thee, and thy soul received
The light reflected, as a light bestowed –
Of fancies fair, and milder hours of youth,
Hyblean murmurs of poetic thought
Industrious in its joy, in vales and glens
Native or outland, lakes and famous hills!
Or on the lonely high-road, when the stars
Were rising; or by secret mountain-streams,
The guides and the companions of thy way!

  Of more than Fancy, of the Social Sense
Distending wide, and man beloved as man,
Where France in all her towns lay vibrating
Like some becalmed bark beneath the burst
Of Heaven's immediate thunder, when no cloud
Is visible, or shadow on the main.
For thou wert there, thine own brows garlanded,
Amid the tremor of a realm aglow,
Amid a mighty nation jubilant,
When from the general heart of human kind
Hope sprang forth like a full-born Deity!
– Of that dear Hope afflicted and struck down,
So summoned homeward, thenceforth calm and sure

From the dread watch-tower of man's absolute self,
With light unwaning on her eyes, to look
Far on – herself a glory to behold,
The Angel of the vision! Then (last strain)
Of Duty, chosen laws controlling choice,
Action and joy! – An Orphic song indeed,
A song divine of high and passionate thoughts
To their own music chanted!

                                    O great Bard!
Ere yet that last strain dying awed the air,
With steadfast eye I viewed thee in the choir
Of ever-enduring men. The truly great
Have all one age, and from one visible space
Shed influence! They, both in power and act,
Are permanent, and Time is not with them,
Save as it worketh for them, they in it.
Nor less a sacred roll, than those of old,
And to be placed, as they, with gradual fame
Among the archives of mankind, thy work
Makes audible a linked lay of Truth,
Of Truth profound a sweet continuous lay,
Not learnt, but native, her own natural notes!
Ah! as I listened with a heart forlorn,
The pulses of my being beat anew:
And even as life returns upon the drowned,
Life's joy rekindling roused a throng of pains –
Keen pangs of Love, awakening as a babe
Turbulent, with an outcry in the heart;
And fears self-willed, that shunned the eye of hope:
And hope that scarce would know itself from fear;
Sense of past youth, and manhood come in vain,
And genius given, and knowledge won in vain;
And all which I had culled in wood-walks wild,
And all which patient toil had reared, and all,
Commune with thee had opened out – but flowers
Strewed on my corse, and borne upon my bier,
In the same coffin, for the self-same grave!

That way no more! and ill beseems it me,
Who came a welcomer in herald's guise,
Singing of glory, and futurity,
To wander back on such unhealthful road,
Plucking the poisons of self-harm! And ill
Such intertwine beseems triumphal wreaths
Strewed before thy advancing!

                                        Nor do thou,
Sage Bard! impair the memory of that hour
Of thy communion with my nobler mind
By pity or grief, already felt too long!
Nor let my words import more blame than needs.
The tumult rose and ceased: for peace is nigh
Where wisdom's voice has found a listening heart.
Amid the howl of more than wintry storms,
The halcyon hears the voice of vernal hours
Already on the wing.

                                        Eve following eve,
Dear tranquil time, when the sweet sense of Home
Is sweetest! moments for their own sake hailed
And more desired, more precious for thy song,
In silence listening, like a devout child,
My soul lay passive, by thy various strain
Driven as in surges now beneath the stars,
With momentary stars of my own birth,
Fair constellated foam, still darting off
Into the darkness; now a tranquil sea,
Outspread and bright, yet swelling to the moon.

And when – O Friend! my comforter and guide!
Strong in thyself, and powerful to give strength! –
Thy long sustained Song finally closed,
And thy deep voice had ceased – yet thou thyself
Wert still before my eyes, and round us both
That happy vision of beloved faces –
Scarce conscious, and yet conscious of its close

I sate, my being blended in one thought
(Thought was it? or aspiration? or resolve?)
Absorbed, yet hanging still upon the sound –
And when I rose, I found myself in prayer.

Epitaph

Stop, Christian Passer-by! – Stop, child of God,
And read with gentle breast. Beneath this sod
A poet lies, or that which once seem'd he –
O, lift one thought in prayer for S.T.C.;
That he who many a year with toil of breath
Found death in life, may here find life in death!
Mercy for praise – to be forgiven for fame
He ask'd, and hoped, through Christ. Do thou the same!

ROBERT SOUTHEY
1774–1843

The Pig

A COLLOQUIAL POEM

Jacob! I do not like to see thy nose
Turn'd up in scornful curve at yonder Pig.
It would be well, my friend, if we, like him,
Were perfect in our kind! . . . And why despise
The sow-born grunter? . . . He is obstinate,
Thou answerest; ugly, and the filthiest beast
That banquets upon offal. . . . Now I pray you
Hear the Pig's Counsel.

                    Is he obstinate?
We must not, Jacob, be deceived by words;
We must not take them as unheeding hands
Receive base money at the current worth.
But with a just suspicion try their sound,
And in the even balance weigh them well.
See now to what this obstinacy comes
A poor, mistreated, democratic beast,
He knows that his unmerciful drivers seek
Their profit, and not his. He hath not learnt
That Pigs were made for Man, . . . born to be brawn'd
And baconized: that he must please to give
Just what his gracious masters please to take;
Perhaps his tusks, the weapons Nature gave
For self-defence, the general privilege.
Perhaps . . . hark Jacob! dost thou hear that horn?
Woe to the young posterity of Pork!
Their enemy is at hand.

                    Again thou say'st
The Pig is ugly. Jacob, look at him!

Those eyes have taught the Lover flattery.
His face . . . nay Jacob, Jacob! were it fair
To judge a Lady in her dishabille?
Fancy it drest, and with saltpetre rouged.
Behold his tail, my friend; with curls like that
The wanton hop marries her stately spouse:
So crisp in beauty Amoretta's hair
Rings round her lover's soul the chains of love.
And what is beauty, but the aptitude
Of parts harmonious? Give thy fancy scope,
And thou wilt find that no imagined change
Can beautify this beast. Place at his end
The starry glories of the Peacock's pride,
Give him the Swan's white breast; for his horn-hoofs
Shape such a foot and ankle as the waves
Crowded in eager rivalry to kiss
When Venus from the enamour'd sea arose; . . .
Jacob, thou canst but make a monster of him!
All alteration man could think, would mar
His Pig-perfection.

                    The last charge, . . . he lives
A dirty life. Here I could shelter him
With noble and right-reverend precedents,
And show by sanction of authority
That 'tis a very honourable thing
To thrive by dirty ways. But let me rest
On better ground the unanswerable defence.
The Pig is a philosopher, who knows
No prejudice. Dirt? . . . Jacob, what is dirt?
If matter, . . . why the delicate dish that tempts
An o'ergorged Epicure to the last morsel
That stuffs him to the throat-gates, is no more.
If matter be not, but as Sages say,
Spirit is all, and all things visible
Are one, the infinitely modified,
Think, Jacob, what that Pig is, and the mire
Wherein he stands knee-deep!

                        And there! the breeze
Pleads with me, and has won thee to a smile
That speaks conviction. O'er yon blossom'd field
Of beans it came, and thoughts of bacon rise.

WALTER SAVAGE LANDOR
1775–1864

Shepherd and Nymph

From *Gebir*

' 'Twas evening, though not sun-set, and spring-tide
Level with these green meadows, seem'd still higher;
'Twas pleasant: and I loosen'd from my neck
The pipe you gave me, and began to play.
O that I ne'er had learnt the tuneful art!
It always brings us enemies or love!
Well, I was playing – when above the waves
Some swimmer's head methought I saw ascend;
I, sitting still, survey'd it, with my pipe
Awkwardly held before my lips half-clos'd.
Gebir! it was a nymph! a nymph divine!
I cannot wait describing how she came,
How I was sitting, how she first assum'd
The sailor: of what happened, there remains
Enough to say, and too much to forget.
The sweet deceiver stept upon this bank
Before I was aware; for, with surprize
Moments fly rapid as with love itself.
Stooping to tune afresh the hoarsen'd reed,
I heard a rustling; and where that arose
My glance first lighted on her nimble feet.
Her feet resembled those long shells explored
By him who to befriend his steeds' dim sight
Would blow the pungent powder in their eye. –
Her eyes too! O immortal Gods! her eyes
Resembled – what could they resemble – what
Ever resemble those! E'en her attire
Was not of wonted woof nor vulgar art:
Her mantle shew'd the yellow samphire-pod,
Her girdle, the dove colour'd wave serene.

198

'Shepherd,' said she, 'and will you wrestle now,
And with the sailor's hardier race engage?'
I was rejoiced to hear it, and contrived
How to keep up contention; – could I fail
By pressing not too strongly, still to press.
'Whether a shepherd, as indeed you seem,
Or whether of the hardier race you boast,
I am not daunted, no: I will engage.'
'But first,' said she, 'what wager will you lay?'
'A sheep,' I answered, 'add what'er you will.'
'I cannot,' she replied, 'make that return:
Our hided vessels, in their pitchy round,
Seldom, unless from rapine, hold a sheep.
But I have sinuous shells, of pearly hue
Within, and they that lustre have imbibed
In the sun's palace porch; where, when unyoked,
His chariot wheel stands midway in the wave.
Shake one, and it awakens; then apply
Its polished lips to your attentive ear,
And it remembers its august abodes,
And murmurs as the ocean murmurs there.
And I have others given me by the nymphs,
Of sweeter sound than any pipe you have. –
But we, by Neptune, for no pipe contend;
This time a sheep I win, a pipe the next.'
Now came she forward, eager to engage;
But, first her dress, her bosom then, survey'd,
And heav'd it, doubting if she could deceive.
Her bosom seem'd, inclos'd in haze like heav'n,
To baffle touch; and rose forth undefined.
Above her knees she drew the robe succinct,
Above her breast, and just below her arms:
'This will preserve my breath, when tightly bound,
If struggle and equal strength should so constrain.'
Thus, pulling hard to fasten it, she spoke,
And, rushing at me, closed. I thrill'd throughout
And seem'd to lessen and shrink up with cold.
Again, with violent impulse gushed my blood;

And hearing nought external, thus absorb'd,
I heard it, rushing through each turbid vein,
Shake my unsteady swimming sight in air.
Yet with unyielding though uncertain arms,
I clung around her neck; the vest beneath
Rustled against our slippery limbs entwined:
Often mine, springing with eluded force,
Started aside, and trembled, till replaced.
And when I most succeeded, as I thought,
My bosom and my throat felt so comprest
That life was almost quivering on my lips,
Yet nothing was there painful! these are signs
Of secret arts, and not of human might,
What arts I cannot tell: I only know
My eyes grew dizzy, and my strength decay'd,
I was indeed o'ercome! – with what regret,
And more, with what confusion, when I reached
The fold, and yielding up the sheep, she cried,
'This pays a shepherd to a conquering maid.'
She smil'd, and more of pleasure than disdain
Was in her dimpled chin, and liberal lip,
And eyes that languished, lengthening, – just like love.
She went away: I, on the wicker gate
Lean'd, and could follow with my eyes alone.
The sheep she carried easy as a cloak,
But when I heard its bleating, as I did,
And saw, she hastening on, its hinder feet
Struggle, and from her snowy shoulder slip,
(One shoulder its poor efforts had unveil'd,)
Then, all my passions mingling fell in tears!
Restless then ran I to the highest ground
To watch her; she was gone; gone down the tide;
And the long moon-beam on the hard wet sand
Lay like a jasper column half uprear'd.'

To Wordsworth

Those who have laid the harp aside
   And turn'd to idler things,
From very restlessness have tried
   The loose and dusty strings;
And, catching back some favourite strain,
Run with it o'er the chords again.

But Memory is not a Muse,
   O Wordsworth! – though 'tis said
They all descend from her, and use
   To haunt her fountain-head:
That other men should work for me
In the rich mines of Poesie,

Pleases me better than the toil,
   Of smoothing under hardened hand,
With attic emery and oil,
   The shining point for Wisdom's wand;
Like those thou temperest 'mid the rills
Descending from thy native hills.

Without his governance, in vain
   Manhood is strong, and youth is bold.
If oftentimes the o'er-piled strain
   Clogs in the furnace, and grows cold,
Beneath his pinions deep and frore,
And swells, and melts, and flows no more,

That is because the heat beneath,
   Pants in its cavern poorly fed.
Life springs not from the couch of Death,
   Nor Muse nor Grace can raise the dead;
Unturn'd then let the mass remain,
Intractable to sun or rain.

A marsh, where only flat leaves lie,
And showing but the broken sky,
Too surely is the sweetest lay
That wins the ear and wastes the day;
Where youthful Fancy pouts alone,
And lets not Wisdom touch her zone.
He who would build his fame up high,
The rule and plummet must apply,
Nor say – I'll do what I have plann'd,
Before he try if loam or sand
Be still remaining in the place
Delved for each polish'd pillar's base.
With skilful eye and fit device,
Thou raisest every edifice:
Whether in sheltered vale it stand
Or overlook the Dardan strand,
Amid those cypresses that mourn
Laodamia's love forlorn.

We both have run o'er half the space
Bounded for mortal's earthly race;
We both have crossed life's fervid line,
And other stars before us shine.
May they be bright and prosperous
As those that have been stars for us!
Our course by Milton's light was sped,
And Shakespeare shining overhead:
Chatting on deck was Dryden too,
The Bacon of the rhyming crew;
None ever crost our mystic sea,
More richly stored with thought than he;
Tho' never tender nor sublime,
He struggles with and conquers Time.
To learn my lore on Chaucer's knee,
I've left much prouder company.
Thee, gentle Spenser fondly led;
But me he mostly sent to bed.
I wish them every joy above

That highly blessed spirits prove,
Save one – and that too shall be theirs,
But after many rolling years,
When 'mid their light, thy light appears.

Hegemon to Praxinoe

Is there any season, O my soul,
When the sources of bitter tears dry up,
And the uprooted flowers take their places again
   Along the torrent-bed?

Could I wish to live, it would be for that season,
To repose my limbs and press my temples there.
But should I not speedily start away
   In the hope to trace and follow thy steps!

Thou art gone, thou art gone, Praxinoe!
And hast taken far from me thy lovely youth,
Leaving me naught that was desirable in mine.
   Alas! alas! what hast thou left me?

The helplessness of childhood, the solitude of age,
The laughter of the happy, the pity of the scorner,
A colourless and broken shadow am I,
   Seen glancing in troubled waters.

My thoughts too are scattered; thou hast cast them off;
They beat against thee, they would cling to thee,
But they are viler than the loose dark weeds,
   Without a place to root or rest in.

I would throw them across my lyre; they drop from it;
My lyre will sound only two measures;
That Pity will never, never come,
   Or come to the sleep that awakeneth not unto her.

THOMAS MOORE.
1779–1852

At the Mid Hour of Night

At the mid hour of night, when stars are weeping, I fly
To the lone vale we loved when life was warm in thine eye,
   And I think that if spirits can steal from the regions of air
    To revisit past scenes of delight, thou wilt come to me
    there,
And tell me our love is remember'd, even in the sky!

Then I sing the wild song it once was rapture to hear,
When our voices, commingling, breathed like one on the
    ear,
   And, as Echo far off through the vale my sad orison rolls,
   I think, oh, my love! 'tis thy voice from the kingdom of
   souls,
Faintly answering still the notes that once were so dear.

A Syrian Evening

From *Lalla Rookh*

Now, upon Syria's land of roses
Softly the light of Eve reposes,
And like a glory, the broad sun
Hangs over sainted Lebanon,
Whose head in wintry grandeur towers,
   And whitens with eternal sleet,
While summer, in a vale of flowers,
   Is sleeping rosy at his feet.

To one who look'd from upper air
O'er all the enchanted regions there,
How beauteous must have been the glow!
The life, the sparkling from below!

THOMAS MOORE

Fair gardens, shining streams, with ranks
Of golden melons on their banks,
More golden where the sun-light falls; –
Gay lizards, glittering on the walls; –
Of ruin'd shrines, busy and bright
As they were all alive with light; –
And, yet more splendid, numerous flocks
Of pigeons, settling on the rocks,
With their rich restless wings, that gleam,
Variously in the crimson beam
Of the warm west – as if inlaid
With brilliants from the mine, or made
Of tearless rainbows, such as span
The unclouded skies of Peristan!
And then, the mingling sounds that come,
Of shepherd's ancient reed, with hum
Of the wild bees of Palestine,
 Banqueting through the flowery vales; –
And, Jordan, those sweet banks of thine;
 And woods, so full of nightingales!

EBENEZER ELLIOT
1781–1849

The Fox-Hunters

What Gods are these? Bright red, or white and green,
Some of them jockey-capp'd and some in hats,
The gods of vermin have their runs, like rats.
Each has six legs, four moving, pendent two,
Like bottled tails, the tilting four between.
Behold Land-Interest's compound Man-and-Horse,
Which so enchants his outraged helot-crew,
Hedge-gapping, with his horn, and view-halloo,
O'er hunter's clover – glorious broom and gorse!
The only crop his godship ever grew:
Except his crop of hate, and smouldering ire,
And cloak'd contempt, of coward insult born,
And hard-faced labour, paid with straw for corn,
And fain to reap it with a scythe of fire.

Epigram

'Prepare to meet the King of Terrors,' cried
To prayerless Want, his plunderer ferret-eyed:
'I am the King of Terrors,' Want replied.

THOMAS LOVE PEACOCK
1785–1866

Chorus

Hail to the Headlong! the Headlong Ap-Headlong!
All hail to the Headlong, the Headlong Ap-Headlong!
    The Headlong Ap-Headlong
    Ap-Breakneck Ap-Headlong
Ap-Cataract Ap-Pistyll Ap-Rhaiader Ap-Headlong!

The bright bowl we steep in the name of the Headlong:
Let the youths pledge it deep to the Headlong Ap-Head-
    long,
    And the rosy-lipped lasses
    Touch the brim as it passes,
And kiss the red tide for the Headlong Ap-Headlong!

The loud harp resounds in the hall of the Headlong:
The light step rebounds in the hall of the Headlong:
    Where shall music invite us,
    Or beauty delight us,
If not in the hall of the Headlong Ap-Headlong?

Huzza! to the health of the Headlong Ap-Headlong!
Fill the bowl, fill in floods, to the health of the Headlong!
    Till the stream ruby-glowing,
    On all sides o'erflowing,
Shall fall in cascades to the health of the Headlong!
    The Headlong Ap-Headlong
    Ap-Breakneck Ap-Headlong
Ap-Cataract Ap-Pistyll Ap-Rhaiader Ap-Headlong!

Seamen Three

Seamen three! What men be ye?
Gotham's three wise men we be.
Whither in your bowl so free?
To rake the moon from out the sea.
The bowl goes trim. The moon doth shine.
And our ballast is old wine;
And your ballast is old wine.

Who art thou, so fast adrift?
I am he they call Old Care,
Here on board we will thee lift.
No: I may not enter there.
Wherefore so? 'Tis Jove's decree,
In a bowl Care may not be;
In a bowl Care may not be.

Fear ye not the waves that roll?
No: in charmed bowl we swim.
What the charm that floats the bowl?
Water may not pass the brim.
The bowl goes trim. The moon doth shine.
And our ballast is old wine;
And your ballast is old wine.

The Brilliancies of Winter

Last of flowers, in tufts around
Shines the gorse's golden bloom:
Milk-white lichens clothe the ground
'Mid the flowerless heath and broom:
Bright are holly-berries, seen
Red, through leaves of glossy green.

Brightly, as on rocks they leap,
Shine the sea-waves, white with spray:
Brightly, in the dingles deep,
Gleams the river's foaming way;
Brightly through the distance show
Mountain-summits clothed in snow.

Brightly, where the torrents bound,
Shines the frozen colonnade,
Which the black rocks, dripping round,
And the flying spray have made:
Bright the ice-drops on the ash
Leaning o'er the cataract's dash.

Bright the hearth, where feast and song
Crown the warrior's hour of peace,
While the snow-storm drives along,
Bidding war's worse tempest cease;
Bright the hearth-flame, flashing clear
On the up-hung shield and spear.

Bright the torchlight of the hall
When the wintry night-winds blow;
Brightest when its splendours fall
On the mead-cup's sparkling flow:
While the maiden's smile of light
Makes the brightness trebly bright.

Close the portals; pile the hearth;
Strike the harp; the feast pursue;
Brim the horns: fire, music, mirth,
Mead and love, are winter's due.
Spring to purple conflict calls
Swords that shine on winter's walls.

Taliesin and Melanghel

Taliesin: Maid of the rock! though loud the flood,
My voice will pierce thy cell:
No foe is in the mountain wood;
No danger in the dell:
The torrents bound along the glade;
Their path is free and bright;
Be thou as they, O mountain maid!
In liberty and light.

Melanghel: The cataracts thunder down the steep;
The woods all lonely wave:
Within my heart the voice sinks deep
That calls me from my cave,
The voice is dear, the song is sweet,
And true the words must be:
Well pleased I quit the dark retreat,
To wend away with thee.

Taliesin: Not yet; not yet; let nightdews fall,
And stars be bright above,
Ere to her long-deserted hall
I guide my gentle love.
When torchlight flashes on the roof,
No foe will near thee stray:
Even now his parting courser's hoof
Rings from the rocky way.

Melanghel: Yet climb the path, and comfort speak,
To cheer the lonely cave,
Where woods are bare, and rocks are bleak,
And wintry torrents rave.
A dearer home my memory knows,
A home I still deplore;
Where firelight glows, while winds and snows
Assail the guardian door.

GEORGE GORDON,
LORD BYRON
1788–1824

Lines Inscribed upon a Cup Formed from a Skull

Start not – nor deem my spirit fled;
   In me behold the only skull,
From which, unlike a living head,
   Whatever flows is never dull.

I lived, I loved, I quaff'd, like thee:
   I died: let earth my bones resign;
Fill up – thou canst not injure me;
   The worm hath fouler lips than thine.

Better to hold the sparkling grape,
   Than nurse the earth-worm's slimy brood;
And circle in the goblet's shape
   The drink of gods, than reptile's food.

Where once my wit, perchance, hath shone,
   In aid of others' let me shine;
And when, alas! our brains are gone,
   . What nobler substitute than wine?

Quaff while thou canst: another race,
   When thou and thine, like me, are sped,
May rescue thee from earth's embrace,
   And rhyme and revel with the dead.

Why not? since through life's little day
   Our heads such sad effects produce;
Redeem'd from worms and wasting clay,
   This chance is theirs, to be of use.

Fare Thee Well

Fare thee well! and if for ever,
  Still for ever, fare thee well:
Even though unforgiving, never
  'Gainst thee shall my heart rebel.
Would that breast were bared before thee
  Where thy head so oft hath lain,
While that placid sleep came o'er thee
  Which thou ne'er canst know again:
Would that breast, by thee glanced over,
  Every inmost thought could show!
Then thou wouldst at last discover
  'T was not well to spurn it so.
Though the world for this commend thee –
  Though it smile upon the blow,
Even its praises must offend thee,
  Founded on another's woe:
Though my many faults defaced me,
  Could no other arm be found,
Than the one which once embraced me,
  To inflict a cureless wound?
Yet, oh yet, thyself deceive not;
  Love may sink by slow decay,
But by sudden wrench, believe not
  Hearts can thus be torn away:
Still thine own its life retaineth,
  Still must mine, though bleeding, beat;
And the undying thought which paineth
  Is – that we no more may meet.
These are words of deeper sorrow
  Than the wail above the dead;
Both shall live, but every morrow
  Wake us from a widow'd bed.
And when thou wouldst solace gather,
  When our child's first accents flow,
Wilt thou teach her to say 'Father!'

Though his care she must forego?
When her little hands shall press thee,
   When her lip to thine is press'd,
Think of him whose prayer shall bless thee
   Think of him thy love had bless'd!
Should her lineaments resemble
   Those thou never more may'st see,
Then thy heart will softly tremble
   With a pulse yet true to me.
All my faults perchance thou knowest,
   All my madness none can know;
All my hopes, where'er thou goest,
   Wither, yet with *thee* they go.
Every feeling hath been shaken;
   Pride, which not a world could bow,
Bows to thee – by thee forsaken,
   Even my soul forsakes me now:
But 'tis done – all words are idle –
   Words from me are vainer still;
But the thoughts we cannot bridle
   Force their way without the will.
Fare thee well! thus disunited,
   Torn from every nearer tie,
Sear'd in heart, and lone, and blighted,
   More than this I scarce can die.

So We'll Go no more *A Roving*

So, we'll go no more a roving
   So late into the night,
Though the heart be still as loving,
   And the moon be still as bright.

For the sword outwears its sheath,
   And the soul wears out the breast,
And the heart must pause to breathe,
   And love itself have rest.

Though the night was made for loving,
    And the day returns too soon,
Yet we'll go no more a roving
    By the light of the moon.

From *Don Juan*

FRAGMENT
On the back of the Poet's MS. of Canto I

I would to heaven that I were so much clay,
    As I am blood, bone, marrow, passion, feeling –
Because at least the past were pass'd away –
    And for the future – (but I write this reeling,
Having got drunk exceedingly to-day,
    So that I seem to stand upon the ceiling)
I say – the future is a serious matter –
And so – for God's sake – hock and soda-water!

(i)

Man's a strange animal, and makes strange use
    Of his own nature, and the various arts,
And likes particularly to produce
    Some new experiment to show his parts;
This is the age of oddities let loose,
    Where different talents find their different marts;
You'd best begin with truth, and when you've lost your
Labour, there's a sure market for imposture.

What opposite discoveries we have seen!
    (Signs of true genius, and of empty pockets.)
One makes new noses, one a guillotine,
    One breaks your bones, one sets them in their sockets;
But vaccination certainly has been
    A kind of antithesis to Congreve's rockets,
With which the Doctor paid off an old pox,
By borrowing a new one from an ox.

Bread has been made (indifferent) from potatoes;
  And galvanism has set some corpses grinning,
But has not answer'd like the apparatus
  Of the Humane Society's beginning,
By which men are unsuffocated gratis:
  What wondrous new machines have late been spinning!
I said the small pox has gone out of late;
Perhaps it may be follow'd by the great.

'Tis said the great came from America;
  Perhaps it may set out on its return, –
The population there so spreads, they say
  'Tis grown high time to thin it in its turn,
With war, or plague, or famine, any way,
  So that civilisation they may learn;
And which in ravage the more loathsome evil is –
Their real lues, or our pseudo-syphilis?

This is the patent age of new inventions
  For killing bodies, and for saving souls,
All propagated with the best intentions;
  Sir Humphrey Davy's lantern, by which coals
Are safely mined for in the mode he mentions,
  Tombuctoo travels, voyages to the Poles,
Are ways to benefit mankind, as true,
Perhaps, as shooting them at Waterloo.

Man's a phenomenon, one knows not what,
  And wonderful, beyond all wondrous measure;
'Tis pity, though, in this sublime world, that
  Pleasure's a sin, and sometimes sin's a pleasure;
Few mortals know what end they would be at,
  But whether glory, power, or love, or treasure,
The path is through perplexing ways, and when
The goal is gain'd, we die, you know – and then –

What then? – I do not know, no more do you –
  And so good night. – Return we to our story:
'Twas in November, when fine days are few,
  And the far mountains wax a little hoary,

And clap a white cape on their mantles blue;
  And the sea dashes round the promontory,
And the loud breaker boils against the rock,
And sober suns must set at five o'clock.

'Twas, as the watchmen say, a cloudy night;
  No moon, no stars, the wind was low or loud
By gusts, and many a sparkling hearth was bright
  With the piled wood round which the family crowd;
There's something cheerful in that sort of light,
  Even as a summer sky's without a cloud
I'm fond of fire, and crickets, and all that,
A lobster salad, and champagne, and chat.

'Twas midnight – Donna Julia was in bed,
  Sleeping, most probably – when at her door
Arose a clatter might awake the dead,
  If they had never been awoke before,
And that they have been so we all have read,
  And are to be so, at the least, once more; –
The door was fasten'd, but with voice and fist
First knocks were heard, then 'Madam – Madam – hist!

'For God's sake, Madam – Madam – here's my master.
  With more than half the city at his back –
Was ever heard of such a curst disaster!
  'Tis not my fault – I kept good watch – Alack!
Do pray undo the bolt a little faster –
  They're on the stair just now, and in a crack
Will all be here; perhaps he yet may fly –
Surely the window's not so *very* high!'

By this time Don Alfonso was arrived,
  With torches, friends, and servants in great number;
The major part of them had long been wived,
  And therefore paused not to disturb the slumber
Of any wicked woman, who contrived
  By stealth her husband's temples to encumber:
Examples of this kind are so contagious,
Were *one* not punish'd, *all* would be outrageous.

I can't tell how, or why, or what suspicion
   Could enter into Don Alfonso's head;
But for a cavalier of his condition
   It surely was exceedingly ill-bred,
Without a word of previous admonition,
   To hold a levée round his lady's bed,
And summon lackeys, arm'd with fire and sword,
To prove himself the thing he most abhorr'd.

Poor Donna Julia! starting as from sleep
   (Mind – that I do not say – she had not slept),
Began at once to scream, and yawn, and weep;
   Her maid, Antonia, who was an adept,
Contrived to fling the bed-clothes in a heap,
   As if she had just now from out them crept;
I can't tell why she should take all this trouble
To prove her mistress had been sleeping double.

But Julia mistress, and Antonia maid,
   Appear'd like two poor harmless women, who
Of goblins, but still more of men afraid,
   Had thought one man might be deterr'd by two,
And therefore side by side were gently laid,
   Until the hours of absence should run through,
And truant husband should return, and say,
'My dear, I was the first who came away.'

Now Julia found at length a voice, and cried,
   'In heaven's name, Don Alfonso, what d'ye mean?
Has madness seized you? would that I had died
   Ere such a monster's victim I had been!
What may this midnight violence betide,
   A sudden fit of drunkenness or spleen?
Dare you suspect me, whom the thought would kill?
Search, then, the room!' – Alfonso said, 'I will.'

He search'd, *they* search'd, and rummaged everywhere,
   Closet and clothes press, chest and window-seat,
And found much linen, lace, and several pair
   Of stockings, slippers, brushes, combs, complete,

With other articles of ladies fair,
  To keep them beautiful, or leave them neat:
Arras they prick'd and curtains with their swords,
And wounded several shutters, and some boards.

Under the bed they search'd, and there they found –
  No matter what – it was not that they sought;
They open'd the windows, gazing if the ground
  Had signs of footmarks, but the earth said naught;
And then they stared each other's faces round:
  'Tis odd, not one of all these seekers thought,
And seems to me almost a sort of blunder,
Of looking *in* the bed as well as under.

During this inquisition Julia's tongue
  Was not asleep – 'Yes, search and search,' she cried,
'Insult on insult heap, and wrong on wrong!
  It was for this that I became a bride!
For this in silence I have suffer'd long
  A husband like Alfonso at my side;
But now I'll bear no more, nor here remain,
If there be law or lawyers in all Spain.

'Yes, Don Alfonso! husband now no more,
  If ever you indeed deserved the name,
Is't worthy of your years? – you have three-score –
  Fifty, or sixty, it is all the same –
Is't wise or fitting, causeless to explore
  For facts against a virtuous woman's fame?
Ungrateful, perjured, barbarous Don Alfonso,
How dare you think your lady would go on so?

'Is it for this I have disdain'd to hold
  The common privileges of my sex?
That I have chosen a confessor so old
  And deaf, that any other it would vex.
And never once he has had cause to scold,
  But found my very innocence perplex

218

So much, he always doubted I was married –
How sorry you will be when I've miscarried!

'Was it for this that no Cortejo e'er
  I yet have chosen from out the youth of Seville?
Is it for this I scarce went anywhere,
  Except to bull-fights, mass, play, rout and revel?
Is it for this, what'er my suitors were,
  I favour'd none – nay, was almost uncivil?
Is it for this that General Count O'Reilly,
Who took Algiers, declares I used him vilely?

'Did not the Italian Musico Cazzani
  Sing at my heart six months at least in vain?
Did not his countryman, Count Corniani,
  Call me the only virtuous wife in Spain?
Were there not also Russians, English, many?
  The Count Strongstroganoff I put in pain,
And Lord Mount Coffeehouse, the Irish peer,
Who kill'd himself for love (with wine) last year.

'Have I not had two bishops at my feet?
  The Duke of Ichar, and Don Fernan Nunez?
And is it thus a faithful wife you treat?
  I wonder in what quarter now the moon is:
I praise your vast forbearance not to beat
  Me also, since the time so opportune is –
Oh, valiant man! with sword drawn and cock'd trigger,
Now, tell me, don't you cut a pretty figure?

'Was it for this you took your sudden journey,
  Under pretence of business indispensable,
With that sublime of rascals your attorney,
  Whom I see standing there, and looking sensible
Of having play'd the fool? though both I spurn, he
  Deserves the worst, his conduct's less defensible,

Because, no doubt, 'twas for his dirty fee,
And not from any love to you nor me.

'If he comes here to take a deposition,
    By all means let the gentleman proceed;
You've made the apartment in a fit condition: –
    There's pen and ink for you, sir, when you need –
Let everything be noted with precision,
    I would not you for nothing should be fee'd –
But as my maid's undrest, pray turn your spies out.'
'Oh!' sobb'd Antonia, 'I could tear their eyes out.'

'There is the closet, there the toilet, there
    The antechamber – search them under, over;
There is the sofa, there the great-arm-chair,
    The chimney – which would really hold a lover.
I wish to sleep, and beg you will take care
    And make no further noise, till you discover
The secret cavern of this lurking treasure –
And when 'tis found, let me, too, have that pleasure.

'And now, Hidalgo! now that you have thrown
    Doubt upon me, confusion over all,
Pray have the courtesy to make it known
    Who is the man you search for? how d'ye call
Him? what's his lineage? let him but be shown –
    I hope he's young and handsome – is he tall?
Tell me – and be assured, that since you stain
Mine honour thus; it shall not be in vain.

'At least, perhaps, he has not sixty years,
    At that age he would be too old for slaughter,
Or for so young a husband's jealous fears –
    (Antonia! let me have a glass of water.)
I am ashamed of having shed these tears,
    They are unworthy of my father's daughter;
My mother dream'd not in my natal hour,
That I should fall into a monster's power.

220

'Perhaps 'tis of Antonia you are jealous,
   You saw that she was sleeping by my side,
When you broke in upon us with your fellows;
   Look where you please – we've nothing, sir, to hide;
Only another time, I trust, you'll tell us,
   Or for the sake of decency abide
A moment at the door, that we may be
Drest to receive so much good company.

'And now, sir, I have done, and say no more;
   The little I have said may serve to show
The guileless heart in silence may grieve o'er
   The wrongs to whose exposure it is slow: –
I leave you to your conscience as before,
   'Twill one day ask you, *why* you used me so?
God grant you feel not then the bitterest grief!
Antonia! where's my pocket handkerchief?'

She ceased, and turn'd upon her pillow; pale
   She lay, her dark eyes flashing through their tears,
Like skies that rain and lighten; as a veil,
   Waved and o'ershading her wan cheek, appears
Her streaming hair; the black curls strive, but fail,
   To hide the glossy shoulder, which uprears
Its snow through all; – her soft lips lie apart,
And louder than her breathing beats her heart.

The Senhor Don Alfonso stood confused;
   Antonia bustled round the ransack'd room,
And, turning up her nose, with looks abused
   Her master, and his myrmidons, of whom
Not one, except the attorney, was amused;
   He, like Achates, faithful to the tomb,
So there were quarrels, cared not for the cause,
Knowing they must be settled by the laws.

With prying snub-nose, all small eyes, he stood.
   Following Antonia's motions here and there,
With much suspicion in his attitude;
   For reputations he had little care;

So that a suit or action were made good,
  Small pity had he for the young and fair,
And ne'er believed in negatives, till these
Were proved by competent false witnesses.

But Don Alfonso stood with downcast looks,
  And, truth to say, he made a foolish figure;
When, after searching in five hundred nooks,
  And treating a young wife with so much rigour,
He gain'd no point, except some self-rebukes,
  Added to those his lady with such vigour
Had pour'd upon him for the last half-hour,
Quick, thick, and heavy – as a thunder-shower.

At first he tried to hammer an excuse,
  To which the sole reply was tears and sobs,
And indications of hysterics, whose
  Prologue is always certain throes, and throbs,
Gasps, and whatever else the owners choose;
  Alfonso saw his wife, and thought of Job's;
He saw too, in perspective, her relations,
And then he tried to muster all his patience.

He stood in act to speak, or rather stammer,
  But sage Antonia cut him short before
The anvil of his speech received the hammer,
  With 'Pray, sir, leave the room, and say no more,
Or madam dies.' – Alfonso mutter'd, 'D—n her.'
  But nothing else, the time of words was o'er;
He cast a rueful look or two, and did,
He knew not wherefore, that which he was bid.

With him retired his '*posse comitatus*,'
  The attorney last, who linger'd near the door
Reluctantly, still tarrying there as late as
  Antonia let him – not a little sore
At this most strange and unexplained '*hiatus*'
  In Don Alfonso's facts, which just now wore
An awkward look; as he revolved he case,
The door was fasten'd in his legal face.

No sooner was it bolted, than – O shame!
   Oh sin! Oh sorrow! and Oh womankind!
How can you do such things and keep your fame,
   Unless this world, and t'other too, be blind?
Nothing so dear as an unfilch'd good name!
   But to proceed – for there is more behind:
With much heartfelt reluctance be it said,
Young Juan slipp'd, half-smother'd, from the bed.

He had been hid – I don't pretend to say
   How, nor can I indeed describe the where –
Young, slender, and pack'd easily, he lay,
   No doubt, in little compass, round or square;
But pity him I neither must nor may
   His suffocation by that pretty pair;
'Twere better, sure, to die so, than be shut
With maudlin Clarence in his Malmsey butt.

And secondly, I pity not, because
   He had no business to commit a sin,
Forbid by heavenly, fined by human laws,
   At least 'twas rather early to begin;
But at sixteen the conscience rarely gnaws
   So much as when we call our old debts in
At sixty years, and draw the accompts of evil,
And find a deuced balance with the devil.

Of his position I can give no notion;
   'Tis written in the Hebrew Chronicle,
How the physicians, leaving pill and potion,
   Prescribed, by way of blister, a young belle,
When old King David's blood grew dull in motion,
   And that the medicine answer'd very well;
Perhaps 'twas in a different way applied,
For David lived, but Juan nearly died.

What's to be done? Alfonso will be back
   The moment he has sent his fools away.
Antonia's skill was put upon the rack,
   But no device could be brought into play –

And how to parry the renew'd attack?
  Besides, it wanted but few hours of day:
Antonia puzzled; Julia did not speak,
But press'd her bloodless lip to Juan's cheek.

He turn'd his lip to hers, and with his hand
  Call'd back the tangles of her wandering hair;
Even then their love they could not all command,
  And half forgot their danger and despair:
Antonia's patience now was at a stand –
  'Come, come, 'tis no time now for fooling there,'
She whisper'd, in great wrath – 'I must deposit
This pretty gentleman within the closet:

'Pray, keep your nonsense for some luckier night –
  Who can have put my master in this mood?
What will become on't – I'm in such a fright,
  The devil's in the urchin, and no good –
Is this a time for giggling? this a plight?
  Why, don't you know that it may end in blood?
You'll lose your life, and I shall lose my place,
My mistress all, for the half-girlish face.

'Had it but been for a stout cavalier
  Of twenty-five or thirty – (come, make haste)
But for a child, what piece of work is here!
  I really, madam, wonder at your taste –
(Come, sir, get in) – my master must be near:
  There, for the present, at the least, he's fast,
And if we can but till the morning keep
Our counsel – Juan, mind, you must not sleep.'

Now, Don Alfonso entering, but alone,
  Closed the oration of the trusty maid:
She loiter'd, and he told her to be gone,
  An order somewhat sullenly obey'd;
However, present remedy was none,
  And no great good seem'd answer'd if she staid;
Retarding both with slow and sidelong view,
She snuff'd the candle, curtsied, and withdrew.

Alfonso paused a minute – then begun
   Some strange excuses for his late proceeding;
He would not justify what he had done,
   To say the best, it was extreme ill-breeding;
But there were ample reasons for it, none
   Of which he specified in this his pleading:
His speech was a fine sample, on the whole
Of rhetoric, which the learn'd call '*rigmarole.*'

Julia said nought; though all the while there rose
   A ready answer, which at once enables
A matron, who her husband's foible knows,
   By a few timely words to turn the tables,
Which, if it does not silence, still must pose, –
   Even if it should comprise a pack of fables;
'Tis to retort with firmness, and when he
Suspects with *one,* do you reproach with *three.*

Julia, in fact had tolerable grounds, –
   Alfonso's loves with Inez were well known;
But whether 'twas that one's own guilt confounds –
   But that can't be, as has been often shown,
A lady with apologies abounds; –
   It might be that her silence sprang alone
From delicacy to Don Juan's ear,
To whom she knew his mother's fame was dear.

There might be one more motive, which makes two,
   Alfonso ne'er to Juan had alluded, –
Mentioned his jealousy, but never who
   Had been the happy lover, he concluded,
Conceal'd amongst his premises; 'tis true,
   His mind the more o'er this its mystery brooded
To speak of Inez now were, one may say,
Like throwing Juan in Alfonso's way.

A hint in tender cases, is enough;
   Silence is best: besides there is a *tact* –
(That modern phrase appears to me sad stuff,
   But it will serve to keep my verse compact) –

Which keeps, when push'd by questions rather rough,
　A lady always distant from the fact:
The charming creatures lie with such a grace,
There's nothing so becoming to the face.

They blush, and we believe them, at least I
　Have always done so; 'tis of no great use,
In any case, attempting a reply,
　For then their eloquence grows quite profuse;
And when at length they're out of breath, they sigh,
　And cast their languid eyes down, and let loose
A tear or two, and then we make it up;
And then – and then – and then – sit down and sup.

Alfonso closed his speech, and begg'd her pardon,
　Which Julia half withheld, and then half granted,
And laid conditions, he thought very hard, on,
　Denying several little things he wanted:
He stood like Adam lingering near his garden,
　With useless penitence perplex'd and haunted,
Beseeching she no further would refuse,
When lo! he stumbled o'er a pair of shoes.

A pair of shoes! – what then? not much, if they
　Are such as fit with ladies' feet, but these
(No one can tell how much I grieve to say)
　Were masculine; to see them, and to seize,
Was but a moment's act. – Ah! well-a-day!
　My teeth begin to chatter, my veins freeze –
Alfonso first examined well their fashion,
And then flew out into another passion.

He left the room for his relinquish'd sword,
　And Julia instant to the closet flew.
'Fly, Juan, fly! for heaven's sake – not a word –
　The door is open – you may yet slip through
The passage you so often have explored –
　Here is the garden-key – Fly – fly – Adieu!
Haste – haste! I hear Alfonso's hurrying feet –
Day has not broke – there's no one in the street.'

None can say that this was not good advice,
   The only mischief was, it came too late;
Of all experience 'tis the usual price,
   A sort of income-tax laid on by fate:
Juan had reach'd the room-door in a trice,
   And might have done so by the garden-gate,
But met Alfonso in his dressing-gown,
Who threaten'd death – so Juan knock'd him down.

Dire was the scuffle, and out went the light;
   Antonia cried out 'Rape!' and Julia 'Fire!'
But not a servant stirr'd to aid the fight.
   Alfonso, pommell'd to his heart's desire,
Swore lustily he'd be revenged this night;
   And Juan, too, blasphemed an octave higher;
His blood was up; though young, he was a Tartar,
And not at all disposed to prove a martyr.

Alfonso's sword had dropp'd ere he could draw it,
   And they continued battling hand to hand,
For Juan very luckily ne'er saw it;
   His temper not being under great command,
If at that moment he had chanced to claw it,
   Alfonso's days had not been in the land
Much longer. – Think of husbands', lovers' lives!
And how ye may be doubly widows – wives!

Alfonso grappled to detain the foe,
   And Juan throttled him to get away,
And blood ('twas from the nose) began to flow;
   At last, as they more faintly wrestling lay,
Juan contrived to give an awkward blow,
   And then his only garment quite gave way;
He fled, like Joseph, leaving it; but there,
I doubt, all likeness ends between the pair.

Lights came at length, and men, and maids, who found
   An awkward spectacle their eyes before;
Antonia in hysterics, Julia swoon'd,
   Alfonso leaning, breathless, by the door;

Some half-torn drapery scatter'd on the ground,
  Some blood, and several footsteps, but no more:
Juan the gate gain'd, turn'd the key about,
And liking not the inside, lock'd the out.

Here ends this canto – Need I sing, or say,
  How Juan, naked, favour'd by the night,
Who favours what she should not, found his way,
  And reach'd his home in an unseemly plight?
The pleasant scandal which arose next day,
  The nine days' wonder which was brought to light,
And how Alfonso sued for a divorce,
Were in the English newspapers, of course.

Canto I, cxxviii–clxxxviii

(ii)

No more – no more – Oh! never more, my heart,
  Canst thou be my sole world, my universe!
Once all in all, but now a thing apart,
  Thou canst not be my blessing or my curse:
The illusion's gone for ever, and thou art
  Insensible, I trust, but none the worse,
And in thy stead I've got a deal of judgment,
Though heaven knows how it ever found a lodgment.

My days of love are over; me no more
  The charms of maid, wife, and still less of widow,
Can make the fool of which they made before, –
  In short, I must not lead the life I did do;
The credulous hope of mutual minds is o'er,
  The copious use of claret is forbid too,
So for a good old-gentlemanly vice,
I think I must take up with avarice.

Ambition was my idol, which was broken
  Before the shrines of Sorrow, and of Pleasure;
And the two last have left me many a token
  O'er which reflection may be made at leisure;

Now, like Friar Bacon's brazen head, I've spoken,
  'Time is, Time was, Time's past:' – a chymic treasure
Is glittering youth, which I have spent betimes –
My heart in passion, and my head on rhymes.

What is the end of fame? 'tis but to fill
  A certain portion of uncertain paper:
Some liken it to climbing up a hill,
  Whose summit, like all hills, is lost in vapour;
For this men write, speak, preach, and heroes kill,
  And bards burn what they call their 'midnight taper,'
To have, when the original is dust,
A name, a wretched picture, and worst bust.

What are the hopes of man? Old Egypt's King
  Cheops erected the first pyramid
And largest, thinking it was just the thing
  To keep his memory whole, and mummy hid:
But somebody or other rummaging,
  Burglariously broke his coffin's lid.
Let not a monument give you or me hopes,
Since not a pinch of dust remains of Cheops.

But I, being fond of true philosophy,
  Say very often to myself, 'Alas!
All things that have been born were born to die,
  And flesh (which Death mows down to hay) is grass;
You've pass'd your youth not so unpleasantly.
  And if you had it o'er again – 'twould pass –
So thank your stars that matters are no worse,
And read your Bible, sir, and mind your purse.'

But for the present, gentle reader! and
  Still gentler purchaser! the bard – that's I –
Must, with permission, shake you by the hand,
  And so your humble servant, and good-bye!
We meet again, if we should understand
  Each other; and if not, I shall not try
Your patience further than by this short sample –
'Twere well if others follow'd my example.

'Go, little book, from this my solitude!
　I cast thee on the waters – go thy ways!
And if, as I believe, thy vein be good,
　The world will find thee after many days.'
When Southey's read, and Wordsworth understood,
　I can't help putting in my claim to praise –
The four first rhymes are Southey's, every line:
For God's sake, reader! take them not for mine!

Canto I, ccxv–ccxxii

(iii)

Oh, Wellington! (or 'Villainton') – for Fame
　Sounds the heroic syllables both ways;
France could not even conquer your great name,
　But punn'd it down to this facetious phrase –
(Beating or beaten she will laugh the same,)
　You have obtain'd great pensions and much praise:.
Glory like yours should any dare gainsay,
Humanity would rise, and thunder 'Nay!'

I don't think that you used Kinnaird quite well
　In Marinèt's affair – in fact 'twas shabby,
And like some other things won't do to tell
　Upon your tomb in Westminster's old abbey.
Upon the rest 'tis not worth while to dwell,
　Such tales being for the tea-hours of some tabby;
But though your years as *man* tend fast to *zero*,
In fact your grace is still but a *young hero*.

Though Britain owes (and pays you too) so much,
　Yet Europe doubtless owes you greatly more:
You have repair'd Legitimacy's crutch,
　A prop not quite so certain as before:
The Spanish, and the French, as well as Dutch,
　Have seen, and felt, how strongly you *restore*;
And Waterloo has made the world your debtor
(I wish your bards would sing it rather better).

You are 'the best of cut-throats:' – do not start;
　The phrase is Shakespeare's, and not misapplied: –
War's a brain-spattering, windpipe-slitting art,
　Unless her cause by right be sanctified.
If you have acted *once* a generous part,
　The world, not the world's masters, will decide,
And I shall be delighted to learn who,
Save you and yours, have gain'd by Waterloo?

I am no flatterer – you've supp'd full of flattery:
　They say you like it too – 'tis no great wonder.
He whose whole life has been asssault and battery,
　At last may get a little tired of thunder;
And swallowing eulogy much more than satire, he
　May like being praised for every lucky blunder,
Call'd 'Saviour of the Nations' – not yet saved,
And 'Europe's Liberator' – still enslaved.

I've done. Now go and dine from off the plate
　Presented by the Prince of the Brazils,
And send the sentinel before your gate
　A slice or two from your luxurious meals:
He fought, but has not fed so well of late.
　Some hunger, too, they say the people feels: –
There is no doubt that you deserve your ration,
But pray give back a little to the nation.

I don't mean to reflect – a man so great as
　You, my lord duke! is far above reflection:
The high Roman fashion, too, of Cincinnatus,
　With modern history has but small connexion:
Though as an Irishman you love potatoes,
　You need not take them under your direction;
And half a million for your Sabine farm
Is rather dear! – I'm sure I mean no harm.

Great men have always scorn'd great recompenses:
　Epaminondas saved his Thebes, and died,
Not leaving even his funeral expenses:
　George Washington had thanks, and nought beside,

Except the all-cloudless glory (which few men's is)
  To free his country: Pitt too had his pride,
And as a high-soul'd minister of state is
Renown'd for ruining Great Britain gratis.

Never had mortal man such opportunity,
  Except Napoleon, or abused it more:
You might have freed fallen Europe from the unity
  Of tyrants, and been blest from shore to shore:
And *now* – what *is* your fame? Shall the Muse tune it ye?
  Now – that the rabble's first vain shouts are o'er?
Go! hear it in your famish'd country's cries!
Behold the world! and curse your victories!

Canto IX, i–ix

On This Day I Complete My Thirty-Sixth Year

'Tis time this heart should be unmoved,
  Since others it hath ceased to move:
Yet, though I cannot be beloved,
  Still let me love!

My days are in the yellow leaf;
  The flowers and fruits of love are gone;
The worm, the canker, and the grief
  Are mine alone!

The fire that on my bosom preys
  Is lone as some volcanic isle;
No torch is kindled at its blaze –
  A funeral pile.

The hope, the fear, the jealous care,
  The exalted portion of the pain
And power of love, I cannot share,
  But wear the chain.

But 'tis not *thus* – and 'tis not *here* –
   Such thoughts should shake my soul, nor *now*,
Where glory decks the hero's bier,
      Or binds his brow.

The sword, the banner, and the field,
   Glory and Greece, around me see!
The Spartan, borne upon his shield,
      Was not more free.

Awake! (not Greece – she *is* awake!)
   Awake, my spirit! Think through *whom*
Thy life-blood tracks its parent lake,
      And then strike home!

Tread those reviving passions down,
   Unworthy manhood! – unto thee
Indifferent should the smile or frown
      Of beauty be.

If thou regrett'st thy youth, *why live?*
   The land of honourable death
Is here: – up to the field, and give
      Away thy breath!

Seek out – less often sought than found –
   A soldier's grave, for thee the best;
Then look around, and choose thy ground,
      And take thy rest.

                 MISSOLONGHI, Jan. 22, 1824

PERCY BYSSHE SHELLEY
1792–1822

From *The Daemon of the World*

How wonderful is Death,
   Death and his brother Sleep!
One pale as yonder wan and hornèd moon,
   With lips of lurid blue,
The other growing like the vital morn,
   When throned on ocean's wave
   It breathes over the world:
Yet both so passing strange and wonderful!

Hath then the iron-sceptred Skeleton,
Whose reign is in the tainted sepulchres,
To the hell dogs that couch beneath his throne
Cast that fair prey? Must that divinest form,
Which love and admiration cannot view
Without a beating heart, whose azure veins
Steal like dark streams along a field of snow,
Whose outline is as fair as marble clothed
In light of some sublimest mind, decay?
   Nor putrefaction's breath
Leave aught of this pure spectacle
   But loathsomeness and ruin? –
   Spare aught but a dark theme,
On which the lightest heart might moralize?
Or is it but that downy-wingèd slumbers
Have charmed their nurse coy Silence near her lids
   To watch their own repose?
   Will they, when morning's beam
   Flows through those wells of light,
Seek far from noise and day some western cave,
Where woods and streams with soft and pausing winds
   A lulling murmur weave? –
   Ianthe doth not sleep

The dreamless sleep of death:
Nor in her moonlight chamber silently
Doth Henry hear her regular pulses throb,
    Or mark her delicate cheek
With interchange of hues mock the broad moon,
    Outwatching weary night,
    Without assured reward.
    Her dewy eyes are closed;
On their translucent lids, whose texture fine
Scarce hides the dark blue orbs that burn below
    With unapparent fire,
    The baby Sleep is pillowed:
    Her golden tresses shade
    The bosom's stainless pride,
Twining like tendrils of the parasite
    Around a marble column.

From *The Mask of Anarchy*

WRITTEN ON THE OCCASION OF THE MASSACRE AT MANCHESTER

As I lay asleep in Italy
There came a voice from over the Sea,
And with great power it forth led me
To walk in the visions of Poesy.

I met Murder on the way –
He had a mask like Castlereagh –
Very smooth he looked, yet grim;
Seven blood-hounds followed him:

All were fat; and well they might
Be in admirable plight,
For one by one, and two by two,
He tossed them human hearts to chew
Which from his wide cloak he drew.

Next came Fraud, and he had on,
Like Eldon, an ermined gown;
His big tears, for he wept well,
Turned to mill-stones as they fell.

And the little children who
Round his feet played to and fro,
Thinking every tear a gem,
Had their brains knocked out by them.

Clothed with the Bible, as with light
And the shadows of the night,
Like Sidmouth, next, Hypocrisy
On a crocodile rode by.

And many more Destructions played
In this ghastly masquerade,
All disguised, even to the eyes,
Like Bishops, lawyers, peers, or spies.

Last came Anarchy: he rode
On a white horse, splashed with blood;
He was pale even to the lips,
Like Death in the Apocalypse.

And he wore a kingly crown;
And in his grasp a sceptre shone;
On his brow this mark I saw –
'I am GOD, AND KING, AND LAW!'

With a pace stately and fast,
Over English land he passed,
Trampling to a mire of blood
The adoring multitude.

And a mighty troop around,
With their trampling shook the ground,
Waving each a bloody sword,
For the service of their Lord.

And with glorious triumph, they
Rode through England proud and gay,
Drunk as with intoxication
Of the wine of desolation.

O'er fields and towns, from sea to sea,
Passed the Pageant swift and free,
Tearing up, and trampling down;
Till they came to London town.

And each dweller, panic-stricken,
Felt his heart with terror sicken
Hearing the tempestuous cry
Of the triumph of Anarchy.

For with pomp to meet him came,
Clothed in arms like blood and flame,
The hired murderers, who did sing
'Thou art God and Law, and King.

'We have waited, weak and lone
For thy coming, Mighty One!
Our purses are empty, our swords are cold,
Give us glory, and blood, and gold.'

Lawyers and priests, a motley crowd,
To the earth their pale brows bowed;
Like a bad prayer not over loud,
Whispering – 'Thou art Law and God.' –

Then all cried with one accord,
'Thou art King, and God, and Lord;
Anarchy, to thee we bow,
Be thy name made holy now!'

And Anarchy, the Skeleton,
Bowed and grinned to every one,
As well as if his education
Had cost ten millions to the nation.

For he knew the Palaces
Of our Kings were rightly his;
His the sceptre, crown, and globe,
And the gold-inwoven robe.

So he sent his slaves before
To seize upon the Bank and Tower,
And was proceeding with intent
To meet his pensioned Parliament

When one fled past, a maniac maid,
And her name was Hope, she said:
But she looked more like Despair,
And she cried out in the air:

'My father Time is weak and gray
With waiting for a better day;
See how idiot-like he stands,
Fumbling with his palsied hands!

'He has had child after child,
And the dust of death is piled
Over every one but me –
Misery, oh, Misery!'

Then she lay down in the street,
Right before the horses' feet,
Expecting, with a patient eye,
Murder, Fraud, and Anarchy.

When between her and her foes
A mist, a light, an image rose,
Small at first, and weak and frail
Like the vapour of a vale:

Till as clouds grow on the blast,
Like tower-crowned giants striding fast,
And glare with lightnings as they fly,
And speak in thunder to the sky,

It grew – a Shape arrayed in mail
Brighter than the viper's scale,
And upborne on wings whose grain
Was as the light of sunny rain.

On its helm, seen far away,
A planet, like the Morning's, lay;
And those plumes its light rained through
Like a shower of crimson dew.

With step as soft as wind it passed
O'er the heads of men – so fast,
That they knew the presence there,
And looked, —but all was empty air.

As flowers beneath May's footstep waken,
As stars from Night's loose hair are shaken,
As waves arise when loud winds call,
Thoughts sprung where'er that step did fall.

And the prostrate multitude
Looked—and ankle-deep in blood,
Hope, that maiden most serene,
Was walking with a quiet mien:

And Anarchy, the ghastly birth,
Lay dead earth upon the earth;
The Horse of Death tameless as wind
Fled, and with his hoofs did grind
To dust the murderers thronged behind.

From *Letter to Maria Gisborne*

You are now
In London, that great sea, whose ebb and flow
At once is deaf and loud, and on the shore
Vomits its wrecks, and still howls on for more.

Yet in its depth what treasures! You will see
That which was Godwin, – greater none than he
Though fallen – and fallen on evil times – to stand
Among the spirits of our age and land,
Before the dread tribunal of *to come*
The foremost, – while Rebuke cowers pale and dumb.
You will see Coleridge – he who sits obscure
In the exceeding lustre and the pure
Intense irradiation of a mind,
Which, with its own internal lightning blind,
Flags wearily through darkness and despair –
A cloud-encircled meteor of the air,
A hooded eagle among blinking owls. –
You will see Hunt – one of those happy souls
Which are the salt of the earth, and without whom
This world would smell like what it is – a tomb;
Who is, what others seem; his room no doubt
Is still adorned with many a cast from Shout,
With graceful flowers tastefully placed about;
And coronals of bay from ribbons hung
And brighter wreaths in neat disorder flung;
The gifts of the most learned among some dozens
Of female friends, sisters-in-law, and cousins.
And there is he with his eternal puns,
Which beat the dullest brain for smiles, like duns
Thundering for money at a poet's door;
Alas! it is no use to say, 'I'm poor!'
Or oft in graver mood, when he will look
Things wiser than were ever read in book,
Except in Shakespeare's wisest tenderness. –
You will see Hogg, – and I cannot express
His virtues, – though I know that they are great,
Because he locks, then barricades the gate
Within which they inhabit; – of his wit
And wisdom, you'll cry out when you are bit.
He is a pearl within an oyster shell,
One of the richest of the deep; – and there
Is English Peacock, with his mountain Fair,

Turned into a Flamingo; – that shy bird
That gleams i' the Indian air – have you not heard
When a man marries, dies, or turns Hindoo,
His best friends hear no more of him? – but you
Will see him, and will like him too, I hope,
With the milk-white Snowdonian Antelope
Matched with this cameleopard – his fine wit
Makes such a wound, the knife is lost in it;
A strain too learnèd for a shallow age,
Too wise for selfish bigots; let his page,
Which charms the chosen spirits of the time,
Fold itself up for the serener clime
Of years to come, and find its recompense
In that just expectation. – Wit and sense,
Virtue and human knowledge; all that might
Make this dull world a business of delight,
Are all combined in Horace Smith. – And these,
With some exceptions, which I need not tease
Your patience by descanting on, – are all
You and I know in London.

From *Adonais*

He has outsoared the shadow of our night;
Envy and calumny and hate and pain,
And that unrest which men miscall delight,
Can touch him not and torture not again;
From the contagion of the world's slow stain
He is secure, and now can never mourn
A heart grown cold, a head grown gray in vain;
Nor, when the spirit's self has ceased to burn,
With sparkless ashes load an unlamented urn.

He lives, he wakes – 'tis Death is dead, not he;
Mourn not for Adonais. – Thou young Dawn,
Turn all thy dew to splendour, for from thee
The spirit thou lamentest is not gone:

Ye caverns and ye forests, cease to moan!
Cease, ye faint flowers and fountains, and thou Air,
Which like a mourning veil thy scarf hadst thrown
O'er the abandoned Earth, now leave it bare
Even to the joyous stars which smile on its despair!

He is made one with Nature: there is heard
His voice in all her music, from the moan
Of thunder, to the song of night's sweet bird;
He is a presence to be felt and known
In darkness and in light, from herb and stone,
Spreading itself where'er that Power may move
Which has withdrawn his being to its own;
Which wields the world with never-wearied love,
Sustains it from beneath, and kindles it above.

He is a portion of the loveliness
Which once he made more lovely: he doth bear
His part while the one Spirit's plastic stress
Sweeps through the dull dense world, compelling there,
All new successions to the forms they wear;
Torturing th' unwilling dross that checks its flight
To its own likeness, as each mass may bear;
And bursting in its beauty and its might
From trees and beasts and men into the Heaven's light.

Stanzas xl-xliii

'The cold earth slept below'

The cold earth slept below,
　　Above the cold sky shone;
And all around, with a chilling sound,
　　From caves of ice and fields of snow,
　　The breath of night like death did flow
　　　Beneath the sinking moon.

The wintry hedge was black,
    The green grass was not seen,
The birds did rest on the bare thorn's breast,
    Whose roots, beside the pathway track,
    Had bound their folds o'er many a crack
        Which the frost had made between.

Thine eyes glowed in the glare
    Of the moon's dying light;
As a fen-fire's beam on a sluggish stream
    Gleams dimly, so the moon shone there,
    And it yellowed the strings of thy raven hair,
        That shook in the wind of night.

The moon made thy lips pale, beloved –
    The wind made thy bosom chill –
The night did shed on thy dear head
    Its frozen dew, and thou didst lie
    Where the bitter breath of the naked sky
        Might visit thee at will.

Stanzas Written in Dejection, near Naples

The sun is warm, the sky is clear,
    The waves are dancing fast and bright,
Blue isles and snowy mountains wear
    The purple noon's transparent might,
    The breath of the moist earth is light,
Around its unexpanded buds;
    Like many a voice of one delight,
The winds, the birds, the ocean floods,
The City's voice itself, is soft like Solitude's.

I see the Deep's untrampled floor
    With green and purple seaweeds strown;
I see the waves upon the shore,
    Like light dissolved in star-showers, thrown:

I sit upon the sands alone, –
    The lightning of the noontide ocean
        Is flashing round me, and a tone
    Arises from its measured motion,
How sweet! did any heart now share in my emotion.

Alas! I have nor hope nor health,
    Nor peace within nor calm around,
Nor that content surpassing wealth
    The sage in meditation found,
        And walked with inward glory crowned –
Nor fame, nor power, nor love, nor leisure.
    Others I see whom these surround –
Smiling they live, and call life pleasure; –
To me that cup has been dealt in another measure.

Yet now despair itself is mild,
    Even as the winds and waters are;
I could lie down like a tired child,
    And weep away the life of care
        Which I have borne and yet must bear,
Till death like sleep might steal on me,
    And I might feel in the warm air
My cheek grow cold, and hear the sea
Breathe o'er my dying brain its last monotony.

Some might lament that I were cold,
    As I, when this sweet day is gone,
Which my lost heart, too soon grown old,
    Insults with this untimely moan;
        They might lament – for I am one
Whom men love not, – and yet regret,
    Unlike this day, which when the sun
Shall on its stainless glory set,
Will linger, though enjoyed, like joy in memory yet.

Song to the Men of England

Men of England, wherefore plough
For the lords who lay ye low?
Wherefore weave with toil and care
The rich robes your tyrants wear?

Wherefore feed, and clothe, and save,
From the cradle to the grave,
Those ungrateful drones who would
Drain your sweat – nay, drink your blood?

Wherefore, Bees of England, forge
Many a weapon, chain, and scourge,
That these stingless drones may spoil
The forced produce of your toil?

Have ye leisure, comfort, calm,
Shelter, food, love's gentle balm?
Or what is it ye buy so dear
With your pain and with your fear?

The seed ye sow, another reaps:
The wealth ye find, another keeps;
The robes ye weave, another wears;
The arms ye forge, another bears.

Sow seed, – but let no tyrant reap;
Find wealth, – let no impostor heap;
Weave robes, – let not the idle wear;
Forge arms, – in your defence to bear.

Shrink to your cellars, holes, and cells;
In halls ye deck another dwells.
Why shake the chains ye wrought? Ye see
The steel ye tempered glance on ye.

With plough and spade, and hoe and loom,
Trace your grave, and build your tomb,
And weave your winding-sheet, till fair
England be your sepulchre.

Similes for Two Political Characters

As from an ancestral oak
    Two empty ravens sound their clarion,
Yell by yell, and croak by croak,
When they scent the noonday smoke
        Of fresh human carrion: –

As two gibbering night-birds flit
    From their bowers of deadly yew
Through the night to frighten it,
When the moon is in a fit,
        And the stars are none, or few: –

As a shark and dog-fish wait
    Under an Atlantic isle,
For the negro-ship, whose freight
Is the theme of their debate,
        Wrinkling their red gills the while –

Are ye, two vultures sick for battle,
    Two scorpions under one wet stone,
Two bloodless wolves whose dry throats rattle,
Two crows perched on the murrained cattle,
        Two vipers tangled into one.

Ode to the West Wind

O wild West Wind, thou breath of Autumn's being,
Thou, from whose unseen presence the leaves dead
Are driven, like ghosts from an enchanter fleeing,

Yellow, and black, and pale, and hectic red,
Pestilence-stricken multitudes: O thou,
Who chariotest to their dark wintry bed

The wingèd seeds, where they lie cold and low,
Each like a corpse within its grave, until
Thine azure sister of the Spring shall blow

Her clarion o'er the dreaming earth and fill
(Driving sweet buds like flocks to feed in air)
With living hues and odours plain and hill:

Wild Spirit, which art moving everywhere;
Destroyer and preserver; hear, oh, hear!

Thou on whose stream, mid the steep sky's commotion,
Loose clouds like earth's decaying leaves are shed,
Shook from the tangled boughs of Heaven and Ocean,

Angels of rain and lightning: there are spread
On the blue surface of thine aëry surge,
Like the bright hair uplifted from the head

Of some fierce Maenad, even from the dim verge
Of the horizon to the zenith's height,
The locks of the approaching storm. Thou dirge

Of the dying year, to which this closing night
Will be the dome of a vast sepulchre,
Vaulted with all thy congregated might

Of vapours, from whose solid atmosphere
Black rain, and fire, and hail will burst: oh, hear!

Thou who didst waken from his summer dreams
The blue Mediterranean, where he lay,
Lulled by the coil of his crystàlline streams,

Beside a pumice isle in Baiae's bay,
And saw in sleep old palaces and towers
Quivering within the wave's intenser day,

All overgrown with azure moss and flowers
So sweet, the sense faints picturing them! Thou
For whose path the Atlantic's level powers

Cleave themselves into chasms, while far below
The sea-blooms and the oozy woods which wear
The sapless foliage of the ocean, know

Thy voice, and suddenly grow gray with fear,
And tremble and despoil themselves: oh, hear!

If I were a dead leaf thou mightest bear;
If I were a swift cloud to fly with thee;
A wave to pant beneath thy power, and share

The impulse of thy strength, only less free
Than thou, O uncontrollable! If even
I were as in my boyhood, and could be

The comrade of thy wanderings over Heaven,
As then, when to outstrip thy skiey speed
Scarce seemed a vision; I would ne'er have striven

As thus with thee in prayer in my sore need.
Oh, lift me as a wave, a leaf, a cloud!
I fall upon the thorns of life! I bleed!

A heavy weight of hours has chained and bowed
One too like thee: tameless, and swift, and proud.

Make me thy lyre, even as the forest is:
What if my leaves are falling like its own!
The tumult of thy mighty harmonies

Will take from both a deep, autumnal tone,
Sweet though in sadness. Be thou, Spirit fierce,
My spirit! Be thou me, impetuous one!

Drive my dead thoughts over the universe
Like withered leaves to quicken a new birth!
And, by the incantation of this verse,

Scatter, as from an unextinguished hearth
Ashes and sparks, my words among mankind!
Be through my lips to unawakened earth

The trumpet of a prophecy! O, Wind,
If Winter comes, can Spring be far behind?

The Question

I dreamed that, as I wandered by the way,
　Bare Winter suddenly was changed to Spring,
And gentle odours led my steps astray,
　Mixed with a sound of waters murmuring
Along a shelving bank of turf, which lay
　Under a copse, and hardly dared to fling
Its green arms round the bosom of the stream,
But kissed it and then fled, as thou mightest in dream.

There grew pied wind-flowers and violets,
　Daisies, those pearled Arcturi of the earth,
The constellated flower that never sets;
　Faint oxslips; tender bluebells, at whose birth
The sod scarce heaved; and that tall flower that wets –
　Like a child, half in tenderness and mirth –
Its mother's face with Heaven's collected tears,
When the low wind, its playmate's voice, it hears.

And in the warm hedge grew lush eglantine,
　Green cowbind and the moonlight-coloured may,
And cherry-blossoms and white cups, whose wine
　Was the bright dew, yet drained not by the day;

And wild roses, and ivy serpentine,
　　With its dark buds and leaves, wandering astray;
And flowers azure, black, and streaked with gold,
Fairer than any wakened eyes behold.

And nearer to the river's trembling edge
　　There grew broad flag-flowers, purple pranked with
　　　white,
And starry river buds among the sedge,
　　And floating water-lilies, broad and bright,
Which lit the oak that overhung the hedge
　　With moonlight beams of their own watery light;
And bulrushes, and reeds of such deep green
As soothed the dazzled eye with sober sheen.

Methought that of these visionary flowers
　　I made a nosegay, bound in such a way
That the same hues, which in their natural bowers
　　Were mingled or opposed, the like array
Kept these imprisoned children of the Hours
　　Within my hand, – and then, elate and gay,
I hastened to the spot whence I had come,
That I might there present it! – Oh! to whom?

The Aziola

'Do you not hear the Aziola cry?
　　Methinks she must be nigh,'
　　　Said Mary, as we sate
In dusk, ere stars were lit, or candles brought;
　　　And I, who thought
This Aziola was some tedious woman,
　　Asked, 'Who is Aziola?' How elate
I felt to know that it was nothing human,
　　No mockery of myself to fear or hate:
　　　And Mary saw my soul,
And laughed, and said, 'Disquiet yourself not;
'Tis nothing but a little downy owl.'

Sad Aziola! many an eventide
    Thy music I had heard
By wood and stream, meadow and mountain-side,
    And fields and marshes wide, –
Such as nor voice, nor lute, nor wind, nor bird,
    The soul ever stirred;
Unlike and far sweeter than them all.
Sad Aziola! from that moment I
    Loved thee and thy sad cry.

To Edward Williams

The serpent is shut out from Paradise.
    The wounded deer must seek the herb no more
        In which its heart-cure lies:
    The widowed dove must cease to haunt a bower
Like that from which its mate with feignèd sighs
        Fled in the April hour.
    I too must seldom seek again
Near happy friends a mitigated pain.

Of hatred I am proud, – with scorn content;
    Indifference, that once hurt me, now is grown
        Itself indifferent;
    But, not to speak of love, pity alone
Can break a spirit already more than bent.
        The miserable one
    Turns the mind's poison into food, –
Its medicine is tears, – its evil good.

Therefore, if now I see you seldomer
    Dear friends, dear *friend*! know that I only fly
        Your looks, because they stir
    Griefs that should sleep and hopes that cannot die:
The very comfort that they minister
        I scarce can bear, yet I,
    So deeply is the arrow gone,
Should quickly perish if it were withdrawn.

When I return to my cold home, you ask
    Why I am not as I have ever been.
      You spoil me for the task
    Of acting a forced part in life's dull scene, –
Of wearing on my brow the idle mask
      Of author, great or mean,
    In the world's carnival. I sought
Peace thus, and but in you I found it not.

Full half an hour, to-day, I tried my lot
    With various flowers, and every one still said,
      'She loves me – loves me not.'
    And if this meant a vision long since fled –
If it meant fortune, fame or peace of thought –
      If it meant, – but I dread
    To speak what you may know too well:
Still there was truth in the sad oracle.

The crane o'er seas and forests seeks her home;
    No bird so wild but has its quiet nest,
      When it no more would roam;
    The sleepless billows on the ocean's breast
Break like a bursting heart, and die in foam,
      And thus at length find rest:
    Doubtless there is a place of peace
Where *my* weak heart and all its throbs will cease.

I asked her, yesterday, if she believed
    That I had resolution. One who *had*
      Would ne'er have thus relieved
    His heart with words, – but what his judgement bade
Would do, and leave the scorner unrelieved.
      These verses are too sad
    To send to you, but that I know,
Happy yourself, you feel another's woe.

JOHN CLARE
1793–1864

The Nightingale's Nest

Up this green woodland-ride let's softly rove,
And list the nightingale – she dwells just here.
Hush! let the wood-gate softly clap, for fear
The noise might drive her from her home of love;
For here I've heard her many a merry year –
At morn, at eve, nay, all the livelong day,
As though she lived on song. This very spot,
Just where that old man's beard all wildly trails
Rude arbours o'er the road and stops the way –
And where that child its bluebell flowers hath got,
Laughing and creeping through the mossy rails –
There have I hunted like a very boy,
Creeping on hands and knees through matted thorn
To find her nest and see her feed her young.
And vainly did I many hours employ:
All seemed as hidden as a thought unborn.
And where those crimping fern-leaves ramp among
The hazel's under-boughs, I've nestled down
And watch'd her while she sung; and her renown
Hath made me marvel that so famed a bird
Should have no better dress than russet brown.
Her wings would tremble in her ecstasy,
And feathers stand on end, as 'twere with joy,
And mouth wide open to release her heart
Of its out-sobbing songs. The happiest part
Of summer's fame she shared, for so to me
Did happy fancies shapen her employ;
But if I touched a bush or scarcely stirred,
All in a moment stopt. I watched in vain:
The timid bird had left the hazel bush,
And at a distance hid to sing again.
Lost in a wilderness of listening leaves,

Rich ecstasy would pour its luscious strain,
Till envy spurred the emulating thrush
To start less wild and scarce inferior songs;
For while of half the year care him bereaves,
To damp the ardour of his speckled breast,
The nightingale to summer's life belongs,
And naked trees and winter's nipping wrongs
Are strangers to her music and her rest.
Her joys are evergreen, her world is wide –
Hark! there she is as usual – let's be hush –
For in this blackthorn-clump, if rightly guessed,
Her curious house is hidden. Part aside
These hazel branches in a gentle way
And stoop right cautious 'neath the rustling boughs,
For we will have another search to-day
And hunt this fern-strewn thorn clump round and round;
And where this reeded wood-grass idly bows,
We'll wade right through, it is a likely nook:
In such like spots and often on the ground,
They'll build, where rude boys never think to look.
Ay, as I live! her secret nest is here,
Upon this whitethorn stump! I've searched about
For hours in vain. There! put that bramble by –
Nay, trample on its branches and get near.
How subtle is the bird! she started out,
And raised a plaintive note of danger nigh,
Ere we were past the brambles; and now, near
Her nest, she sudden stops – as choking fear
That might betray her home. So even now
We'll leave it as we found it: safety's guard
Of pathless solitudes shall keep it still.
See there! she's sitting on the old oak bough,
Mute in her fears; our presence doth retard
Her joys, and doubt turns every rapture chill.
Sing on, sweet bird! may no worse hap befall
Thy visions than the fear that now deceives.
We will not plunder music of its dower,
Nor turn this spot of happiness to thrall;

For melody seems hid in every flower
That blossoms near thy home. These harebells all
Seem bowing with the beautiful in song;
And gaping cuckoo, with its spotted leaves,
Seems blushing with the singing it has heard.
How curious is the nest! no other bird
Uses such loose materials, or weaves
Its dwelling in such spots: dead oaken leaves
Are placed without and velvet moss within,
And little scraps of grass, and – scant and spare,
Of what seem scarce materials – down and hair;
For from men's haunts she nothing seems to win.
Yet nature is the builder, and contrives
Homes for her children's comfort even here,
Where solitude's disciples spend their lives
Unseen, save when a wanderer passes near
Who loves such pleasant places. Deep adown
The nest is made, a hermit's mossy cell.
Snug lie her curious eggs in number five,
Of deadened green, or rather olive-brown;
And the old prickly thorn-bush guards them well.
So here we'll leave them, still unknown to wrong,
As the old woodland's legacy of song.

Remembrances

Summer's pleasures they are gone like to visions every one,
And the cloudy days of autumn and of winter cometh on.
I tried to call them back, but unbidden they are gone
Far away from heart and eye and for ever far away.
Dear heart, and can it be that such raptures meet decay?
I thought them all eternal when by Langley Bush I lay,
I thought them joys eternal when I used to shout and play
On its bank at 'clink and bandy', 'chock' and 'taw' and
        'ducking-stone',
Where silence sitteth now on the wild heath as her own
Like a ruin of the past all alone.

When I used to lie and sing by old Eastwell's boiling spring,
When I used to tie the willow boughs together for a swing,
And fish with crooked pins and thread and never catch a
    thing,
With heart just like a feather, now as heavy as a stone;
When beneath old Lea Close Oak I the bottom branches
    broke
To make our harvest cart like so many working folk,
And then to cut a straw at the brook to have a soak.
Oh, I never dreamed of parting or that trouble had a sting,
Or that pleasures like a flock of birds would ever take to
    wing,
Leaving nothing but a little naked spring.

When jumping time away on old Crossberry Way,
And eating haws like sugarplums ere they had lost the may,
And skipping like a leveret before the peep of day
On the roly-poly up and downs of pleasant Swordy Well,
When in Round Oak's narrow lane as the south got black
    again
We sought the hollow ash that was shelter from the rain,
With our pockets full of peas we had stolen from the grain;
How delicious was the dinner-time on such a showery day!
Oh, words are poor receipts for what time hath stole away,
The ancient pulpit trees and the play.

When for school o'er Little Field with its brook and
    wooden brig,
Where I swaggered like a man though I was not half so big,
While I held my little plough though 'twas but a willow
    twig,
And drove my team along made of nothing but a name,
'Gee hep' and 'hoit' and 'woi' – oh, I never call to mind
These pleasant names of places but I leave a sigh behind,
While I see the little mouldiwarps hang sweeing to the
    wind
On the only aged willow that in all the field remains,

mouldiwarps: moles. *sweeing*: swaying.

And nature hides her face while they're sweeing in their
    chains
And in a silent murmuring complains.

Here was commons for their hills, where they seek for
    freedom still,
Though every common's gone and though traps are set to
    kill
The little homeless miners – oh, it turns my bosom chill
When I think of old Sneap Green, Puddock's Nook and
    Hilly Snow,
Where bramble bushes grew and the daisy gemmed in dew
And the hills of silken grass like to cushions to the view,
Where we threw the pismire crumbs when we'd nothing
    else to do,
All levelled like a desert by the never-weary plough,
All vanish'd like the sun where that cloud is passing now
And settled here for ever on its brow.

Oh, I never thought that joys would run away from boys,
Or that boys would change their minds and forsake such
    summer joys;
But alack, I never dreamed that the world had other toys
To petrify first feeling like the fable into stone,
Till I found the pleasure past and a winter come at last,
Then the fields were sudden bare and the sky got overcast,
And boyhood's pleasing haunts, like a blossom in the blast,
Was shrivelled to a withered weed and trampled down and
    done,
Till vanished was the morning spring and set the summer
    sun,
And winter fought her battle strife and won.

By Langley Bush I roam, but the bush hath left its hill,
On Cowper Green I stray, 'tis a desert strange and chill,
And the spreading Lea Close Oak, ere decay had penned its
    will,

pismire: ant.

To the axe of the spoiler and self-interest fell a prey,
And Crossberry Way and old Round Oak's narrow lane
With its hollow trees like pulpits I shall never see again,
Enclosure like a Buonaparte let not a thing remain,
It levelled every bush and tree and levelled every hill
And hung the moles for traitors – though the brook is
    running still
It runs a naked stream, cold and chill.

Oh, had I known as then joy had left the paths of men,
I had watched her night and day, be sure, and never slept
    agen,
And when she turned to go, oh, I'd caught her mantle then,
And wooed her like a lover by my lonely side to stay;
Ay, knelt and worshipped on, as love in beauty's bower,
And clung upon her smiles as a bee upon a flower,
And gave her heart my posies, all cropt in a sunny hour,
As keepsakes and pledges all to never fade away;
But love never heeded to treasure up the may,
So it went the common road to decay.

Love and Solitude

I hate the very noise of troublous man
Who did and does me all the harm he can.
Free from the world I would a prisoner be
And my own shadow all my company;
And lonely see the shooting stars appear,
Worlds rushing into judgment all the year.
Oh, lead me onward to the loneliest shade,
The dearest place that quiet ever made,
Where kingcups grow most beauteous to behold,
And shut up green and open into gold.
Farewell to poesy – and leave the will;
Take all the world away – and leave me still
The mirth and music of a woman's voice,
That bids the heart be happy and rejoice.

From *Child Harold*

(i)

My life hath been one love – no blot it out
My life hath been one chain of contradictions –
Madhouses Prisons wh-re shops – never doubt
But that my life hath had some strong convictions
That such was wrong – religion makes restrictions
I would have followed – but life turned a bubble
& clumb the giant stile of maledictions
They took me from my wife & to save trouble
I wed again & made the error double

Yet abscence claims them both & keeps them too
& locks me in a shop in spite of law
Among a low lived set & dirty crew
Here let the Muse oblivions curtain draw
& let man think – for God hath often saw
Things here too dirty for the light of day
For in a madhouse there exists no law –
Now stagnant grows my too refined clay
I envy birds their wings to flye away

How servile is the task to please alone
Though beauty woo & love inspire the song
Mere painted beauty with her heart of stone
Thinks the world worships while she flaunts along
The flower of sunshine butterflye of song
Give me the truth of heart in womans life
The love to cherish one – & do no wrong
To none – O peace of every care & strife
Is true love in an estimable wife

How beautiful this hill of fern swells on
So beautiful the chappel peeps between
The hornbeams – with its simple bell – Alone
I wander here hid in a palace green

Mary is abscent – but the forest queen
Nature is with me – morning noon & gloaming
I write my poems in these paths unseen
& when among these brakes & beeches roaming
I sigh for truth & home & love & woman

I sigh for one & two – & still I sigh
For many are the whispers I have heard
From beautys lips – loves soul in many an eye
Hath pierced my heart with such intense regard
I looked for joy & pain was the reward
I think of them I love each girl & boy
Babes of two mothers – on this velvet sward
& nature thinks – in her so sweet employ
While dews fall on each blossom weeping joy

Here is the chappel yard enclosed with pales
& oak trees nearly top its little bell
Here is the little bridge with guiding rail
That leads me on to many a pleasant dell
The fern owl chitters like a startled knell
To nature – yet tis sweet at evening still –
A pleasant road curves round the gentle swell
Where nature seems to have her own sweet will
Planting her beech & thorn about the sweet fern hill

I have had many loves – & seek no more
These solitudes my last delights shall be
The leaf hid forest – & the lonely shore
Seem to my mind like beings that are free
Yet would I had some eye to smile on me
Some heart where I could make a happy home in
Sweet Susan that was wont my love to be
& Bessey of the glen – for I've been roaming
With both at morn & noon & dusky gloaming

Cares gather round – I snap their chains in two
& smile in agony & laugh in tears
Like playing with a deadly serpent – who
Stings to the death – there is no room for fears

Where death would bring me happiness – his sheers
Kills cares that hiss to poison many a vein
The thought to be extinct my fate endears
Pale death the grand phisician cures all pain
The dead rest well – who lived for joys in vain

(ii)

The blackbird startles from the homestead hedge
Raindrops & leaves fall yellow as he springs
Such images are natures sweetest pledge
For me there's music in his rustling wings
'Prink prink' he cries & loud the robin sings
The small hawk like a shot drops from the sky
Close to my feet for mice & creeping things
Then swift as thought again he suthers bye
& hides among the clouds from the pursuing eye

The lightnings vivid flashes rend the cloud
That rides like castled crags along the sky
& splinters them to fragments – while aloud
The thunder, heaven's artillery vollies bye
Trees crash earth trembles – beast prepare to flye
Almighty what a crash – yet man is free
& walks unhurt while danger seems so nigh –
Heaven's archway now the rainbow seems to be
That spans the eternal round of earth & sky & sea

A shock a moment in the wrath of God
Is long as hell's eternity to all
His thunderbolts leave life but as the clod
Cold & inanimate – their temples fall
Beneath his frown to ashes – the eternal pall
Of wrath sleeps o'er the ruins where they fell
& nought of memory may their creeds recall
The sin of Sodom was a moments yell
Fire's deathbed theirs their first grave the last hell

suthers: whirs.

The towering willow with its pliant boughs
Sweeps its grey foliage to the autumn wind
The level grounds where oft a group of cows
Huddled together close – or propped behind
An hedge or hovel ruminate & find
The peace – as walks & health & I pursue
For natures every place is still resigned
To happiness – new life's in every view
& here I comfort seek & early joys renew

The lake that held a mirror to the sun
Now curves with wrinkles in the stillest place
The autumn wind sounds hollow as a gun
& water stands in every swampy place
Yet in these fens peace harmony & grace
The attributes of nature are allied
The barge with naked mast in sheltered place
Beside the brig close to the bank is tied
While small waves plashes by its bulky side

Song

The floods come o'er the meadow leas
The dykes & full & brimming
Field furrows reach the horses knees
Where wild ducks oft are swimming
The skyes are black the fields are bare
The trees their coats are loosing
The leaves are dancing in the air
The sun its warmth refusing

Brown are the flags & fading sedge
& tanned the meadow plains
Bright yellow is the osier hedge
Beside the brimming drains
The crows sit on the willow tree
The lake is full below
But still the dullest thing I see
Is self that wanders slow

The dullest scenes are not so dull
As thoughts I cannot tell
The brimming dykes are not so full
As my hearts silent swell
I leave my troubles to the winds
With none to share a part
The only joy my feeling finds
Hides in an aching heart

Abscence in love is worse than any fate
Summer is winter's desert & the spring
Is like a ruined city desolate
Joy dies & hope retires on feeble wing
Nature sinks heedless – birds unheeded sing
'Tis solitude in citys – crowds all move
Like living death—though all to life still cling –
The strangest bitterest thing that life can prove
Is woman's undisguise of hate & love

The Pale Sun

Pale sunbeams gleam
That nurtur a few flowers
Pilewort & daisey & a sprig o' green
On whitethorn bushes
In the leaf strewn hedge

These harbingers
Tell spring is coming fast
& these the schoolboy marks
& wastes an hour from school
Agen the old pasture hedge

Cropping the daisey
& the pilewort flowers
Pleased with the Spring & all he looks upon
He opes his spelling book
& hides her blossoms there

Shadows fall dark
Like black in the pale sun
& lye the bleak day long
Like black stock under hedges
& bare wind rocked trees

'Tis chill but pleasant –
In the hedge bottom lined
With brown seer leaves the last
Year littered there & left
Mopes the hedge sparrow

With trembling wings & cheeps
Its welcome to pale sunbeams
Creeping through – & further on
Made of green moss
The nest & green-blue eggs are seen

All token spring & every day
Green & more green hedges & close
& everywhere appears –
Still tis but March
But still that March is Spring

Love Lies Beyond the Tomb

Love lies beyond
The tomb, the earth, which fades like dew!
I love the fond,
The faithful, and the true.

Love lives in sleep,
The happiness of healthy dreams:
Eve's dews may weep,
But love delightful seems.

'Tis seen in flowers,
And in the even's pearly dew;
On earth's green hours,
And in the heaven's eternal blue.

'Tis heard in spring
When light and sunbeams, warm and kind,
   On angel's wing
Bring love and music to the mind.

   And where is voice,
So young, so beautifully sweet
   As nature's choice,
When spring and lovers meet?

   Love lies beyond
The tomb, the earth, the flowers, and dew.
   I love the fond,
The faithful, young, and true.

Mary

It is the evening hour,
   How silent all doth lie:
The horned moon she shows her face
   In the river with the sky.
Just by the path on which we pass
The flaggy lake lies still as glass.

Spirit of her I love,
   Whispering to me
Stories of sweet visions as I rove,
   Here stop, and crop with me
Sweet flowers that in the still hour grew –
We'll take them home, nor shake off the bright dew.

Mary, or sweet spirit of thee,
   As the bright sun shines to-morrow
Thy dark eyes these flowers shall see,
   Gathered by me in sorrow,
In the still hour when my mind was free
To walk alone – yet wish I walked with thee.

Cowper

Cowper, the poet of the fields
   Who found the muse on common ground –
The homesteads that each cottage shields
   He loved – and made them classic ground.

The lonely house, the rural walk
   He sang so musically true,
E'en now they share the people's talk
   Who love the poet Cowper too.

Who has not read the 'Winter Storm,'
   And does not feel the falling snow
And woodmen keeping noses warm
   With pipes wherever forests grow?

The 'Winter's Walk' and 'Summer's Noon' –
   We meet together by the fire
And think the walks are o'er too soon
   When books are read and we retire.

Who travels o'er those sweet fields now
   And brings not Cowper to his mind?
Birds sing his name in every bough,
   Nature repeats it in the wind.

And every place the poet trod
   And every place the poet sung
Are like the Holy Land of God,
   In every mouth, on every tongue.

Love's Story

I do not love thee
So I'll not deceive thee.
I do love thee,
Yet I'm loth to leave thee.

I do not love thee
Yet joy's very essence
Comes with thy footstep,
Is complete in thy presence.

I do not love thee
Yet when gone, I sigh
And think about thee
Till the stars all die

I do not love thee
Yet thy bright black eyes
Bring to my heart's soul
Heaven and paradise

I do not love thee
Yet thy handsome ways
Bring me in absence
Almost hopeless days

I cannot hate thee
Yet my love seems debtor
To love thee more
So hating, love thee better.

Death

Flowers shall hang upon the palls,
Brighter than patterns upon shawls,
And blossoms shall be in the coffin lids,
Sadder than tears on grief's eyelids,
Garlands shall hide pale corpses' faces
When beauty shall rot in charnel places,
Spring flowers shall come in tears of sorrow
For the maiden goes down to her grave to-morrow.

Last week she went walking and stepping along,
Gay as first flowers of spring or the tune of a song;

Her eye was as bright as the sun in its calm,
Her lips they were rubies, her bosom was warm,
And white as the snowdrop that lies on her breast;
Now death like a dream is her bedfellow guest,
And white as the sheets – ay, and paler than they –
Now her face in its beauty has perished to clay.

Spring flowers they shall hang on her pall,
More bright than the pattern that bloom'd on her shawl,
And blooms shall be strewn where the corpse lies hid,
More sad than the tears upon grief's eyelid;
And ere the return of another sweet May
She'll be rotting to dust in the coffined clay,
And the grave whereon the bright snowdrops grow
Shall be the same soil as the beauty below.

Meet Me in the Green Glen

Love, meet me in the green glen,
  Beside the tall elm-tree,
Where the sweetbrier smells so sweet agen;
  There come with me,
    Meet me in the green glen.

Meet me at the sunset
  Down in the green glen,
Where we've often met
  By hawthorn-tree and foxes' den,
    Meet me in the green glen.

Meet me in the green glen,
  By sweetbrier bushes there;
Meet me by your own sen,
  Where the wild thyme blossoms fair
    Meet me in the green glen.

Meet me by the sweetbrier,
  By the mole-hill swelling there,
When the west glows like a fire
  God's crimson bed is there.
    Meet me in the green glen.

Now is Past

Now is past – the happy now
  When we together roved
Beneath the wildwood's oak-tree bough
  And nature said we loved.
    Winter's blast
The now since then has crept between,
  And left us both apart.
Winters that withered all the green
  Have froze the beating heart.
    Now is past.

Now is past since last we met
  Beneath the hazel bough;
Before the evening sun was set
  Her shadow stretched below.
    Autumn's blast
Has stained and blighted every bough;
  Wild strawberries like her lips
Have left the mosses green below,
  Her bloom's upon the hips.
    Now is past.

Now is past, is changed agen,
  The woods and fields are painted new.
Wild strawberries which both gathered then,
  None know now where they grew.
    The sky's o'ercast,

Wood strawberries faded from wood-sides,
　　Green leaves have all turned yellow;
No Adelaide walks the wood-rides,
　　True love has no bed-fellow.
　　　Now is past.

'I peeled bits of straw'

I peeled bits of straw and I got switches too
From the grey peeling willow as idlers do,
And I switched at the flies as I sat all alone
Till my flesh, blood and marrow was turned to dry bone.
My illness was love, though I knew not the smart,
But the beauty of love was the blood of my heart.
Crowded places, I shunned them as noises too rude
And fled to the silence of sweet solitude,
Where the flower in green darkness buds, blossoms, and
　　fades,
Unseen of all shepherds and flower-loving maids –
The hermit bees find them but once and away;
There I'll bury alive and in silence decay.
I looked on the eyes of fair woman too long,
Till silence and shame stole the use of my tongue:
When I tried to speak to her I'd nothing to say,
So I turned myself round and she wandered away.
When she got too far off, why, I'd something to tell,
So I sent sighs behind her and walked to my cell.
Willow switches I broke and peeled bits of straws,
Ever lonely in crowds, in nature's own laws –
My ball-room the pasture, my music the bees,
My drink was the fountain, my church the tall trees.
Who ever would love or be tied to a wife
When it makes a man mad all the days of his life?

I Hid My Love

I hid my love when young while I
Couldn't bear the buzzing of a fly;
I hid my love to my despite
Till I could not bear to look at light:
I dare not gaze upon her face
But left her memory in each place;
Where'er I saw a wild flower lie
I kissed and bade my love good-bye.

I met her in the greenest dells,
Where dewdrops pearl the wood bluebells;
The lost breeze kissed her bright blue eye,
The bee kissed and went singing by,
A sunbeam found a passage there,
A gold chain round her neck so fair;
As secret as the wild bee's song
She lay there all the summer long.

I hid my love in field and town
Till e'en the breeze would knock me down;
The Bees seemed singing ballads o'er,
The flyes buzz turned a Lion's roar;
And even silence found a tongue,
To haunt me all the summer long;
The riddle nature could not prove
Was nothing else but secret love.

An Invite, to Eternity

Wilt thou go with me, sweet maid,
Say, maiden, wilt thou go with me
Through the valley-depths of shade,
Of night and dark obscurity;

Where the path has lost its way,
Where the sun forgets the day,
Where there's nor life nor light to see,
Sweet maiden, wilt thou go with me?

Where stones will turn to flooding streams,
Where plains will rise like ocean waves,
Where life will fade like visioned dreams
And mountains darken into caves,
Say, maiden, wilt thou go with me
Through this sad non-identity,
Where parents live and are forgot,
And sisters live and know us not?

Say, maiden, wilt thou go with me
In this strange death of life to be,
To live in death and be the same,
Without this life or home or name,
At once to be and not to be –
That was and is not – yet to see
Things pass like shadows, and the sky
Above, below, around us lie?

The land of shadows wilt thou trace,
And look – nor know each other's face;
The present mixed with reason gone,
And past and present all as one?
Say, maiden, can thy life be led
To join the living with the dead?
Then trace thy footsteps on with me;
We're wed to one eternity.

I Am

I am – yet what I am none cares or knows,
    My friends forsake me like a memory lost;
I am the self-consumer of my woes,

They rise and vanish in oblivions host,
Like shadows in love – frenzied stifled throes
And yet I am, and live like vapours tost

Into the nothingness of scorn and noise,
  Into the living sea of waking dreams,
Where there is neither sense of life or joys,
  But the vast shipwreck of my life's esteems;
And e'en the dearest – that I love the best –
Are strange – nay, rather stranger than the rest.

I long for scenes where man has never trod,
  A place where woman never smiled or wept;
There to abide with my Creator, God,
  And sleep as I in childhood sweetly slept;
Untroubling and untroubled where I lie,
The grass below – above the vaulted sky.

A Vision

I lost the love of heaven above,
  I spurned the lust of earth below,
I felt the sweets of fancied love,
  And hell itself my only foe.

I lost earth's joys, but felt the glow
  Of heaven's flame abound in me,
Till loveliness and I did grow
  The bard of immortality.

I loved, but woman fell away;
  I hid me from her faded flame.
I snatched the sun's eternal ray
  And wrote till earth was but a name.

In every language upon earth,
  On every shore, o'er every sea,
I gave my name immortal birth
  And kept my spirit with the free.

JOHN KEATS

1795-1821

Sonnet *Addressed to Haydon*

Great spirits now on earth are sojourning;
   He of the cloud, the cataract, the lake,
   Who on Helvellyn's summit, wide awake,
Catches his freshness from Archangel's wing:
He of the rose, the violet, the spring,
   The social smile, the chain for Freedom's sake:
   And lo! – whose steadfastness would never take
A meaner sound than Raphael's whispering.
And other spirits there are standing apart
   Upon the forehead of the age to come;
These, these will give the world another heart,
And other pulses. Hear ye not the hum
Of mighty workings? –
   Listen awhile ye nations, and be dumb.

Hymn to *Pan*

From *Endymion*

'O thou, whose mighty palace roof doth hang
From jagged trunks, and overshadoweth
Eternal whispers, glooms, the birth, life, death
Of unseen flowers in heavy peacefulness;
Who lov'st to see the hamadryads dress
Their ruffled locks where meeting hazels darken;
And through whole solemn hours dost sit, and hearken
The dreary melody of bedded reeds –
In desolate places, where dank moisture breeds
The pipy hemlock to strange overgrowth;
Bethinking thee, how melancholy loth
Thou wast to lose fair Syrinx – do thou now,

By thy love's milky brow!
By all the trembling mazes that she ran,
Hear us, great Pan!

'O thou, for whose soul-soothing quiet, turtles
Passion their voices cooingly 'mong myrtles,
What time thou wanderest at eventide
Through sunny meadows, that outskirt the side
Of thine enmossed realms; O thou, to whom
Broad leaved fig trees even now foredoom
Their ripen'd fruitage; yellow girted bees
Their golden honeycombs; our village leas
Their fairest blossom'd beans and poppied corn;
The chuckling linnet its five young unborn,
To sing for thee; low creeping strawberries
Their summer coolness; pent up butterflies
Their freckled wings; yea, the fresh budding year
All its completions – be quickly near,
By every wind that nods the mountain pine,
O forester divine!

'Thou, to whom every faun and satyr flies
For willing service; whether to surprise
The squatted hare while in half sleeping fit;
Or upward ragged precipices flit
To save poor lambkins from the eagle's maw;
Or by mysterious enticement draw
Bewildered shepherds to their path again;
Or to tread breathless round the frothy main,
And gather up all fancifullest shells
For thee to tumble into Naiad's cells,
And, being hidden, laugh at their out-peeping;
Or to delight thee with fantastic leaping,
The while they pelt each other on the crown
With silvery oak apples, and fir cones brown –
By all the echoes that about thee ring,
Hear us, O satyr king!

'O Hearkener to the loud clapping shears,
While ever and anon to his shorn peers
A ram goes bleating: Winder of the horn,
When snouted wild-boars routing tender corn
Anger our huntsmen: Breather round our farms,
To keep off mildews, and all weather harms:
Strange ministrant of undescribed sounds,
That comes a swooning over hollow grounds,
And wither drearily on barren moors:
Dread opener of the mysterious doors
Leading to universal knowledge – see,
Great son of Dryope,
The many that are come to pay their vows
With leaves about their brows!

'Be still the unimaginable lodge
For solitary thinkings; such as dodge
Conception to the very bourne of heaven,
Then leave the naked brain: be still the leaven,
That spreading in this dull and clodded earth
Gives it a touch ethereal – a new birth:
Be still a symbol of immensity;
A firmament reflected in a sea;
An element filling the space between,
An unknown – but no more; we humbly screen
With uplift hands our foreheads, lowly bending,
And giving out a shout most heaven rending,
Conjure thee to receive our humble Paean,
Upon thy Mount Lycean!'

Ode to a Nightingale

My heart aches, and a drowsy numbness pains
   My sense, as though of hemlock I had drunk,
Or emptied some dull opiate to the drains
   One minute past, and Lethe-wards had sunk:

'Tis not through envy of thy happy lot,
　But being too happy in thine happiness, –
　　That thou, light-winged Dryad of the trees,
　　　In some melodious plot
　Of beechen green, and shadows numberless,
　　Singest of summer in full-throated ease.

O, for a draught of vintage! that hath been
　Cool'd a long age in the deep-delved earth,
Tasting of Flora and the country green,
　Dance, and Provençal song, and sunburnt mirth!
O for a beaker full of the warm South,
　Full of the true, the blushful Hippocrene,
　　With beaded bubbles winking at the brim,
　　　And purple-stained mouth;
　That I might drink, and leave the world unseen,
　　And with thee fade away into the forest dim:

Fade far away, dissolve, and quite forget
　What thou among the leaves hast never known,
The weariness, the fever, and the fret
　Here, where men sit and hear each other groan;
Where palsy shakes a few, sad, last gray hairs,
　Where youth grows pale, and spectre-thin, and dies;
　　Where but to think is to be full of sorrow
　　　And leaden-eyed despairs,
　Where Beauty cannot keep her lustrous eyes,
　　Or new Love pine at them beyond to-morrow.

Away! away! for I will fly to thee,
　Not charioted by Bacchus and his pards,
But on the viewless wings of Poesy,
　Though the dull brain perplexes and retards:
Already with thee! tender is the night,
　And haply the Queen-Moon is on her throne,
　　Cluster'd around by all her starry Fays;
　　　But here there is no light,
　Save what from heaven is with the breezes blown
　　Through verdurous glooms and winding mossy ways.

I cannot see what flowers are at my feet,
  Nor what soft incense hangs upon the boughs,
But, in embalmed darkness, guess each sweet
  Wherewith the seasonable month endows
The grass, the thicket, and the fruit-tree wild;
  White hawthorn, and the pastoral eglantine;
    Fast fading violets cover'd up in leaves;
      And mid-May's eldest child,
  The coming musk-rose, full of dewy wine,
    The murmurous haunt of flies on summer eves.

Darkling I listen; and, for many a time
  I have been half in love with easeful Death,
Call'd him soft names in many a mused rhyme,
  To take into the air my quiet breath;
Now more than ever seems it rich to die,
  To cease upon the midnight with no pain,
    While thou art pouring forth thy soul abroad
      In such an ecstasy!
  Still wouldst thou sing, and I have ears in vain –
    To thy high requiem become a sod.

Thou wast not born for death, immortal Bird!
  No hungry generations tread thee down;
The voice I hear this passing night was heard
  In ancient days by emperor and clown:
Perhaps the self-same song that found a path
  Through the sad heart of Ruth, when, sick for home,
    She stood in tears amid the alien corn;
      The same that oft-times hath
  Charm'd magic casements, opening on the foam
    Of perilous seas, in faery lands forlorn.

Forlorn! the very word is like a bell
  To toll me back from thee to my sole self!
Adieu! the fancy cannot cheat so well
  As she is fam'd to do, deceiving elf.

Adieu! adieu! thy plaintive anthem fades
  Past the near meadows, over the still stream,
    Up the hill-side; and now 'tis buried deep
      In the next valley-glades:
  Was it a vision, or a waking dream?
  Fled is that music: – Do I wake or sleep?

Ode on a Grecian Urn

Thou still unravish'd bride of quietness,
  Thou foster-child of silence and slow time,
Sylvan historian, who canst thus express
  A flowery tale more sweetly than our rhyme:
What leaf-fring'd legend haunts about thy shape
  Of deities or mortals, or of both,
    In Tempe or the dales of Arcady?
  What men or gods are these? What maidens loth?
What mad pursuit? What struggle to escape?
    What pipes and timbrels? What wild ecstasy?

Heard melodies are sweet, but those unheard
  Are sweeter; therefore, ye soft pipes, play on;
Not to the sensual ear, but, more endear'd,
  Pipe to the spirit ditties of no tone:
Fair youth, beneath the trees, thou canst not leave
  Thy song, nor ever can those trees be bare;
    Bold Lover, never, never canst thou kiss,
Though winning near the goal – yet, do not grieve;
  She cannot fade, though thou hast not thy bliss,
    For ever wilt thou love, and she be fair!

Ah, happy, happy boughs! that cannot shed
  Your leaves, nor ever bid the Spring adieu;
And, happy melodist, unwearied,
  For ever piping songs for ever new;
More happy love! more happy, happy love!
  For ever warm and still to be enjoy'd,

For ever panting, and for ever young;
All breathing human passion far above,
    That leaves a heart high-sorrowful and cloy'd,
        A burning forehead, and a parching tongue.

Who are these coming to the sacrifice?
    To what green altar, O mysterious priest,
Lead'st thou that heifer lowing at the skies,
    And all her silken flanks with garlands drest?
What little town by river or sea shore,
    Or mountain-built with peaceful citadel,
        Is emptied of this folk, this pious morn?
And, little town, thy streets for evermore
    Will silent be; and not a soul to tell
        Why thou art desolate, can e'er return.

O Attic shape! Fair attitude! with brede
    Of marble men and maidens overwrought,
With forest branches and the trodden weed;
    Thou, silent form, dost tease us out of thought
As doth eternity: Cold Pastoral!
    When old age shall this generation waste,
        Thou shalt remain, in midst of other woe
Than ours, a friend to man, to whom thou say'st,
    'Beauty is truth, truth beauty,' – that is all
        Ye know on earth, and all ye need to know.

Ode to Psyche

O Goddess! hear these tuneless numbers, wrung
    By sweet enforcement and remembrance dear,
And pardon that thy secrets should be sung
    Even into thine own soft-conched ear:
Surely I dreamt to-day, or did I see
    The winged Psyche with awaken'd eyes?
I wander'd in a forest thoughtlessly,
    And, on the sudden, fainting with surprise,

Saw two fair creatures, couched side by side
  In deepest grass, beneath the whisp'ring roof
  Of leaves and trembled blossoms, where there ran
    A brooklet, scarce espied:

'Mid hush'd, cool-rooted flowers, fragrant-eyed,
  Blue, silver-white, and budded Tyrian,
They lay calm-breathing on the bedded grass;
  Their arms embraced, and their pinions too;
  Their lips touch'd not, but had not bade adieu,
As if disjoined by soft-handed slumber,
And ready still past kisses to outnumber
  At tender eye-dawn of aurorean love:
    The winged boy I knew;
  But who wast thou, O happy, happy dove?
    His Psyche true!

O latest born and loveliest vision far
  Of all Olympus' faded hierarchy!
Fairer than Phoebe's sapphire-region'd star,
  Or Vesper, amorous glow-worm of the sky;
Fairer than these, though temple thou hast none.
    Nor altar heap'd with flowers;
Nor virgin-choir to make delicious moan
    Upon the midnight hours;
No voice, no lute, no pipe, no incense sweet
  From chain-swung censer teeming;
No shrine, no grove, no oracle, no heat
  Of pale-mouth'd prophet dreaming.

O brightest! though too late for antique vows,
  Too, too late for the fond believing lyre,
When holy were the haunted forest boughs,
  Holy the air, the water, and the fire;
Yet even in these days so far retir'd
  From happy pieties, thy lucent fans,
  Fluttering among the faint Olympians,
I see, and sing, by my own eyes inspir'd.

So let me be thy choir, and make a moan
    Upon the midnight hours;
Thy voice, thy lute, thy pipe, thy incense sweet
  From swinged censer teeming;
Thy shrine, thy grove, thy oracle, thy heat
  Of pale-mouth'd prophet dreaming.

Yes, I will be thy priest, and build a fane
  In some untrodden region of my mind,
Where branched thoughts, new grown with pleasant pain,
  Instead of pines shall murmur in the wind:
Far, far around shall those dark-cluster'd trees
  Fledge the wild-ridged mountains steep by steep;
And there by zephyrs, streams, and birds, and bees,
  The moss-lain Dryads shall be lull'd to sleep;
And in the midst of this wide quietness
A rosy sanctuary will I dress
With the wreath'd trellis of a working brain,
  With buds, and bells, and stars without a name,
With all the gardener Fancy e'er could feign,
  Who breeding flowers, will never breed the same:
And there shall be for thee all soft delight
  That shadowy thought can win,
A bright torch, and a casement ope at night,
  To let the warm Love in!

To Autumn

Season of mists and mellow fruitfulness,
  Close bosom-friend of the maturing sun;
Conspiring with him how to load and bless
  With fruit the vines that round the thatch-eves run;
To bend with apples the moss'd cottage-trees,
  And fill all fruit with ripeness to the core;
    To swell the gourd, and plump the hazel shells

With a sweet kernel; to set budding more,
And still more, later flowers for the bees,
Until they think warm days will never cease,
    For Summer has o'er-brimm'd their clammy cells.

Who hath not seen thee oft amid thy store?
    Sometimes whoever seeks abroad may find
Thee sitting careless on a granary floor,
    Thy hair soft-lifted by the winnowing wind;
Or on a half-reap'd furrow sound asleep,
    Drows'd with the fume of poppies, while thy hook
        Spares the next swath and all its twined flowers:
And sometimes like a gleaner thou dost keep
    Steady thy laden head across a brook;
    Or by a cyder-press, with patient look,
        Thou watchest the last oozings hours by hours.

Where are the songs of Spring? Ay, where are they?
    Think not of them, thou hast thy music too, –
While barred clouds bloom the soft-dying day,
    And touch the stubble-plains with rosy hue;
Then in a wailful choir the small gnats mourn
    Among the river sallows, borne aloft
        Or sinking as the light wind lives or dies;
And full-grown lambs loud bleat from hilly bourn;
    Hedge-crickets sing; and now with treble soft
    The red-breast whistles from a garden-croft;
        And gathering swallows twitter in the skies.

Ode on Melancholy

No, no, go not to Lethe, neither twist
    Wolf's-bane, tight-rooted, for its poisonous wine;
Nor suffer thy pale forehead to be kiss'd
    By nightshade, ruby grape of Proserpine;
Make not your rosary of yew-berries,
    Nor let the beetle, nor the death-moth be

Your mournful Psyche, nor the downy owl
A partner in your sorrow's mysteries;
  For shade to shade will come too drowsily,
    And drown the wakeful anguish of the soul.

But when the melancholy fit shall fall
  Sudden from heaven like a weeping cloud,
That fosters the droop-headed flowers all,
  And hides the green hill in an April shroud;
Then glut thy sorrow on a morning rose,
  Or on the rainbow of the salt sand-wave,
    Or on the wealth of globed peonies;
Or if thy mistress some rich anger shows,
  Emprison her soft hand, and let her rave,
    And feed deep, deep upon her peerless eyes.

She dwells with Beauty – Beauty that must die;
  And Joy, whose hand is ever at his lips
Bidding adieu; and aching Pleasure nigh,
  Turning to Poison while the bee-mouth sips;
Ay, in the very temple of delight
  Veil'd Melancholy has her sovran shrine,
    Though seen of none save him whose strenuous
      tongue
Can burst Joy's grape against his palate fine;
His soul shall taste the sadness of her might,
    And be among her cloudy trophies hung.

Fragment of an Ode to Maia, Written on May Day, 1818

Mother of Hermes! and still youthful Maia!
    May I sing to thee
As thou wast hymned on the shores of Baiae?
    Or may I woo thee
In earlier Sicilian? or thy smiles
Seek as they once were sought, in Grecian isles,

By bards who died content on pleasant sward,
  Leaving great verse unto a little clan?
O, give me their old vigour, and unheard
  Save of the quiet Primrose, and the span
      Of heaven and few ears,
Rounded by thee, my song should die away
      Content as theirs,
Rich in the simple worship of a day.

What the Thrush Said

O thou whose face hath felt the Winter's wind,
  Whose eye has seen the snow-clouds hung in mist,
  And the black elm tops 'mong the freezing stars,
  To thee the spring will be a harvest-time.
O thou, whose only book has been the light
  Of supreme darkness which thou feddest on
  Night after night when Phoebus was away,
  To thee the Spring shall be a triple morn.
O fret not after knowledge – I have none,
  And yet my song comes native with the warmth.
O fret not after knowledge – I have none,
  And yet the Evening listens. He who saddens
At thought of idleness cannot be idle,
And he's awake who thinks himself asleep.

From *Hyperion*

A FRAGMENT

Deep in the shady sadness of a vale
Far sunken from the healthy breath of morn,
Far from the fiery noon, and eve's one star,
Sat gray-hair'd Saturn, quiet as a stone,
Still as the silence round about his lair;
Forest on forest hung about his head
Like cloud on cloud. No stir of air was there,

Not so much life as on a summer's day
Robs not one light seed from the feather'd grass,
But where the dead leaf fell, there did it rest.
A stream went voiceless by, still deadened more
By reason of his fallen divinity
Spreading a shade: the Naiad 'mid her reeds
Press'd her cold finger closer to her lips.

Along the margin-sand large foot-marks went,
No further than to where his feet had stray'd,
And slept there since. Upon the sodden ground
His old right hand lay nerveless, listless, dead,
Unsceptred; and his realmless eyes were closed;
While his bow'd head seem'd list'ning to the Earth,
His ancient mother, for some comfort yet.

It seem'd no force could wake him from his place;
But there came one, who with a kindred hand
Touch'd his wide shoulders, after bending low
With reverence, though to one who knew it not.
She was a Goddess of the infant world;
By her in stature the tall Amazon
Had stood a pigmy's height: she would have ta'en
Achilles by the hair and bent his neck;
Or with a finger stay'd Ixion's wheel.
Her face was large as that of Memphian sphinx,
Pedestal'd haply in a palace court,
When sages look'd to Egypt for their lore.
But oh! how unlike marble was that face:
How beautiful, if sorrow had not made
Sorrow more beautiful than Beauty's self.
There was a listening fear in her regard,
As if calamity had but begun;
As if the vanward clouds of evil days
Had spent their malice, and the sullen rear
Was with its stored thunder labouring up.
One hand she press'd upon that aching spot
Where beats the human heart, as if just there,

Though an immortal, she felt cruel pain:
The other upon Saturn's bended neck
She laid, and to the level of his ear
Leaning with parted lips, some words she spake
In solemn tenour and deep organ tone:
Some mourning words, which in our feeble tongue
Would come in these like accents; O how frail
To that large utterance of the early Gods!
'Saturn, look up! – though wherefore, poor old King?
I have no comfort for thee, no not one:
I cannot say, "O wherefore sleepest thou?"
For heaven is parted from thee, and the earth
Knows thee not, thus afflicted, for a God;
And ocean too, with all its solemn noise,
Has from thy sceptre pass'd; and all the air
Is emptied of thine hoary majesty.
Thy thunder, conscious of the new command,
Rumbles reluctant o'er our fallen house;
And thy sharp lightning in unpractis'd hands
Scorches and burns our once serene domain.
O aching time! O moments big as years!
All as ye pass swell out the monstrous truth,
And press it so upon our weary griefs
That unbelief has not a space to breathe.
Saturn, sleep on: – O thoughtless, why did I
Thus violate thy slumbrous solitude?
Why should I ope thy melancholy eyes?
Saturn, sleep on! while at thy feet I weep.'

Book I, lines 1–71

Sonnet on the Sea

It keeps eternal whisperings around
    Desolate shores, and with its mighty swell
    Gluts twice ten thousand Caverns, till the spell
Of Hecate leaves them their old shadowy sound.

Often 'tis in such gentle temper found,
  That scarcely will the very smallest shell
  Be mov'd for days from where it sometime fell,
When last the winds of Heaven were unbound.
Oh ye! who have your eye-balls vex'd and tir'd,
  Feast them upon the wideness of the Sea;
    Oh ye! whose ears are dinn'd with uproar rude,
Or fed too much with cloying melody –
    Sit ye near some old Cavern's Mouth, and brood
Until ye start, as if the sea-nymphs quir'd!

The Poet

A FRAGMENT

Where's the Poet? show him! show him,
Muses nine! that I may know him!
'Tis the man who with a man
  Is an equal, be he King,
Or poorest of the beggar-clan
  Or any other wondrous thing
A man may be 'twixt ape and Plato;
  'Tis the man who with a bird,
Wren or Eagle, finds his way to
  All its instincts; he hath heard
The Lion's roaring, and can tell
  What his horny throat expresseth,
And to him the Tiger's yell
  Comes articulate and presseth
On his ear like mother-tongue.

Teignmouth

Here all the summer could I stay,
  For there's Bishop's teign
  And King's teign

288

And Coomb at the clear teign head –
 Where close by the stream
 You may have your cream
All spread upon barley bread.

 There's arch Brook
 And there's larch Brook
Both turning many a mill;
 And cooling the drouth
 Of the salmon's mouth
And fattening his silver gill.

 There is Wild wood,
 A Mild hood
To the sheep on the lea o' the down,
 Where the golden furze,
 With its green, thin spurs,
Doth catch at the maiden's gown.

 There is Newton marsh
 With its spear grass harsh –
A pleasant summer level
 Where the maidens sweet
 Of the Market Street,
Do meet in the dusk to revel.

 There's the Barton rich
 With dyke and ditch
And hedge for the thrush to live in
 And the hollow tree
 For the buzzing bee
And bank for the wasp to hive in.

 And O, and O
 The daisies blow
And the primroses are awaken'd,
 And violets white
 Sit in silver plight,
And the green bud's as long as the spike end.

Then who would go
Into dark Soho,
And chatter with dack'd hair'd critics,
When he can stay
For the new-mown hay,
And startle the dappled Prickets?

La Belle Dame Sans Merci

O what can ail thee, knight-at-arms,
Alone and palely loitering?
The sedge is wither'd from the lake,
And no birds sing.

O what can ail thee, knight-at-arms,
So haggard and so woe-begone?
The squirrel's granary is full,
And the harvest's done.

I see a lily on thy brow
With anguish moist and fever dew;
And on thy cheek a fading rose
Fast withereth too.

I met a lady in the meads,
Full beautiful – a faery's child,
Her hair was long, her foot was light,
And her eyes were wild.

I made a garland for her head,
And bracelets too, and fragrant zone;
She look'd at me as she did love,
And made sweet moan.

I set her on my pacing steed,
And nothing else saw all day long,
For sideways would she lean, and sing
A faery's song.

She found me roots of relish sweet,
  And honey wild, and manna dew;
And sure in language strange she said –
  'I love thee true!'

She took me to her elfin grot,
  And there she gazed and sigh'd full sore,
And there I shut her wild wild eyes
  With kisses four.

And there she lulled me asleep,
  And there I dream'd – ah! woe betide!
The latest dream I ever dream'd
  On the cold hill side.

I saw pale kings and princes too,
  Pale warriors, death-pale were they all;
They cried – 'La Belle Dame sans merci
  Thee hath in thrall!'

I saw their starv'd lips in the gloam,
  With horrid warning gaped wide,
And I awoke, and found me here,
  On the cold hill side.

And this is why I sojourn here,
  Alone and palely loitering,
Though the sedge is wither'd from the lake,
  And no birds sing.

Sonnet on the Sonnet

If by dull rhymes our English must be chain'd,
And, like Andromeda, the Sonnet sweet
Fetter'd, in spite of pained loveliness,
Let us find out, if we must be constrain'd,
Sandals more interwoven and complete
To fit the naked foot of Poesy:

Let us inspect the Lyre, and weigh the stress
Of every chord, and see what may be gain'd
By ear industrious, and attention meet;
Misers of sound and syllable, no less
Than Midas of his coinage, let us be
Jealous of dead leaves in the bay wreath crown;
So, if we may not let the Muse be free,
She will be bound with garlands of her own.

Dawlish Fair

Over the hill and over the dale,
And over the bourn to Dawlish –
Where Gingerbread Wives have a scanty sale
And gingerbread nuts are smallish.

Rantipole Betty she ran down a hill
And kicked up her petticoats fairly
Says I I'll be Jack if you will be Gill.
So she sat on the Grass debonnairly.

Here's somebody coming, here's somebody coming!
  Says I 'tis the Wind at a parley
So without any fuss any hawing and humming
  She lay on the grass debonnairly.

Here's somebody here and here's somebody there!
  Says I hold your tongue you young Gipsey.
So she held her tongue and lay plump and fair
  And dead as a venus tipsy.

O who wouldn't hie to Dawlish fair
  O who wouldn't stop in a Meadow
O who would not rumple the daisies there
  And make the wild fern for a bed do.

Hither Hither Love

Hither hither Love
  Tis a shady Mead.
Hither, hither Love
  Let us feed and feed

Hither hither sweet
  Tis a cowslip bed
Hither, hither sweet
  Tis with dew bespread

Hither hither dear
  By the breath of Life
Hither hither dear
  Be the Summer's wife

Though one moment's pleasure
  In one moment flies
Though the passion's treasure
  In one moment dies.

Yet it has not passed
  Think how near, how near
And while it doth last
  Think how dear how dear

Hither hither hither
  Love this boon hath sent
If I die and wither
  I shall die content.

GEORGE DARLEY
1795–1846

Wherefore, Unlaurelled Boy

Wherefore, unlaurelled Boy,
  Whom the contemptuous Muse will not inspire,
With a sad kind of joy
  Still sing'st thou to thy solitary lyre?

The melancholy winds
  Pour through unnumber'd reeds their idle woes,
And every Naiad finds
  A stream to weep her sorrow as it flows.

Her sighs unto the air
  The Wood-maid's native oak doth broadly tell,
And Echo's fond despair
  Intelligible rocks re-syllable.

Wherefore then should not I,
  Albeit no haughty Muse my heart inspire,
Fated of grief to die,
  Impart it to a solitary lyre?

From *Nepenthe*

(i)

O blest unfabled Incense Tree,
That burns in glorious Araby,
With red scent chalicing the air,
Till earth-life grow Elysian there!

Half buried to her flaming breast
In this bright tree, she makes her nest,
Hundred-sunned Phoenix! when she must
Crumble at length to hoary dust!

Her gorgeous death-bed! her rich pyre
Burnt up with aromatic fire!
Her urn, sight high from spoiler men!
Her birthplace when self-born again!

The mountainless green wilds among,
Here ends she her unechoing song!
With amber tears and odorous sighs
Mourned by the desert where she dies!

Laid like the young fawn mossily
In sun-green vales of Araby,
I woke hard by the Phoenix tree
That with shadeless boughs flamed over me;
And upward called by a dumb cry
With moonbroad orbs of wonder, I
Beheld the immortal Bird on high
Glassing the great sun in her eye.
Stedfast she gazed upon his fire,
Still her destroyer and her sire!
As if to his her soul of flame
Had flown already, whence it came;
Like those that sit and glare so still,
Intense with their death struggle, till
We touch, and curdle at their chill! –
But breathing yet while she doth burn,
   The deathless Daughter of the sun!
Slowly to crimson embers turn
   The beauties of the brightsome one.
O'er the broad nest her silver wings
Shook down their wasteful glitterings;
Her brinded neck high-arched in air
Like a small rainbow faded there;
But brighter glowed her plumy crown
Mouldering to golden ashes down;
With fume of sweet woods, to the skies,
Pure as a Saint's adoring sighs,

Warm as a prayer in Paradise,
Her life-breath rose in sacrifice!
The while with shrill triumphant tone
Sounding aloud, aloft, alone,
Ceaseless her joyful death wail she
Sang to departing Araby!

Deep melancholy wonder drew
Tears from my heartspring at that view;
Like cresset shedding its last flare
Upon some wistful mariner,
The Bird, fast blending with the sky,
Turned on me her dead-gazing eye
Once – and as surge to shallow spray
Sank down to vapoury dust away!

O, fast her amber blood doth flow
From the heart-wounded Incense Tree,
Fast as earth's deep-embosomed woe
In silent rivulets to the sea!

Beauty may weep her fair first-born,
Perchance in as resplendent tears,
Such golden dewdrops bow the corn
When the stern sickleman appears.

But oh! such perfume to a bower
Never allured sweet-seeking bee,
As to sip fast that nectarous shower
A thirstier minstrel drew in me!

(ii)

All hail, green-mantled Ida!
Floodgate of heaven-fall'n streams!
Replenisher of wasteful ocean's store!

Sweetener of his salt effluence! Ever-pure!
Battener of meagre Earth! Bestower
Of their moist breath to vegetable things
That suck their life from thee! –
All hail! –
All hail, green Ida! –
Woody-belted Ida! –
Nurse of the bounding lion! his green lair,
Whence he doth shake afar
The shepherdry with his roar! All hail,
Peaks where the wild ass flings
His Pegasean heels against mankind,
And the more riotous mares
Pawing at heaven, snuff the womb-swelling wind!
Ida, all hail! all hail!
Nature's green, ever-during pyramid
Heaped o'er the behemoth brute-royal bones
Of monstrous Anakim!
All hail, great Ida! throne
Of that old Jove the olden poet sung
Where, from the Gods alone,
He listened to the moan
Of his divine Sarpedon, thousand moans among! –
Ida, all hail! all hail!
Thus on thy pinnacle,
With springy foot like the wild swan that soars
Off to invisible shores,
I stand! with blind Ambition's waxen wings
High o'er my head
Outspread
Plucking me off the Earth to wheel aërial rings!
Lo! as my vision glides
Adown these perilous flowery sides,
Green hanging-gardens only trod
By Nymph or Sylvan god,
And sees o'er what a gulf their eminent glory swells,
I tremble with delight,
Proud of my terrible plight,

And turn me to the hollow caves
Where the hoarse spirit of the Euxine raves,
The melancholy tale of that drown'd Youth he tells
To the fast fleeting waves,
For ever in vast murmurs, as he laves
With foam his sedgy locks loose-floating down the
    Dardanelles!

    Down the Dardanelles!
    What Echo in musical sound repels
    My words, like thunder rolled
    From the high-toppling rocks
    In loud redoublous shocks
    Behold, great Sun, behold!

    Down the Dardanelles!
    Behold the Thunderer where she rides!
    Behold her how she swells
    Like floating clouds her canvas sides!
    Raising with ponderous breast the tides
    On both the shores, as down she strides,
    Down the Dardanelles!

    Down the Dardanelles!
    Each Continent like a caitiff stands,
    As every broadside knells!
    While with a voice that shakes the strands
    She spreads her hundred-mouth'd commands,
    Albion's loud law to both the lands,
    Down the Dardanelles!

    Down the Dardanelles!
    Ye billowy hills before her bowne!
    Wind Caverns! your deep shells
    Ring Ocean and Earth her old Renown,
    Long as that sun from Ida's crown
    Smoothes her broad road with splendour down,
    Down the Dardanelles!

Anthea, ever dear!
I feel, I feel the sharp satyric ear
Thy draught Circean gave me, echoing clear
With that far chime!
Capacious grown enough to hear
The music of the lower sphere,
Tho' fainter than the passing tread of stealthy-
 footed Time.

Be mute, ye summer airs around!
Let not a sigh disturb the sound
That like a shadow climbs the steepy ground
Up from blue Helle's dim profound!
Listen! the roar
Creeps on the ear as on a little shore,
And by degrees
Swells like the rushing sound of many seas,
And now as loud upon the brain doth beat
As Helle's tide in thunderbursts broke foaming at my
 feet.
Hist! ho! – the Spirit sings
While in the cradle of the surge he swings,
Or falling down its sheeted laps,
Speaks to it in thunder-claps
Terrifical, half-suffocated things!
For ever with his furious breath
Keeping a watery storm beneath
Where'er he sinks, that o'er him seethe
The frothy salt-sea surfaces
Dissolving with an icy hiss,
As if the marvellous flood did flow
Over a quenchless fire below!
Hist! ho! the Spirit sings!

In the caves of the deep – lost Youth! lost Youth! –
O'er and o'er, fleeting billows! fleeting billows! –
Rung to his restless everlasting sleep
By the heavy death-bells of the deep,

Under the slimy-dropping sea-green willows,
    Poor Youth! lost Youth!
  Laying his dolorous head, forsooth,
  On Carian reefs uncouth –
    Poor Youth!
On the wild sand's ever-shifting pillows!

In the foam's cold shroud – lost Youth! lost Youth! –
And the lithe waterweed swathing round him! –
Mocked by the surges roaring o'er him loud,
'Will the sun-seeker freeze in his shroud,
Aye, where the deep-wheeling eddy has wound him?'
    Lost Youth! poor Youth!
  Vail him his Dædalian wings, in truth?
  Stretched there without all ruth –
    Poor Youth! –
Weeping fresh torrents into those that drowned him!

(iii)

As from the moist and gelid sleep
Of Death we rise on shuddering bones,
The waste of that long night to weep,
We pined us down to skeletons;
So shuddering, weeping, weltering, worn,
Gleaming with spectral eyes forlorn,
Upon my bleak estate and bare
Greyly I rose; like wan Despair
Slow roused from Dissolution's lair.
But in what dread dominion? Air
Hung like a hell-blue vapour there,
Steaming from some thick ooze, that cold
Over my foot like reptiles rolled
Sluggish, with many a slimy fold;
Lethe's foul self, perchance, or flood
Made slab with gouts of gall and blood
Wept by the woe that wades the mud,
Cocytus, bubbling with drowned sighs,

But lo! what shadowy forms arise,
Far off, to these ferruginous skies?
Mountains, as sharp as squally clouds
When fell winds whistle in the shrouds,
Upcall to Fury, above, before,
My vision by this ominous shore,
Where each a burning pyramid seems,
O'erflown with liquorous fire, that teems
Down the slope edges in four streams.
Most sure the abysmal fen I tread
Shelves to the River of the Dead
That bears unto the eternal sea
Millions of ghastly things like me.
Hark! from slow-floating bier and bier
Murmurs and rueful sobs I hear,
The while from these sepulchring hills
A yewtree wind the valley fills
That whispers with fast-fleeting breath,
'This is the dolorous Valley of Death!
Valley of Dolour – and of Death!'

(iv)

Lo! in the mute mid wilderness,
What wondrous Creature, of no kind,
His burning lair doth largely press,
Gaze fixt, and feeding on the wind?
His fell is of the desert dye,
And tissue adjust, dun-yellow and dry,
Compact of living sands; his eye
Black luminary, soft and mild,
With its dark lustre cools the wild.
From his stately forehead springs,
Piercing to heaven, a radiant horn!
Lo, the compeer of lion-kings,
The steed self-armed, the Unicorn!
Ever heard of, never seen,
With a main of sands between

Him and approach; his lonely pride
To course his arid arena wide,
Free as the hurricane, or lie here,
Lord of his couch as his career!
Wherefore should this foot profane
His sanctuary, still domain?
Let me turn, ere eye so bland
Perchance be fire-shot, like heaven's brand,
To wither my boldness! Northward now,
Behind the white star on his brow
Glittering straight against the Sun,
Far athwart his lair I run.

Queen Eleanor and her Dwarf

From *Thomas à Becket*

Dwerga:

What, am I not thy grandchild? thou that bought'st me
Of my Norse dam, when scarce the size of a crab,
And fed'st me to my present stature with
Dainties of all kinds – cock's eggs, and young frogs
So freshly caught they whistled as they singed,
Like moist wood, on the spit, still bubbling out
Dew from their liquid ribs, to baste themselves,
As they turn'd slowly – then rich snails that slip
My throttle down ere I well savour them;
Most luscious mummy; bat's milk cheese; at times
The sweetbreads of fall'n mooncalves, or the jellies
Scumm'd after shipwreck floating to the shore:
Have I not eat live mandrakes, screaming torn
From their warm churchyard-bed, out of thy hand?
With other roots and fruits cull'd ere their season,–

The yew's green berries, nightshade's livid bugles,
That poison human chits but nourish me, –
False mushrooms, toadstools, oakwarts, hemlock chopt?

Eleanor:

Ay, thou'rt an epicure in such luxuries.

Dwerga:

My fangs still water! – Grandam, thou art good!
Dost thou not give me daily for my draught
Pure sloe-juice, bitter-sweet! or wormwood wine,
Syrup of galls, old coffin-snags boil'd down
Thrice in fat charnel-juice, so strong and hilarious,
I dance to a tub's sound like the charmer's snake,
We at Aleppo saw? What made me, pray you,
All that I am, but this fine food? Thou art,
Then, my creatress; and I am thy creature.

The *Mermaidens' Vesper-Hymn*

Troop home to silent grots and caves!
　Troop home! and mimic as you go
The mournful winding of the waves
　Which to their dark abysses flow.

At this sweet hour, all things beside
　In amorous pairs to covert creep;
The swans that brush the evening tide
　Homeward in snowy couples keep.

In his green den the murmuring seal
　Close by his sleek companion lies;
While singly we to bedward steal,
　And close in fruitless sleep our eyes.

In bowers of love men take their rest,
  In loveless bowers we sigh alone,
With bosom-friends are others blest, –
  But we have none! but we have none!

HARTLEY COLERIDGE
1796–1849

November

The mellow year is hasting to its close;
The little birds have almost sung their last,
Their small notes twitter in the dreary blast –
That shrill-piped harbinger of early snows;
The patient beauty of the scentless rose,
Oft with the Morn's hoar crystal quaintly glass'd,
Hangs, a pale mourner for the summer past,
And makes a little summer where it grows:
In the chill sunbeam of the faint brief day
The dusky waters shudder as they shine,
The russet leaves obstruct the struggling way
Of oozy brooks, which no deep banks define,
And the gaunt woods, in ragged, scant array,
Wrap their old limbs with sombre ivy twine.

From Country to Town

(i)

I left the land where men with Nature dwelling,
Know not how much they love her lovely forms –
Nor heed the history of forgotten storms,
On the blank folds inscribed of drear Helvellyn;
I sought the town, where toiling, buying, selling –
Getting and spending, poising hope and fear,
Make but one season of the live-long year.
Now for the brook from moss-girt fountain welling,
I see the foul stream hot with sleepless trade;
For the slow creeping vapours of the morn,
Black hurrying smoke, in opaque mass up-borne,
O'er dining engines hangs, a stifling shade –
Yet Nature lives e'en here, and will not part
From her best home, the lowly-loving heart.

305

(ii)

'Tis strange to me, who long have seen no face,
That was not like a book, whose every page
I knew by heart, a kindly common-place,
And faithful record of progressive age –
To wander forth, and view an unknown race;
Of all that I have been, to find no trace,
No footstep of my by-gone pilgrimage.
Thousands I pass, and no one stays his pace
To tell me that the day is fair, or rainy;
Each one his object seeks with anxious chase,
And I have not a common hope with any:
Thus like one drop of oil upon a flood,
In uncommunicating solitude,
Single am I amid the countless many.

'Hast thou not seen an aged rifted tower'

Hast thou not seen an aged rifted tower,
Meet habitation for the Ghost of Time,
Where fearful ravage makes decay sublime,
And destitution wears the face of power?
Yet is the fabric deck'd with many a flower
Of fragrance wild, and many-dappled hue,
Gold streak'd with iron-brown and nodding blue,
Making each ruinous chink a fairy bower.
E'en such a thing methinks I fain would be,
Should Heaven appoint me to a lengthen'd age;
So old in look, that Young and Old may see
The record of my closing pilgrimage:
Yet, to the last, a rugged wrinkled thing
To which young sweetness may delight to cling!

THOMAS HOOD
1799–1845

Autumn

I saw old Autumn in the misty morn
Stand shadowless like Silence, listening
To silence, for no lonely bird would sing
Into his hollow ear from woods forlorn,
Nor lowly hedge nor solitary thorn;
Shaking his languid locks all dewy bright
With tangled gossamer that fell by night,
    Pearling his coronet of golden corn.

Where are the songs of Summer? – With the sun,
Oping the dusky eyelids of the south,
Till shade and silence waken up as one,
And Morning sings with a warm odorous mouth.
Where are the merry birds? – Away, away,
On panting wings through the inclement skies,
    Lest owls should prey
    Undazzled at noonday,
And tear with horny beak their lustrous eyes.

Where are the blooms of Summer? – In the west,
Blushing their last to the last sunny hours,
When the mild Eve by sudden Night is prest
Like tearful Proserpine, snatch'd from her flow'rs
    To a most gloomy breast.
Where is the pride of Summer, – the green prime, –
The many, many leaves all twinkling? – Three
    On the mossed elm; three on the naked lime
Trembling, – and one upon the old oak tree!
    Where is the Dryads' immortality?
Gone into mournful cypress and dark yew,
Or wearing the long gloomy Winter through
    In the smooth holly's green eternity.

The squirrel gloats on his accomplished hoard,
The ants have brimmed their garners with ripe grain,
  And honey bees have stored
The sweets of Summer in their luscious cells;
The swallows all have wing'd across the main;
But here the Autumn melancholy dwells,
  And sighs her tearful spells,
Amongst the sunless shadows of the plain.
    Alone, alone,
    Upon a mossy stone,
She sits and reckons up the dead and gone
With the last leaves for a love-rosary,
Whilst all the wither'd world looks drearily,
Like a dim picture of the drowned past
In the hush'd mind's mysterious far away
Doubtful what ghostly thing will steal the last
Into that distance, grey upon the grey.

O go and sit with her, and be o'ershaded
Under the languid downfall of her hair:
She wears a coronal of flowers faded
Upon her forehead, and a face of care;
There is enough of wither'd everywhere
To make her bower, – and enough of gloom;
There is enough of sadness to invite,
If only for the rose that died, – whose doom
Is Beauty's, – she that with the living bloom
Of conscious cheeks most beautifies the light:
There is enough of sorrowing, and quite
Enough of bitter fruits the earth doth bear, –
Enough of chilly droppings for her bowl;
Enough of fear and shadowy despair,
To frame her cloudy prison for the soul!

Silence

There is a silence where hath been no sound,
There is a silence where no sound may be,
In the cold grave – under the deep, deep sea,
Or in wide desert where no life is found,
Which hath been mute, and still must sleep profound;
No voice is hush'd – no life treads silently,
But clouds and cloudy shadows wander free,
That never spoke, over the idle ground:
But in green ruins, in the desolate walls
Of antique palaces, where Man hath been,
Though the dun fox, or wild hyena, calls,
And owls, that flit continually between,
Shriek to the echo, and the low winds moan,
There the true Silence, is self-conscious and alone.

The Sea of Death

A FRAGMENT

Methought I saw
Life swiftly treading over endless space:
And, at her footprint, but a bygone pace,
The ocean-past, which, with increasing wave,
Swallowed her steps like a pursuing grave.

Sad were my thoughts that anchored silently
On the dead waters of that passionless sea,
Unstirred by any touch of living breath:
Silence hung over it, and drowsy death,
Like a gorged sea-bird, slept with folded wings
On crowded carcases – sad passive things
That wore the thin grey surface, like a veil
Over the calmness of their features pale.

And there were spring-faced cherubs that did sleep
Like water-lilies on that motionless deep,
How beautiful! with bright unruffled hair
On sleek unfretted brows, and eyes that were
Buried in marble tombs, a pale eclipse!
And smile-bedimpled cheeks, and pleasant lips,
Meekly apart, as if the soul intense
Spake out in dreams of its own innocence:
And so they lay in loveliness, and kept
The birth-night of their peace, that Life e'en wept
With very envy of their happy fronts;
For there were neighbour brows scarred by the brunts
Of strife and sorrowing – where Care had set
His crooked autograph, and marred the jet
Of glossy locks, with hollow eyes forlorn,
And lips that curled in bitterness and scorn –
Wretched, – as they had breathed of this world's pain,
And so bequeathed it to the world again
Through the beholder's heart in heavy sighs.

So lay they garmented in torpid light,
Under the pall of a transparent night,
Like solemn apparitions lulled sublime
To everlasting rest, – and with them Time
Slept, as he sleeps upon the silent face
Of a dark dial in a sunless place.

JAMES CLARENCE MANGAN
1803-1849

Twenty Golden Years Ago

O the rain, the weary, dreary rain,
How it plashes on the window-sill!
Night, I guess too, must be on the wane,
Strass and Gass around are grown so still.
Here I sit, with coffee in my cup:
Ah! 'twas rarely I beheld it flow
In the tavern where I loved to sup
Twenty golden years ago!

Twenty years ago, alas! – But stay:
On my life, 'tis half-past twelve o'clock!
After all, the hours do slip away.
Come, here goes to burn another block.
For the night, or morn, is wet and cold,
And my fire is dwindling rather low:

Dear! I don't feel well at all, somehow:
Few in Weimar dream how bad I am.
Floods of tears grow common with me now,
High Dutch floods, that reason cannot dam.
Doctors think I'll neither live nor thrive
If I mope at home so; I don't know!
Am I living now? I was alive
Twenty golden years ago.

Wifeless, friendless, flagonless, alone,
Not quite bookless, tho', unless I choose;
Left with naught to do, except to groan,
Not a soul to woo, except the muse;
O but this is hard for me to bear,
Me, who whilom lived so much *en haut*,
Me, who broke all hearts like chinaware,
Twenty golden years ago!

Perhaps 'tis better time's defacing waves
Long have quenched the radiance of my brow;
They who curse me nightly from their graves,
Scarce could love me were they living now.
But my loneliness hath darker ills:
Such dun duns as Conscience, Thought, and Co.,
Awful Gorgons! worse than tailor's bills
Twenty golden years ago!

Did I paint a fifth of what I feel,
O how plaintive you would ween I was!
But I won't, albeit I have a deal
More to wail about than Kerner has!
Kerner's tears are wept for withered flowers,
Mine for withered hopes; my scroll of woe
Dates, alas, from youth's deserted bowers,
Twenty golden years ago!

Yet, may Deutschland bardlings flourish long!
Me, I tweak no beak among them; hawks
Must not pounce on hawks: besides, in song
I could not once beat all of them by chalks.
Though you find me, as I near my goal,
Sentimentalizing like Rousseau,
Ah, I had a grand Byronian soul
Twenty golden years ago!

Tick-tick! tick-tick! – Not a sound save time's,
And the wind-gust as it drives the rain.
Tortured torturer of reluctant rhymes,
Go to bed, and rest thine aching brain!
Sleep! no more the dupe of hopes or schemes.
Soon thou sleepest where the thistles blow:
Curious anticlimax to thy dreams
Twenty golden years ago!

The Saw-Mill

My path lay towards the Mourne again;
But I stopped to rest by the hillside
That glanced adown o'er the sunken glen,
Which the saw- and water-mills hide,
Which now, as then,
The saw- and water-mills hide.

And there, as I lay reclined on the hill,
Like a man made by sudden qualm ill,
I heard the water in the water-mill,
And I saw the saw in the saw-mill,
As I thus lay still,
I saw the saw in the saw-mill.

The saw, the breeze, and the humming bees
Lulled me into a dreamy reverie,
Till the objects round me, hills, mills, trees,
Seemed grown alive all and every;
By slow degrees
Took life, as it were, all and every!

Anon the sound of the waters grew
To a mournful ditty,
And the song of the tree that the saw sawed through
Disturbed my spirit with pity,
Began to subdue
My spirit with tenderest pity!

'O Wanderer! the hour that brings thee back
Is of all meet hours the meetest.
Thou now, in sooth, art on the track,
Art nigher to home than thou weetest;
Thou hast thought time slack,
But his flight has been of the fleetest!

'For thee it is that I dree such pain
As, when wounded, even a plank will;
My bosom is pierced, is rent in twain,
That thine may ever bide tranquil,
May ever remain
Henceforward, untroubled and tranquil.

'In a few days more, most lonely one!
Shall I, as a narrow ark, veil
Thine eyes from the glare of the world and the sun,
'Mong the urns in yonder dark vale,
In the cold and the dun
Recesses of yonder dark vale!

'For this grieve not! Thou knowest what thanks
The weary-souled and the meek owe
To Death!' ... I awoke, and heard four planks
Fall down with a saddening echo.
I heard four planks
Fall down with a hollow echo.

Siberia

In Siberia's wastes
The ice-wind's breath
Woundeth like toothèd steel:
Lost Siberia doth reveal
Only blight and death.

Blight and death alone.
No summer shines;
Night is interblent with day;
In Siberia's wastes, alway
The blood blackens, the heart pines.

In Siberia's wastes
No tears are shed,
For they freeze within the brain,
Naught is felt but dullest pain,
Pain acute, yet dead;

Pain as in a dream,
When years go by
Funeral-paced, yet fugitive;
When man lives and doth not live,
Doth not live, nor die.

In Siberia's wastes
Are sands and rocks.
Nothing blooms of green or soft,
But the snow-peaks rise aloft,
And the gaunt ice-blocks.

And the exile there
Is one with those;
They are part, and he is part!
For the sands are in his heart,
And the killing snows.

Therefore, in those wastes
None curse the Czar.
Each man's tongue is cloven by
The north blast, that heweth nigh
With sharp scimitar.

And such doom each drees,
Till, hunger-gnawn,
Cold-slain, he at length sinks there;
Yet scarce more a corpse than ere
His last breath was drawn.

THOMAS LOVELL BEDDOES
1803-1849

Song by Two Voices

FIRST VOICE

Who is the baby, that doth lie
Beneath the silken canopy
Of thy blue eye?

SECOND

It is young Sorrow, laid asleep
In the crystal deep.

BOTH

Let us sing his lullaby,
Heigho! a sob and a sigh.

FIRST VOICE

What sound is that, so soft, so clear,
Harmonious as a bubbled tear
Bursting, we hear?

SECOND

It is young Sorrow, slumber breaking,
Suddenly awaking.

BOTH

Let us sing his lullaby,
Heigho! a sob and a sigh.

Song by the Deaths

*The Deaths and the figures paired with them come out of the walls: some
seat themselves at the table, and appear to feast, with mocking
gestures others dance fantastically to a rattling music, singing.*

Mummies and skeletons, out of your stones;
  Every age, every fashion, and figure of Death:
The death of the giant with petrified bones:
  The death of the infant who never drew breath.
Little and gristly or bony and big,
  White and clattering, grassy and yellow;
The partners are waiting, so strike up a jig,
  Dance and be merry, for Death's a droll fellow.
The emperor and empress, the king and the queen,
  The knight and the abbot, friar fat, friar thin,
The gipsy and beggar, are met on the green;
  Where's Death and his sweetheart? We want to begin.
In circles and mazes and many a figure,
  Through clouds, over chimneys and corn-fields yellow,
We'll dance and laugh at the red-nosèd grave-digger,
  Who dreams not that Death is so merry a fellow.

The Song that Wolfram Heard in Hell

Old Adam, the carrion crow,
  The old crow of Cairo;
He sat in the shower, and let it flow
Under his tail and over his crest;
    And through every feather
    Leaked the wet weather;
And the bough swung under his nest;
For his beak it was heavy with marrow.
  Is that the wind dying? O no;
  It's only two devils, that blow
Through a murderer's bones, to and fro,
    In the ghosts' moonshine.

Ho! Eve, my grey carrion wife,
   When we have supped on king's marrow,
Where shall we drink and make merry our life?
Our nest it is queen Cleopatra's skull,
     'Tis cloven and cracked,
     And battered and hacked,
But with tears of blue eyes it is full:
Let us drink then, my raven of Cairo.
    Is that the wind dying? O no;
    It's only two devils, that blow
    Through a murderer's bones, to and fro,
     In the ghosts' moonshine.

Mandrake's Song

Folly hath now turned out of door
Mankind and Fate, who were before
   Jove's Harlequin and Clown;
The World's no stage, no tavern more –
   Its sign the Fool's ta'en down.
    With poppy rain and cypress dew
    Weep all, for all, who laughed for you,
For goose grass is no medicine more,
    But the owl's brown eye's the sky's new blue.
     Heigho! Foolscap!

The New Cecilia

Whoever has heard of St Gingo
   Must know that the gipsy
   He married was tipsy
Every day of her life with old Stingo.

And after the death of St Gingo
   The wonders he did do
   Th' incredulous widow
Denied with unladylike lingo:

318

'For St Gingo a fig and a feather-end!
  He no more can work wonder
  Than a clyster-pipe thunder
Or I sing a psalm with my nether-end.'

As she said it, her breakfast beginning on
  A tankard of home-brewed inviting ale,
Lo! the part she was sitting and sinning on
  Struck the old hundredth up like a nightingale.

Loud as psophia in an American forest or
  The mystic Memnonian marble in
A desart at daybreak, that chorister
  Breathed forth his Æolian warbling.

That creature seraphic and spherical,
Her firmament, kept up its clerical
  Thanksgivings, until she did aged die
Cooing and praising and chirping alert in
Her petticoat, swung like a curtain
  Let down o'er the tail of a Tragedy.

Therefore, Ladies, repent and be sedulous
  In praising your lords, lest, ah! well a day!
Such judgement befall the incredulous
  And your latter ends melt into melody.

Song from the Ship

  To sea! To sea! the calm is o'er;
    The wanton water leaps in sport,
  And rattles down the pebbly shore;
    The dolphin wheels, the sea-cows snort,
  And unseen Mermaids' pearly song
  Comes bubbling up the weeds among.
    Fling broad the sail, dip deep the oar:
    To sea! To sea! the calm is o'er.

To sea! To sea! our wide-winged bark
  Shall billowy cleave its sunny way,
And with its shadow fleet and dark
  Break the caved Tritons' azure ray,
Like mighty eagle soaring light
O'er antelopes on Alpine height
  The anchor heaves, the ship swings free,
  The sails swell full. To sea, to sea!

Love-in-Idleness

He: 'Shall I be your first love, lady, shall I be your first?
  Oh! then I'll fall before you down on my velvet knee
  And deeply bend my rosy head and press it upon thee,
And swear that there is nothing more for which my heart
    doth thirst,
    But a downy kiss and pink
    Between your lips' soft chink.'

She: 'Yes, you shall be my first love, boy, and you shall be
    my first,
  And I will raise you up again unto my bosom's fold;
  And when you kisses many one on lip and cheek have
    told,
I'll let you loose upon the grass, to leave me if you durst;
    And so we'll toy away
    The nights besides the day.'

He: 'But let me be your second love, but let me be your
    second,
  For then I'll tap so gently, dear, upon your window pane,
  And creep between the curtains in, where never man has
    lain,
And never leave thy gentle side till the morning star hath
    beckoned,
    Within the silken lace
    Of thy young arms' embrace.'

She: 'Well thou shalt be my second love, yes, gentle boy,
      my second,
  And I will wait at eve for thee within my lonely bower,
  And yield unto thy kisses, like a bud to April's shower,
From moonset till the tower-clock the hour of dawn hath
      reckoned,
          And lock thee with my arms
          All silent up in charms.'

He: 'No, I will be thy third love, lady, aye I will be the
      third,
  And break upon thee, bathing, in woody place alone,
  And catch thee to my saddle and ride o'er stream and
      stone,
And press thee well, and kiss thee well, and never speak a
      word,
          'Till thou hast yielded up
          The margin of love's cup.'

She: 'Then thou shalt not be my first love, boy, nor my
      second, nor my third;
  If thou'rt the first, I'll laugh at thee and pierce thy flesh
      with thorns;
  If the second, from my chamber pelt with jeering laugh
      and scorns;
And if thou darest be the third, I'll draw my dirk unheard
          And cut thy heart in two, –
          And then die, weeping you.'

Song of the Stygian Naiades

'What do you think the mermaids of the Styx were singing as
I watched them bathing the other day'–

          Proserpine may pull her flowers,
            Wet with dew or wet with tears,
            Red with anger, pale with fears;
          Is it any fault of ours,

If Pluto be an amorous king
    And come home nightly, laden
Underneath his broad bat-wing
    With a gentle earthly maiden?
Is it so, Wind, is it so?
All that I and you do know
Is that we saw fly and fix
'Mongst the flowers and reeds of Styx,
            Yesterday,
Where the Furies made their hay
For a bed of tiger cubs,
A great fly of Beelzebub's,
The bee of hearts, which mortals name
Cupid, Love, and Fie for shame.

Proserpine may weep in rage,
    But ere I and you have done
    Kissing, bathing in the sun,
What I have in yonder cage,
    She shall guess and ask in vain,
Bird or serpent, wild or tame;
    But if Pluto does't again,
It shall sing out loud his shame.
    What hast caught then? What hast caught?
Nothing but a poet's thought,
    Which so light did fall and fix
    'Mongst the flowers and reeds of Styx,
            Yesterday,
Where the Furies made their hay
For a bed of tiger cubs,
A great fly of Beelzebub's,
The bee of hearts, which mortals name
Cupid, Love, and Fie for shame.

The Phantom-Wooer

A ghost, that loved a lady fair,
Ever in the starry air
  Of midnight at her pillow stood;
And, with a sweetness skies above
The luring words of human love,
  Her soul the phantom wooed.
Sweet and sweet is their poisoned note,
The little snakes of silver throat,
In mossy skulls that nest and lie,
Ever singing 'die, oh! die.'

Young soul put off your flesh, and come
With me into the quiet tomb,
  Our bed is lovely, dark, and sweet;
The earth will swing us, as she goes,
Beneath our coverlid of snows,
  And the warm leaden sheet.
Dear and dear is their poisoned note,
The little snakes of silver throat,
In mossy skulls that nest and lie,
Ever singing 'die, oh! die.'

CHARLES TENNYSON-TURNER
1808–1879

A Summer Twilight

It is a Summer twilight, balmy-sweet,
A twilight brighten'd by an infant moon,
Fraught with the fairest light of middle June;
The lonely garden echoes to my feet,
And hark! O hear I not the gentle dews,
Fretting the silent forest in his sleep?
Or does the stir of housing insects creep
Thus faintly on mine ear? Day's many hues
Waned with the paling light and are no more,
And none but reptile pinions beat the air:
The bat is hunting softly by my door,
And, noiseless as the snow-flakes, leaves his lair;
O'er the still copses flitting here and there,
Wheeling the self-same circuit o'er and o'er.

A Forest Lake

O lake of sylvan shore! when gentle Spring
Slopes down upon thee from the mountain side,
When birds begin to build and brood and sing;
Or, in maturer season, when the pied
And fragrant turf is throng'd with blossoms rare;
In the frore sweetness of the breathing morn,
When the loud echoes of the herdsman's horn
Do sally forth upon the silent air
Of thy thick forestry, may I be there,
While the wood waits to see its phantom born
At clearing twilight, in thy grassy breast;
Or, when cool eve is busy, on thy shores,
With trails of purple shadow from the West,
Or dusking in the wake of tardy oars.

EDGAR ALLAN POE
1809–1841

Romance

Romance, who loves to nod and sing,
With drowsy head and folded wing,
Among the green leaves as they shake
Far down within some shadowy lake,
To me a painted parroquet
Hath been – a most familiar bird –
Taught me my alphabet to say –
To lisp my very earliest word
While in the wild wood I did lie,
A child – with a most knowing eye.

Of late, eternal Condor years
So shake the very Heaven on high
With tumult as they thunder by,
I have no time for idle cares
Through gazing on the unquiet sky.
And when an hour with calmer wings
Its down upon my spirit flings –
That little time with lyre and rhyme
To while away – forbidden things!
My heart would feel to be a crime
Unless it trembled with the strings.

The City in the Sea

Lo! Death has rear'd himself a throne
In a strange city lying alone
Far down within the dim West,
Where the good and the bad and the worst and the best
Have gone to their eternal rest.

There shrines and palaces and towers
(Time-eaten towers that tremble not!)
Resemble nothing that is ours.
Around, by lifting winds forgot,
Resignedly beneath the sky
The melancholy waters lie.

No rays from the holy heaven come down
On the long night-time of that town;
But light from out of the lurid sea
Streams up the turrets silently –
Gleams up the pinnacles far and free –
Up domes – up spires – up kingly halls –
Up fanes – up Babylon-like walls –
Up shadowy long-forgotten bowers
Of sculptured ivy and stone flowers –
Up many and many a marvellous shrine
Whose wreathèd friezes intertwine
The viol, the violet, and the vine.
Resignedly beneath the sky
The melancholy waters lie.
So blend the turrets and shadows there
That all seem pendulous in air,
While from a proud tower in the town
Death looks gigantically down.

There open fanes and gaping graves
Yawn level with the luminous waves;
But not the riches there that lie
In each idol's diamond eye –
Not the gaily-jewelled dead
Tempt the waters from their bed;
For no ripples curl, alas!
Along that wilderness of glass –
No swellings tell that winds may be
Upon some far-off happier sea –
No heavings hint that winds have been
On seas less hideously serene.

But lo, a stir is in the air!
The wave – there is a movement there!
As if the towers had thrust aside,
In slightly sinking, the dull tide –
As if their tops had feebly given
A void within the filmy Heaven.
The waves have now a redder glow –
The hours are breathing faint and low –
And when, amid no earthly moans,
Down, down that town shall settle hence,
Hell, rising from a thousand thrones,
Shall do it reverence.

Claribel

A MELODY

Where Claribel low-lieth
  The breezes pause and die,
    Letting the rose-leaves fall:
But the solemn oak-tree sigheth,
    Thick-leaved, ambrosial,
  With an ancient melody
  Of an inward agony,
Where Claribel low-lieth.

At eve the beetle boometh
  Athwart the thicket lone:
At noon the wild bee hummeth
  About the moss'd headstone:
At midnight the moon cometh,
  And looketh down alone.
Her song the lintwhite swelleth,
The clear-voiced mavis dwelleth,
  The callow throstle lispeth,
The slumbrous wave outwelleth,
  The babbling runnel crispeth,
The hollow grot replieth
  Where Claribel low-lieth.

The Dying Swan

The plain was grassy, wild and bare,
Wide, wild, and open to the air,
Which had built up everywhere
  An under-roof of doleful gray.
With an inner voice the river ran,

Adown it floated a dying swan,
    And loudly did lament.
  It was the middle of the day.
Ever the weary wind went on,
    And took the reed-tops as it went.

Some blue peaks in the distance rose,
And white against the cold-white sky,
Shone out their crowning snows.
  One willow over the river wept,
And shook the wave as the wind did sigh;
Above in the wind was the swallow,
    Chasing itself at its own wild will,
    And far thro' the marish green and still
    The tangled water-courses slept,
Shot over with purple, and green, and yellow.

The wild swan's death-hymn took the soul
Of that waste place with joy
Hidden in sorrow: at first to the ear
The warble was low, and full and clear;
And floating about the under-sky,
Prevailing in weakness, the coronach stole
Sometimes afar, and sometimes anear;
But anon her awful jubilant voice,
With a music strange and manifold,
Flow'd forth on a carol free and bold;
As when a mighty people rejoice
With shawms, and with cymbals, and harps of gold,
And the tumult of their acclaim is roll'd
Thro' the open gates of the city afar,
To the shepherd who watcheth the evening star.
And the creeping mosses and clambering weeds,
And the willow-branches hoar and dank,
And the wavy swell of the soughing reeds,
And the wave-worn horns of the echoing bank,
And the silvery marish-flowers that throng
The desolate creeks and pools among,
Were flooded over with eddying song.

The Deserted House

Life and Thought have gone away
    Side by side,
    Leaving door and windows wide:
Careless tenants they!

    All within is dark as night:
    In the windows is no light;
    And no murmur at the door,
    So frequent on its hinge before.

Close the door, the shutters close,
    Or thro' the windows we shall see
    The nakedness and vacancy
Of the dark deserted house.

Come away: no more of mirth
    Is here or merry-making sound.
The house was builded of the earth,
    And shall fall again to ground.

Come away: for Life and Thought
  Here no longer dwell;
    But in a city glorious –
A great and distant city – have bought
  A mansion incorruptible.
Would they could have stayed with us!

Song

A spirit haunts the year's last hours
Dwelling amid these yellowing bowers:
    To himself he talks;
For at eventide, listening earnestly,

At his work you may hear him sob and sigh
    In the walks;
      Earthward he boweth the heavy stalks
Of the mouldering flowers:
    Heavily hangs the broad sunflower
      Over its grave i' the earth so chilly;
    Heavily hangs the hollyhock,
      Heavily hangs the tiger-lily.

The air is damp, and hush'd, and close,
As a sick man's room when he taketh repose
    An hour before death;
My very heart faints and my whole soul grieves
At the moist rich smell of the rotting leaves,
    And the breath
    Of the fading edges of box beneath,
And the year's last rose.
    Heavily hangs the broad sunflower
      Over its grave i' the earth so chilly;
    Heavily hangs the hollyhock,
      Heavily hangs the tiger-lily.

A Character

With a half-glance upon the sky
At night he said, 'The wanderings
Of this most intricate Universe
Teach me the nothingness of things.'
Yet could not all creation pierce
Beyond the bottom of his eye.

He spake of beauty: that the dull
Saw no divinity in grass,
Life in dead stones, or spirit in air;
Then looking as 'twere in a glass,
He smooth'd his chin and sleek'd his hair,
And said the earth was beautiful.

ALFRED, LORD TENNYSON

He spake of virtue: not the gods
More purely, when they wish to charm
Pallas and Juno sitting by:
And with a sweeping of the arm,
And a lack-lustre dead-blue eye,
Devolved his rounded periods.

Most delicately hour by hour
He canvass'd human mysteries,
And trod on silk, as if the winds
Blew his own praises in his eyes,
And stood aloof from other minds
In impotence of fancied power.

With lips depress'd as he were meek,
Himself unto himself he sold:
Upon himself himself did feed:
Quiet, dispassionate, and cold,
And other than his form of creed,
With chisell'd features clear and sleek.

The Kraken

Below the thunders of the upper deep;
Far, far beneath in the abysmal sea,
His ancient, dreamless, uninvaded sleep
The Kraken sleepeth: faintest sunlights flee
About his shadowy sides: above him swell
Huge sponges of millennial growth and height;
And far away into the sickly light,
From many a wondrous grot and secret cell
Unnumber'd and enormous polypi
Winnow with giant arms the slumbering green.
There hath he lain for ages and will lie
Battening upon huge seaworms in his sleep,
Until the latter fire shall heat the deep;
Then once by man and angels to be seen,
In roaring he shall rise and on the surface die.

ROBERT BROWNING
1812–1889

Waring

I

What's become of Waring
Since he gave us all the slip,
Chose land-travel or seafaring,
Boots and chest, or staff and scrip,
Rather than pace up and down
Any longer London-town?

Who'd have guessed it from his lip,
Or his brow's accustomed bearing,
On the night he thus took ship,
Or started landward? – little caring
For us, it seems, who supped together,
(Friends of his too, I remember)
And walked home thro' the merry weather,
The snowiest in all December;
I left his arm that night myself
For what's-his-name's, the new prose-poet,
That wrote the book there, on the shelf –
How, forsooth, was I to know it
If Waring meant to glide away
Like a ghost at break of day?
Never looked he half so gay!

He was prouder than the Devil:
How he must have cursed our revel!
Ay, and many other meetings,
Indoor visits, outdoor greetings.
As up and down he paced this London,
With no work done, but great works undone,
Where scarce twenty knew his name.
Why not, then, have earlier spoken,

Written, bustled? Who's to blame
If your silence kept unbroken?
'True, but there were sundry jottings,
'Stray-leaves, fragments, blurrs and blottings,
'Certain first steps were achieved
'Already which' – (is that your meaning?)
'Had well borne out who'er believed
'In more to come!' But who goes gleaning
Hedge-side chance-blades, while full-sheaved
Stand cornfields by him? Pride, o'erweening
Pride alone, puts forth such claims
O'er the day's distinguished names.

Meantime, how much I loved him,
I find out now I've lost him:
I, who cared not if I moved him,
Who could so carelessly accost him,
Henceforth never shall get free
Of his ghostly company,
His eyes that just a little wink
As deep I go into the merit
Of this and that distinguished spirit –
His cheeks' raised colour, soon to sink,
As long I dwell on some stupendous
And tremendous (Heaven defend us!)
Monstr'-inform'-ingens-horrend-ous
Demoniaco-seraphic
Penman's latest piece of graphic.
Nay, my very wrist grows warm
With his dragging weight of arm!
E'en so, swimmingly appears,
Thro' one's after-supper musings,
Some lost Lady of old years,
With her beauteous vain endeavour,
And goodness unrepaid as ever:
The face, accustomed to refusings,
We, puppies that we were ... Oh never
Surely, nice of conscience, scrupled

Being aught like false, forsooth, to?
Telling aught but honest truth to?
What a sin, had we centupled
Its possessor's grace and sweetness!
No! she heard in its completeness
Truth, for truth's a weighty matter,
And, truth at issue, we can't flatter!
Well, 'tis done with: she's exempt
From damning us thro' such a sally;
And so she glides, as down a valley,
Taking up with her contempt,
Past our reach; and in, the flowers
Shut her unregarded hours.

Oh, could I have him back once more,
This Waring, but one half-day more!
Back, with the quiet face of yore,
So hungry for acknowledgment
Like mine! I'd fool him to his bent!
Feed, should not he, to heart's content?
I'd say, 'to only have conceived
'Your great works, tho' they ne'er make progress,
'Surpasses all we've yet achieved!'
I'd lie so, I should be believed.
I'd make such havoc of the claims
Of the day's distinguished names
To feast him with, as feasts an ogress
Her sharp-toothed golden-crowned child!
Or, as one feasts a creature rarely
Captured here, unreconciled
To capture; and completely gives
Its pettish humours licence, barely
Requiring that it lives.

Ichabod, Ichabod,
The glory is departed!
Travels Waring East away?

Who, of knowledge, by hearsay,
Reports a man upstarted
Somewhere as a God,
Hordes grown European-hearted,
Millions of the wild made tame
On a sudden at his fame?
In Vishnu-land what Avatar?
Or who, in Moscow, towards the Czar,
With the demurest of footfalls
Over the Kremlin's pavement, bright
With serpentine and syenite,
Steps, with five other Generals,
That simultaneously take snuff,
For each to have pretext enough
To kerchiefwise unfurl his sash
Which, softness' self, is yet the stuff
To hold fast where a steel chain snaps,
And leave the grand white neck no gash?
Waring, in Moscow, to those rough
Cold northern natures borne, perhaps,
Like the lambwhite maiden dear
From the circle of mute kings,
Unable to repress the tear,
Each as his sceptre down he flings,
To Dian's fane at Taurica,
Where now a captive priestess, she alway
Mingles her tender grave Hellenic speech
With theirs, tuned to the hailstone-beaten beach,
As pours some pigeon, from the myrrhy lands
Rapt by the whirlblast to fierce Scythian strands
Where breed the swallows, her melodious cry
Amid their barbarous twitter!
In Russia? Never! Spain were fitter!
Ay, most likely 'tis in Spain
That we and Waring meet again –
Now, while he turns down that cool narrow lane
Into the blackness, out of grave Madrid
All fire and shine – abrupt as when there's slid

Its stiff gold blazing pall
From some black coffin-lid.
Or, best of all,
I love to think
The leaving us was just a feint;
Back here to London did he slink;
And now works on without a wink
Of sleep, and we are on the brink
Of something great in fresco-paint:
Some garret's ceiling, walls and floor,
Up and down and o'er and o'er
He splashes, as none splashed before
Since great Caldara Polidore:
Or Music means this land of ours
Some favour yet, to pity won
By Purcell from his Rosy Bowers, –
'Give me my so long promised son,
'Let Waring end what I begun!'
Then down he creeps and out he steals
Only when the night conceals
His face – in Kent 'tis cherry-time,
Or, hops are picking; or, at prime
Of March, he wanders as, too happy,
Years ago when he was young,
Some mild eve when woods grew sappy,
And the early moths had sprung
To life from many a trembling sheath
Woven the warm boughs beneath;
While small birds said to themselves
What should soon be actual song,
And young gnats, by tens and twelves,
Made as if they were the throng
That crowd around and carry aloft
The sound they have nursed, so sweet and pure,
Out of a myriad noises soft,
Into a tone that can endure
Amid the noise of a July noon,
When all God's creatures crave their boon,

337

All at once and all in tune,
And get it, happy as Waring then,
Having first within his ken
What a man might do with men,
And far too glad, in the even-glow,
To mix with your world he meant to take
Into his hand, he told you, so –
And out of it his world to make,
To contract and to expand
As he shut or oped his hand.
Oh, Waring, what's to really be?
A clear stage and a crowd to see!
Some Garrick – say – but shall not he
The heart of Hamlet's mystery pluck?
Or, where most unclean beasts are rife,
Some Junius – am I right? – shall tuck
His sleeve, and out with flaying-knife!
Some Chatterton shall have the luck
Of calling Rowley into life!
Some one shall somehow run a muck
With this old world, for want of strife
Sound asleep: contrive, contrive
To rouse us, Waring! Who's alive?
Our men scarce seem in earnest now:
Distinguished names!—but 'tis, somehow,
As if they played at being names
Still more distinguished, like the games
Of children. Turn our sport to earnest
With a visage of the sternest!
Bring the real times back, confessed
Still better than our very best!

II

'When I last saw Waring . . .'
(How all turned to him who spoke –
You saw Waring? Truth or joke?
In land-travel, or sea-faring?)

'We were sailing by Triest,
'Where a day or two we harboured:
'A sunset was in the West,
'When, looking over the vessel's side,
'One of our company espied
'A sudden speck to larboard.
'And, as a sea-duck flies and swims
'At once, so came the light craft up,
'With its sole lateen sail that trims
'And turns (the water round its rims
'Dancing, as round a sinking cup)
'And by us like a fish it curled,
'And drew itself up close beside,
'Its great sail on the instant furled,
'And o'er its planks, a shrill voice cried,
'(A neck as bronzed as a Lascar's)
' "Buy wine of us, you English Brig?
' "Or fruit, tobacco and cigars?
' "A Pilot for you to Triest?
' "Without one, look you ne'er so big,
' "They'll never let you up the bay!
' "We natives should know best."
'I turned, and "just those fellows' way,"
'Our captain said. "The 'long-shore thieves
' "Are laughing at us in their sleeves."
'In truth, the boy leaned laughing back;
'And one, half-hidden by his side
'Under the furled sail, soon I spied,
'With great grass hat, and kerchief black,
'Who looked up, with his kingly throat,
'Said somewhat, while the other shook
'His hair back from his eyes to look
'Their longest at us; then the boat,
'I know not how, turned sharply round,
'Laying her whole side on the sea
'As a leaping fish does; from the lee
'Into the weather, cut somehow
'Her sparkling path beneath our bow;

'And so went off, as with a bound,
'Into the rose and golden half
'Of the sky, to overtake the sun,
'And reach the shore, like the sea-calf
'Its singing cave; yet I caught one
'Glance ere away the boat quite passed,
'And neither time nor toil could mar
'Those features: so I saw the last
'Of Waring!' – You? Oh, never star
Was lost here, but it rose afar!
Look East, where whole new thousands are!
In Vishnu-land what Avatar?

EMILY JANE BRONTË
1818–1848

To a Wreath of Snow
By A. G. Almeda

O transient voyager of heaven!
O silent sign of winter skies!
What adverse wind thy sail has driven
To dungeons where a prisoner lies?

Methinks the hands that shut the sun
So sternly from this mourning brow
Might still their rebel task have done
And checked a thing so frail as thou.

They would have done it had they known
The talisman that dwelt in thee,
For all the suns that ever shone
Have never been so kind to me.

For many a week, and many a day,
My heart was weighed with sinking gloom,
When morning rose in mourning grey
And faintly lit my prison room;

But, angel like, when I awoke,
Thy silvery form so soft and fair,
Shining through darkness, sweetly spoke
Of cloudy skies and mountains bare –

The dearest to a mountaineer,
Who, all life long has loved the snow
That crowned her native summits drear
Better than greenest plains below.

And, voiceless, soulless messenger,
Thy presence waked a thrilling tone
That comforts me while thou art here
And will sustain when thou art gone.

R. Alcona to J. Brenzaida

Cold in the earth, and the deep snow piled above thee!
Far, far removed, cold in the dreary grave!
Have I forgot, my Only Love, to love thee,
Severed at last by Time's all-wearing wave?

Now, when alone, do my thoughts no longer hover
Over the mountains on Angora's shore;
Resting their wings where heath and fern-leaves cover
That noble heart for ever, ever more?

Cold in the earth, and fifteen wild Decembers
From those brown hills have melted into spring –
Faithful indeed is the spirit that remembers
After such years of change and suffering!

Sweet Love of youth, forgive if I forget thee
While the World's tide is bearing me along:
Sterner desires and darker hopes beset me,
Hopes which obscure but cannot do thee wrong.

No other Sun has lightened up my heaven;
No other Star has ever shone for me:
All my life's bliss from thy dear life was given –
All my life's bliss is in the grave with thee.

But when the days of golden dreams had perished
And even Despair was powerless to destroy,
Then did I learn how existence could be cherished,
Strengthened and fed without the aid of joy;

Then did I check the tears of useless passion,
Weaned my young soul from yearning after thine;
Sternly denied its burning wish to hasten
Down to that tomb already more than mine!

And even yet, I dare not let it languish,
Dare not indulge in Memory's rapturous pain;
Once drinking deep of that divinest anguish,
How could I seek the empty world again?

Julian M. and A. G. Rochelle

Silent is the House – all are laid asleep;
One, alone, looks out o'er the snow wreaths deep;
Watching every cloud, dreading every breeze
That whirls the 'wildering drifts and bends the groaning
    trees.

Cheerful is the hearth, soft the matted floor;
Not one shivering gust creeps through pane or door;
The little lamp burns straight, its rays shoot strong and far;
I trim it well to be the Wanderer's guiding-star.

Frown, my haughty sire; chide, my angry dame;
Set your slaves to spy, threaten me with shame;
But neither sire nor dame, nor prying serf shall know
What angel nightly tracks that waste of winter snow.

In the dungeon crypts idly did I stray,
Reckless of the lives wasting there away;
'Draw the ponderous bars; open, Warder stern!'
He dare not say me nay – the hinges harshly turn.

'Our guests are darkly lodged,' I whispered, gazing through
The vault whose grated eye showed heaven more grey than
    blue.
(This was when glad spring laughed in awaking pride.)
'Aye, darkly lodged enough!' returned my sullen guide.

Then, God forgive my youth, forgive my careless tongue!
I scoffed, as the chill chains on the damp flagstones rung;
'Confined in triple walls, art thou so much to fear,
That we must bind thee down and clench thy fetters here?'

The captive raised her face; it was as soft and mild
As sculptured marble saint or slumbering, unweaned child:
It was so soft and mild, it was so sweet and fair,
Pain could not trace a line nor grief a shadow there!

The captive raised her hand and pressed it to her brow:
'I have been struck,' she said, 'and I am suffering now;
Yet these are little worth, your bolts and irons strong;
And were they forged in steel they could not hold me long.'

Hoarse laughed the jailor grim: 'Shall I be won to hear;
Dost think, fond dreaming wretch, that *I* shall grant thy
      prayer?
Or, better still, wilt melt my master's heart with groans?
Ah, sooner might the sun thaw down these granite stones!

'My master's voice is low, his aspect bland and kind,
But hard as hardest flint the soul that lurks behind;
And I am rough and rude, yet not more rough to see
Than is the hidden ghost which has its home in me!'

About her lips there played a smile of almost scorn:
'My friend,' she gently said, 'you have not heard me mourn
When you my parents' lives – *my* lost life, can restore,
Then may I weep and sue – but *never*, Friend, before!'

Her head sank on her hands; its fair curls swept the ground;
The dungeon seemed to swim in strange confusion round –
'Is she so near to death?' I murmured, half aloud,
And, kneeling, parted back the floating golden cloud.

Alas, how former days upon my heart were borne;
How memory mirrored then the prisoner's joyous morn:
Too blithe, too loving child, too warmly, wildly gay!
Was that the wintry close of thy celestial May?

She knew me and she sighed, 'Lord Julian, can it be,
Of all my playmates, you alone remember me?
Nay, start not at my words, unless you deem it shame
To own, from conquered foe, a once familiar name.

'I cannot wonder now at ought the world will do,
And insult and contempt I lightly brook from you,
Since those, who vowed away their souls to win my love,
Around this living grave like utter strangers move!

'Nor has one voice been raised to plead that I might die,
Not buried under earth but in the open sky;
By ball or speedy knife or headsman's skilful blow –
A quick and welcome pang instead of lingering woe!

'Yet, tell them, Julian, all, I am not doomed to wear
Year after year in gloom and desolate despair;
A messenger of Hope comes every night to me;
And offers, for short life, eternal liberty.

He comes with western winds, with evening's wandering
    airs,
With that clear dusk of heaven that brings the thickest
    stars;
Winds take a pensive tone, and stars a tender fire,
And visions rise and change which kill me with desire –

'Desire for nothing known in my maturer years
When joy grew mad with awe at counting future tears,
When, if my spirit's sky was full of flashes warm,
I knew not whence they came, from sun or thunderstorm;

'But first a hush of peace, a soundless calm descends;
The struggle of distress and fierce impatience ends;
Mute music soothes my breast – unuttered harmony
That I could never dream till earth was lost to me.

'Then dawns the Invisible, the Unseen its truth reveals;
My outward sense is gone, my inward essence feels –
Its wings are almost free, its home, its harbour found;
Measuring the gulf it stoops and dares the final bound!

'Oh, dreadful is the check – intense the agony
When the ear begins to hear and the eye begins to see;

When the pulse begins to throb, the brain to think again,
The soul to feel the flesh and the flesh to feel the chain!

'Yet I would lose no sting, would wish no torture less;
The more that anguish racks the earlier it will bless;
And robed in fires of Hell, or bright with heavenly shine,
If it but herald Death, the vision is divine.'

She ceased to speak, and I, unanswering, watched her there,
Not daring now to touch one lock of silken hair –
As I had knelt in scorn, on the dank floor I knelt still,
My fingers in the links of that iron hard and chill.

I heard, and yet heard not, the surly keeper growl;
I saw, yet did not see, the flagstone damp and foul.
The keeper, to and fro, paced by the bolted door
And shivered as he walked and, as he shivered, swore.

While my cheek glowed in flame, I marked that he did rave
Of air that froze his blood, and moisture like the grave –
'We have been two hours good!' he muttered peevishly;
Then, loosing off his belt the rusty dungeon key,

He said, 'You may be pleased, Lord Julian, still to stay,
But duty will not let me linger here all day;
If I might go, I'd leave this badge of mine with you,
Not doubting that you'd prove a jailor stern and true.'

I took the proffered charge; the captive's drooping lid
Beneath its shady lash a sudden lightning hid;
Earth's hope was not so dead, heaven's home was not so
    dear;
I read it in that flash of longing quelled by fear.

Then like a tender child whose hand did just enfold,
Safe in its eager grasp, a bird it wept to hold,
When pierced with one wild glance from the troubled hazel
    eye,
It gushes into tears and lets its treasure fly,

Thus ruth and selfish love together striving tore
The heart all newly taught to pity and adore;

If I should break the chain, I felt my bird would go;
Yet I must break the chain or seal the prisoner's woe.

Short strife, what rest could soothe – what peace could
    visit me
While she lay pining there for Death to set her free ?
'Rochelle, the dungeons teem with foes to gorge our hate –
Thou art too young to die by such a bitter fate!'

With hurried blow on blow, I struck the fetters through,
Regardless how that deed my after hours might rue.
Oh, I was over-blest by the warm unasked embrace –
By the smile of grateful joy that lit her angel face!

And I was over-blest – aye, more than I could dream
When, faint, she turned aside from noon's unwonted
    beam;
When though the cage was wide – the heaven around it
    lay –
Its pinion would not waft my wounded dove away.

Through thirteen anxious weeks of terror-blent delight
I guarded her by day and guarded her by night,
While foes were prowling near and Death gazed greedily
And only Hope remained a faithful friend to me.

Then oft with taunting smile I heard my kindred tell
'How Julian loved his hearth and sheltering roof-tree well;
How the trumpet's voice might call, the battle-standard
    wave,
But Julian had no heart to fill a patriot's grave.'

And I, whom am so quick to answer sneer with sneer;
So ready to condemn, to scorn, a coward's fear,
I held my peace like one whose conscience keeps him
    dumb,
And saw my kinsmen go – and lingered still at home.

Another hand than mine my rightful banner held
And gathered my renown on Freedom's crimson field;

Yet I had no desire the glorious prize to gain –
It needed braver nerve to face the world's disdain.

And by that patient strength that could that world defy,
By suffering, with calm mind, contempt and calumny;
By never-doubting love, unswerving constancy,
Rochelle, I earned at last an equal love from thee!

Last Lines

Why ask to know what date, what clime?
There dwelt our own humanity,
Power-worshippers from earliest time,
Foot-kissers of triumphant crime
Crushers of helpless misery,
Crushing down Justice, honouring Wrong:
If that be feeble, this be strong.

Shedders of blood, shedders of tears:
Self-cursers avid of distress;
Yet mocking heaven with senseless prayers
For mercy on the merciless.

It was the autumn of the year
When grain grows yellow in the ear;
Day after day, from noon to noon,
The August sun blazed bright as June.

But we with unregarding eyes
Saw panting earth and glowing skies;
No hand the reaper's sickle held,
Nor bound the ripe sheaves in the field.

Our corn was garnered months before,
Threshed out and kneaded-up with gore;
Ground when the ears were milky sweet
With furious toil of hoofs and feet;
I, doubly cursed on foreign sod,
Fought neither for my home nor God.

13 May, 1848

INDEX OF AUTHORS

INDEX OF FIRST LINES